Kobayashi's
...on Maid

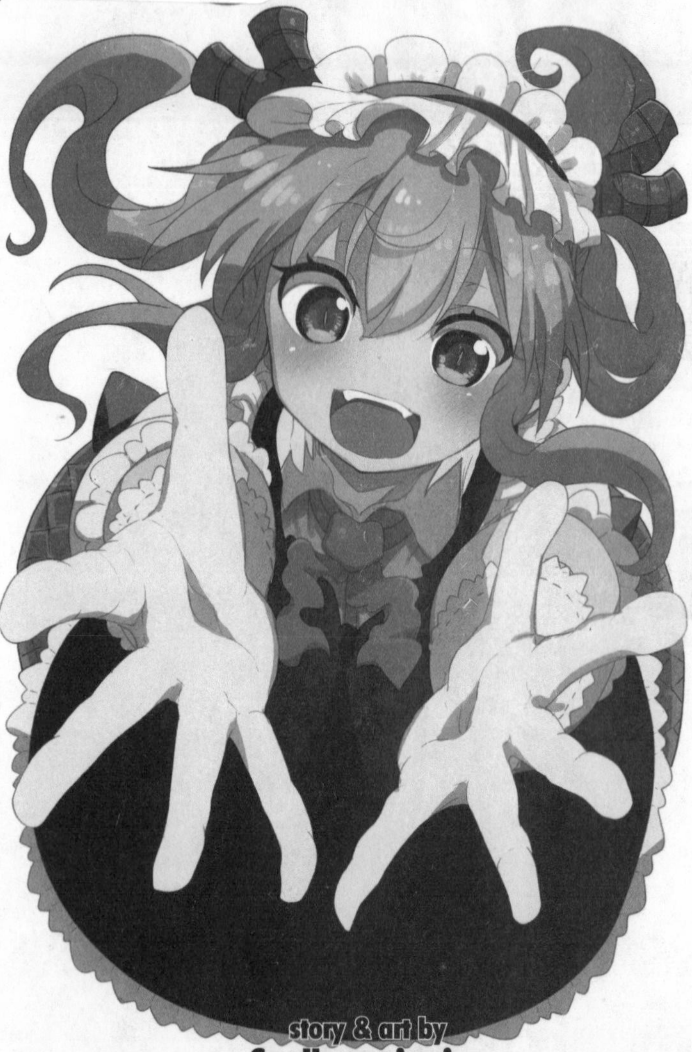

story & art by
Coolkyousinnjya

Miss Kobayashi's Dragon Maid

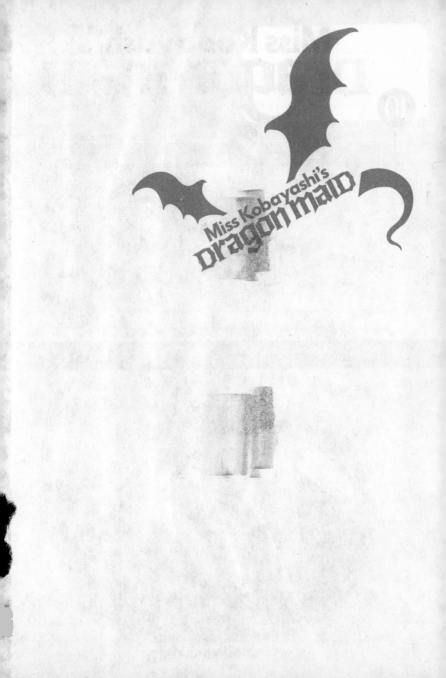

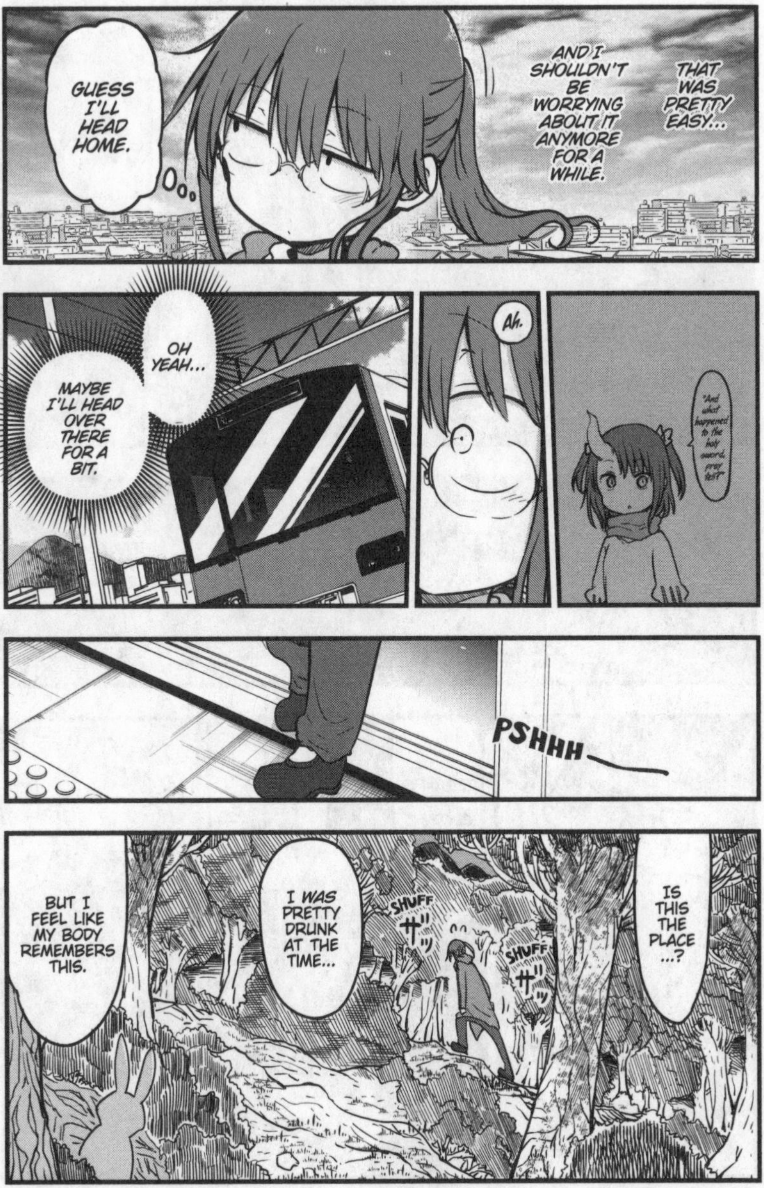
THAT WAS PRETTY EASY...
AND I SHOULDN'T BE WORRYING ABOUT IT ANYMORE FOR A WHILE.
GUESS I'LL HEAD HOME.
"And what happened to the holy sword, pray tell?"
Ah.
OH YEAH...
MAYBE I'LL HEAD OVER THERE FOR A BIT.
PSHHH—
IS THIS THE PLACE...?
SHUFF ザッ
SHUFF ザッ
I WAS PRETTY DRUNK AT THE TIME...
BUT I FEEL LIKE MY BODY REMEMBERS THIS.

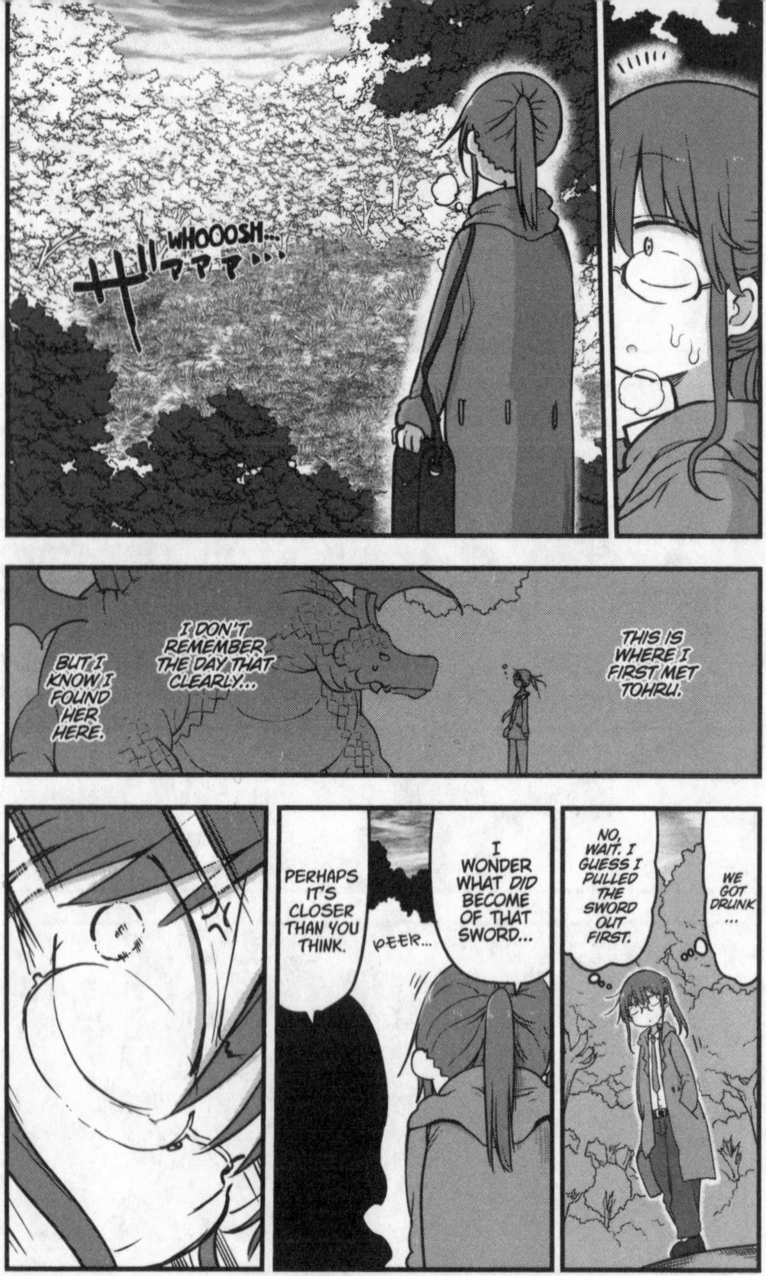
WHOOOSH...
ザァァァ…
THIS IS WHERE I FIRST MET TOHRU.
I DON'T REMEMBER THE DAY THAT CLEARLY...
BUT I KNOW I FOUND HER HERE.
WE GOT DRUNK...
NO, WAIT. I GUESS I PULLED THE SWORD OUT FIRST.
I WONDER WHAT DID BECOME OF THAT SWORD...
PEER...
PERHAPS IT'S CLOSER THAN YOU THINK.

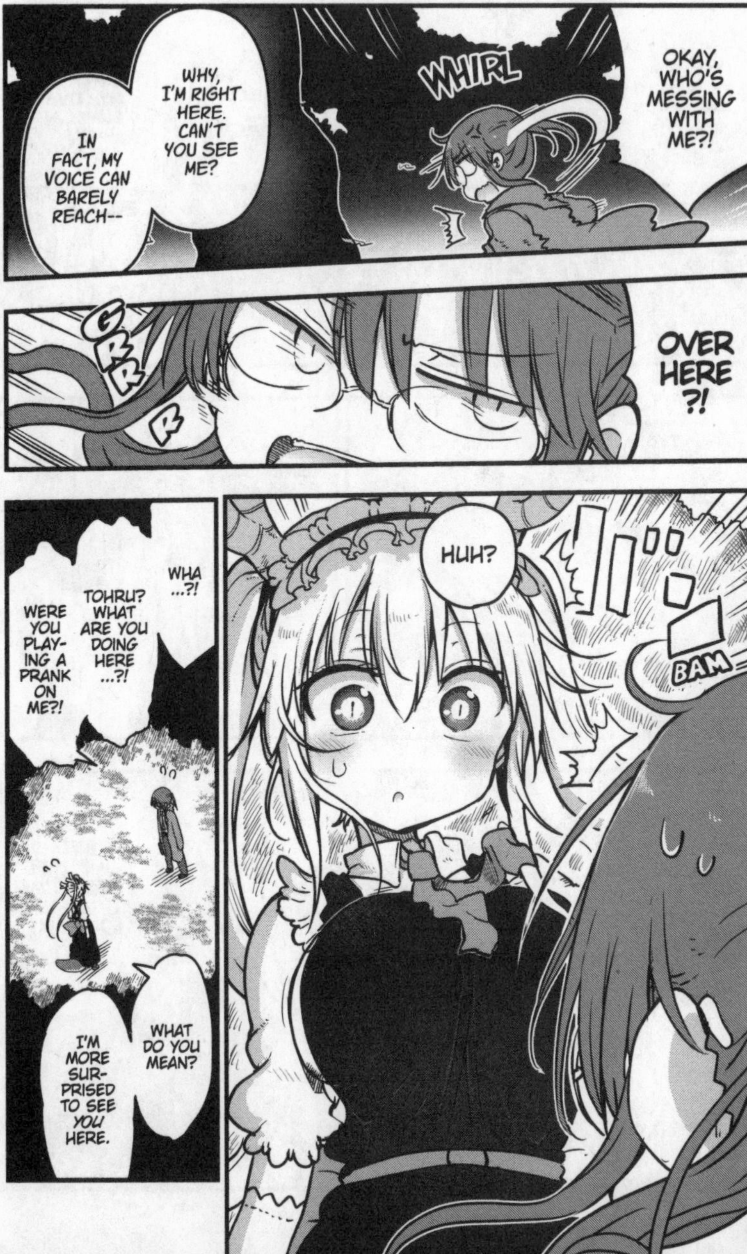
OKAY, WHO'S MESSING WITH ME?!
WHIRL
WHY, I'M RIGHT HERE. CAN'T YOU SEE ME?
IN FACT, MY VOICE CAN BARELY REACH--
OVER HERE?!
GRRR
BAM
HUH?
WHA ...?!
TOHRU? WHAT ARE YOU DOING HERE ...?!
WERE YOU PLAYING A PRANK ON ME?!
WHAT DO YOU MEAN?
I'M MORE SURPRISED TO SEE *YOU* HERE.

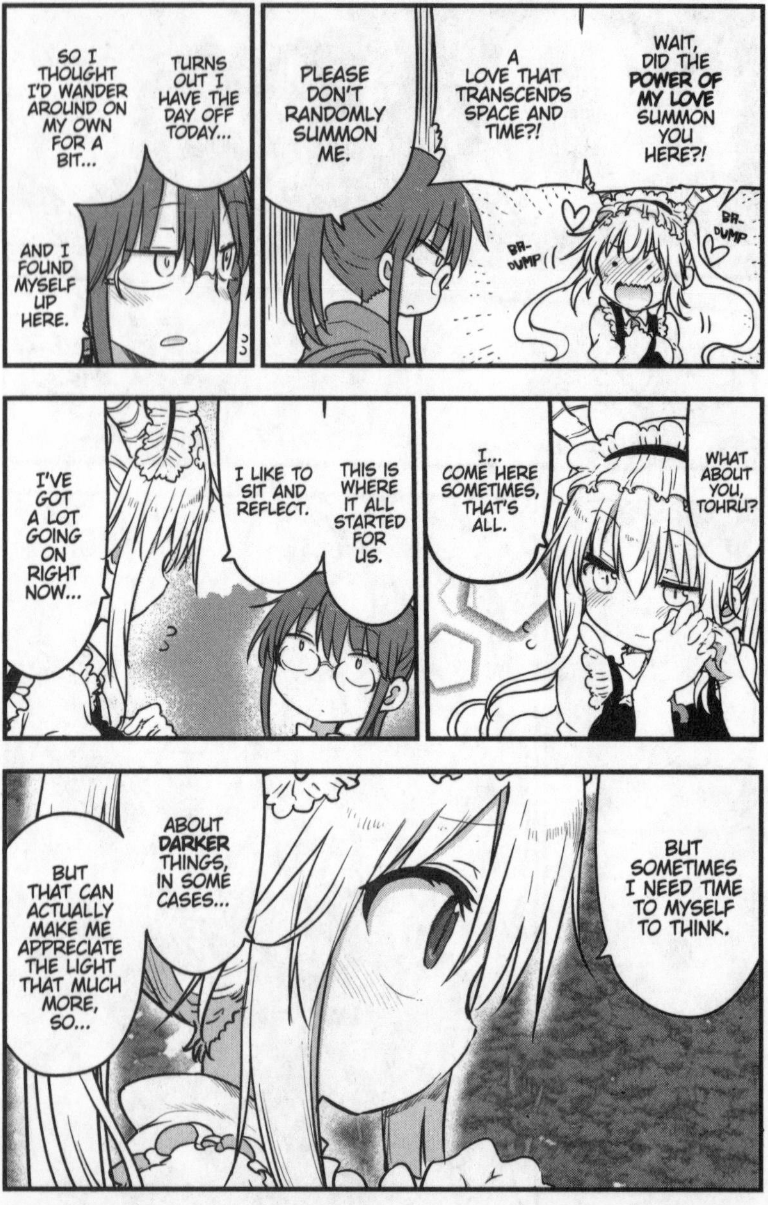
WAIT, DID THE **POWER OF MY LOVE** SUMMON YOU HERE?!
A LOVE THAT TRANSCENDS SPACE AND TIME?!
BA-DUMP
BA-DUMP
PLEASE DON'T RANDOMLY SUMMON ME.
TURNS OUT I HAVE THE DAY OFF TODAY...
SO I THOUGHT I'D WANDER AROUND ON MY OWN FOR A BIT...
AND I FOUND MYSELF UP HERE.
WHAT ABOUT YOU, TOHRU?
I... COME HERE SOMETIMES, THAT'S ALL.
THIS IS WHERE IT ALL STARTED FOR US.
I LIKE TO SIT AND REFLECT.
I'VE GOT A LOT GOING ON RIGHT NOW...
BUT SOMETIMES I NEED TIME TO MYSELF TO THINK.
ABOUT **DARKER** THINGS, IN SOME CASES...
BUT THAT CAN ACTUALLY MAKE ME APPRECIATE THE LIGHT THAT MUCH MORE, SO...

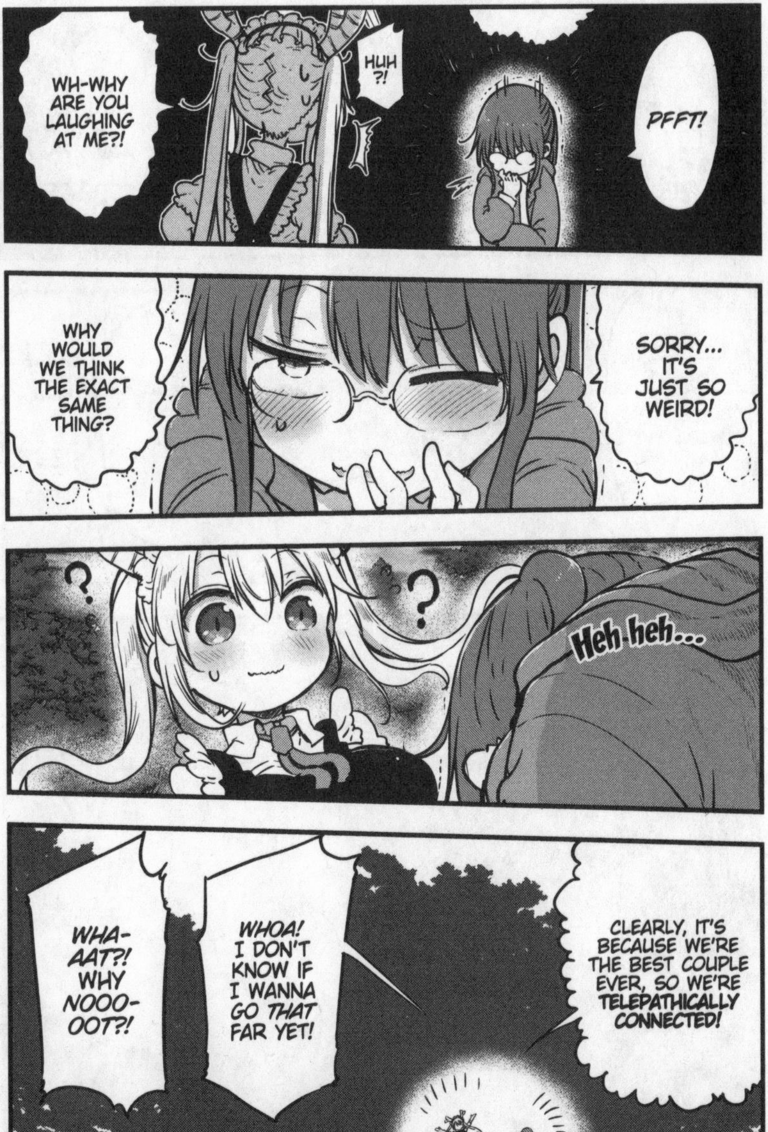
PFFT!
HUH?!
WH-WHY ARE YOU LAUGHING AT ME?!
SORRY... IT'S JUST SO WEIRD!
WHY WOULD WE THINK THE EXACT SAME THING?
Heh heh...
CLEARLY, IT'S BECAUSE WE'RE THE BEST COUPLE EVER, SO WE'RE TELEPATHICALLY CONNECTED!
WHOA! I DON'T KNOW IF I WANNA GO THAT FAR YET!
WHA-AAT?! WHY NOOOO-OOT?!

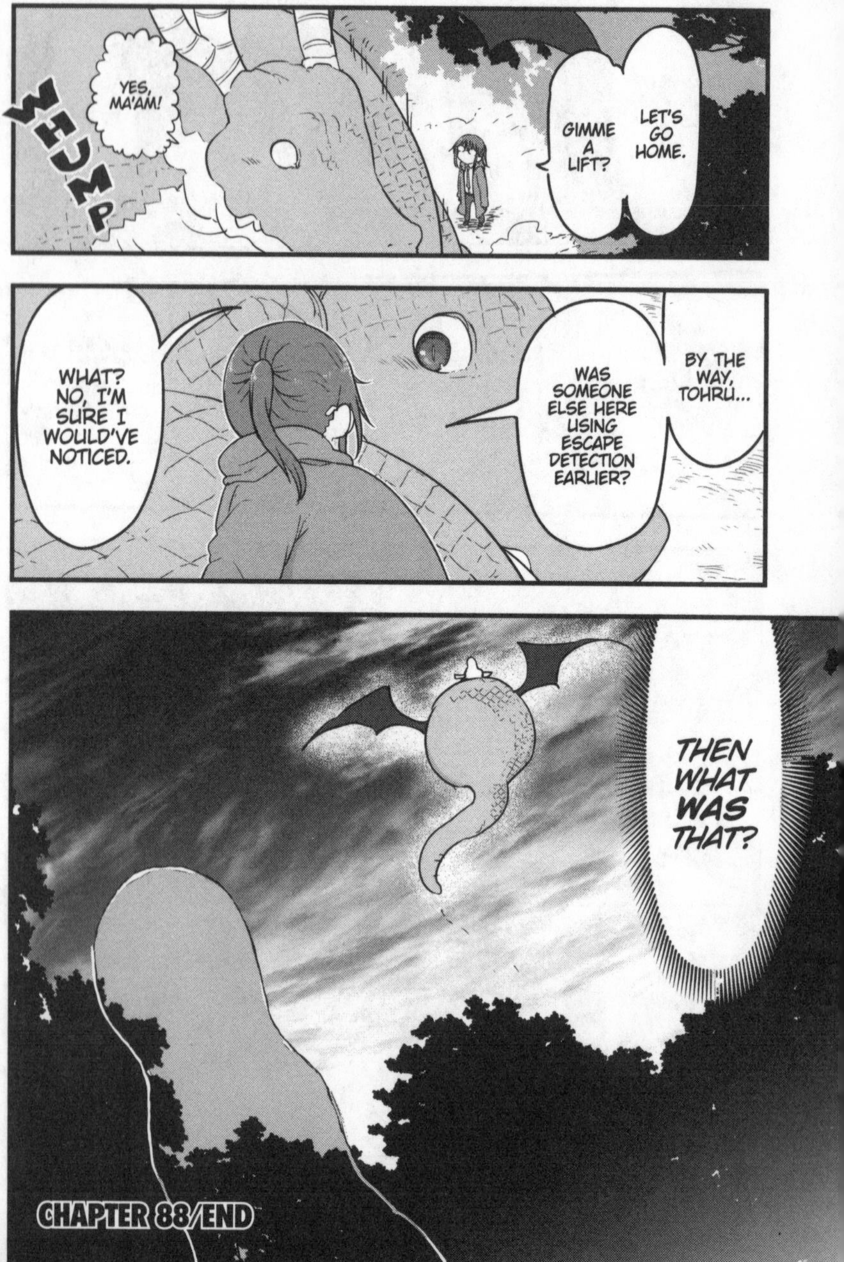
LET'S GO HOME.
GIMME A LIFT?
YES, MA'AM!
WHUMP
BY THE WAY, TOHRU...
WAS SOMEONE ELSE HERE USING ESCAPE DETECTION EARLIER?
WHAT? NO, I'M SURE I WOULD'VE NOTICED.
THEN WHAT WAS THAT?
CHAPTER 88/END

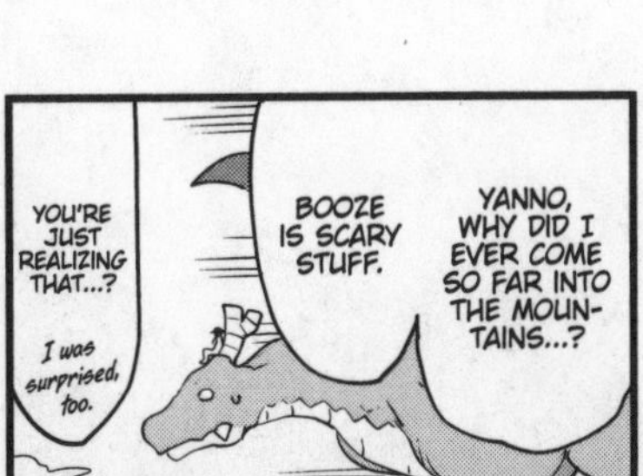
YANNO, WHY DID I EVER COME SO FAR INTO THE MOUN-TAINS...?
BOOZE IS SCARY STUFF.
YOU'RE JUST REALIZING THAT...?
I was surprised, too.

Miss Kobayashi's
DRAGON MAID

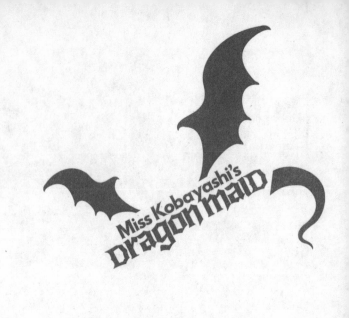

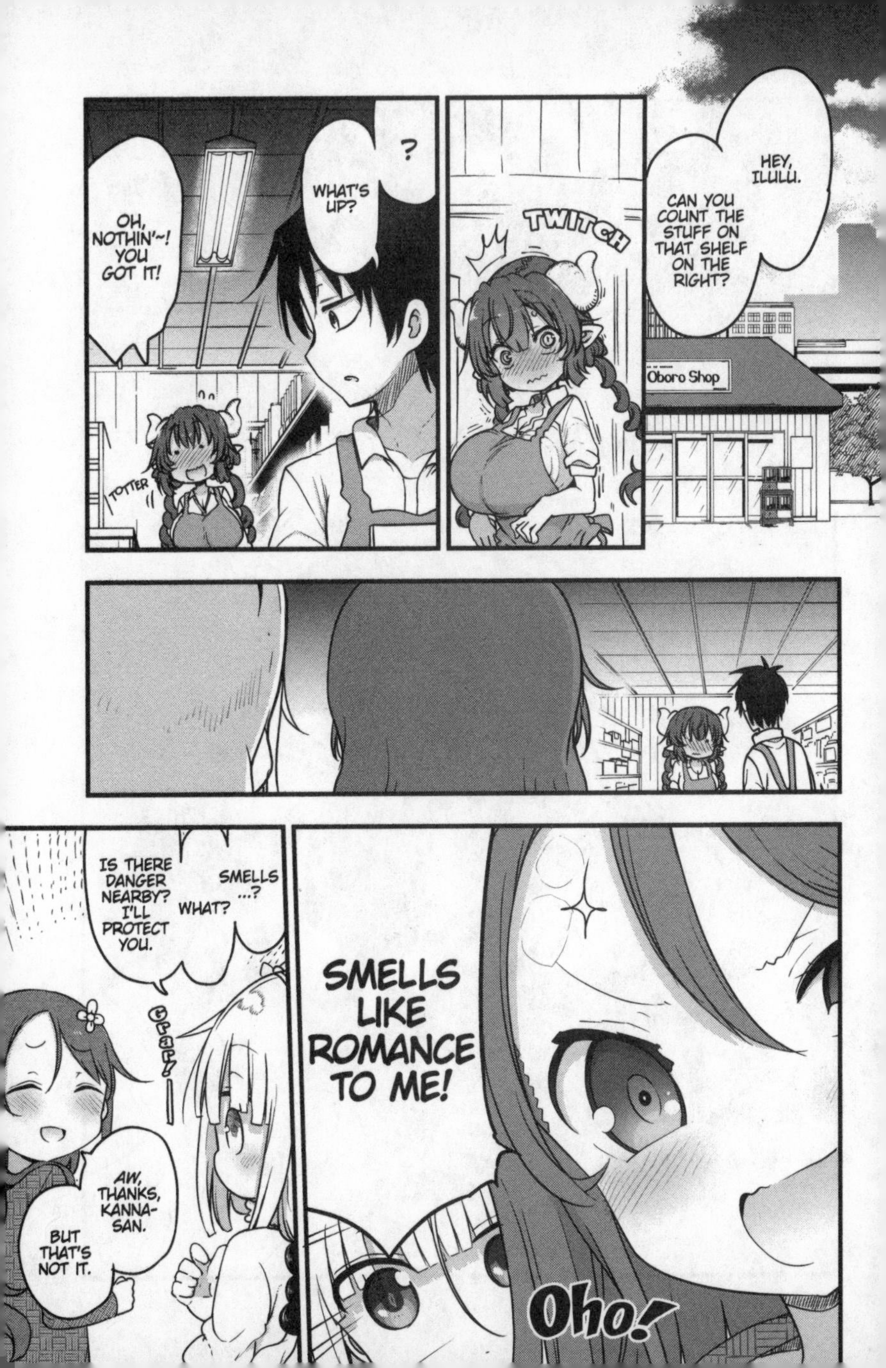

HEY, ILULU.
CAN YOU COUNT THE STUFF ON THAT SHELF ON THE RIGHT?
Oboro Shop
TWITCH
?
WHAT'S UP?
OH, NOTHIN'~! YOU GOT IT!
TOTTER
SMELLS LIKE ROMANCE TO ME!
Oho!
SMELLS ...? WHAT?
IS THERE DANGER NEARBY? I'LL PROTECT YOU.
Grar!
AW, THANKS, KANNA-SAN.
BUT THAT'S NOT IT.

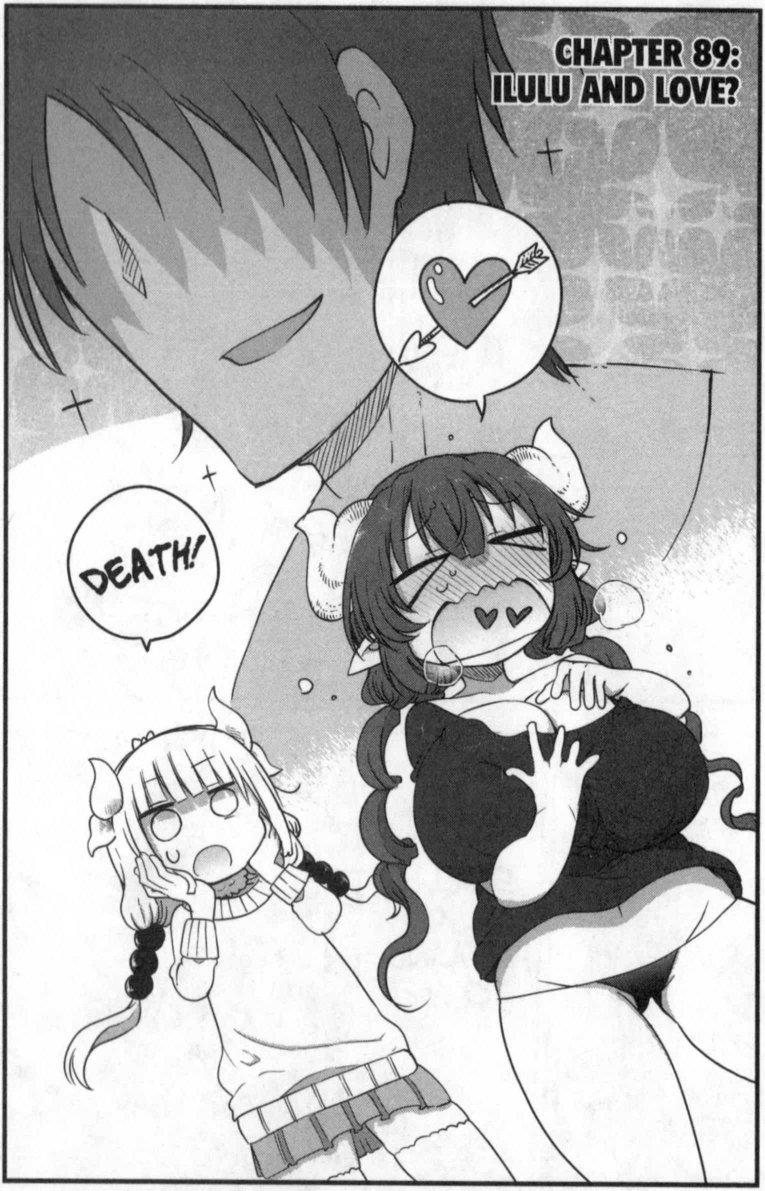
CHAPTER 89:
ILULU AND LOVE?
DEATH!

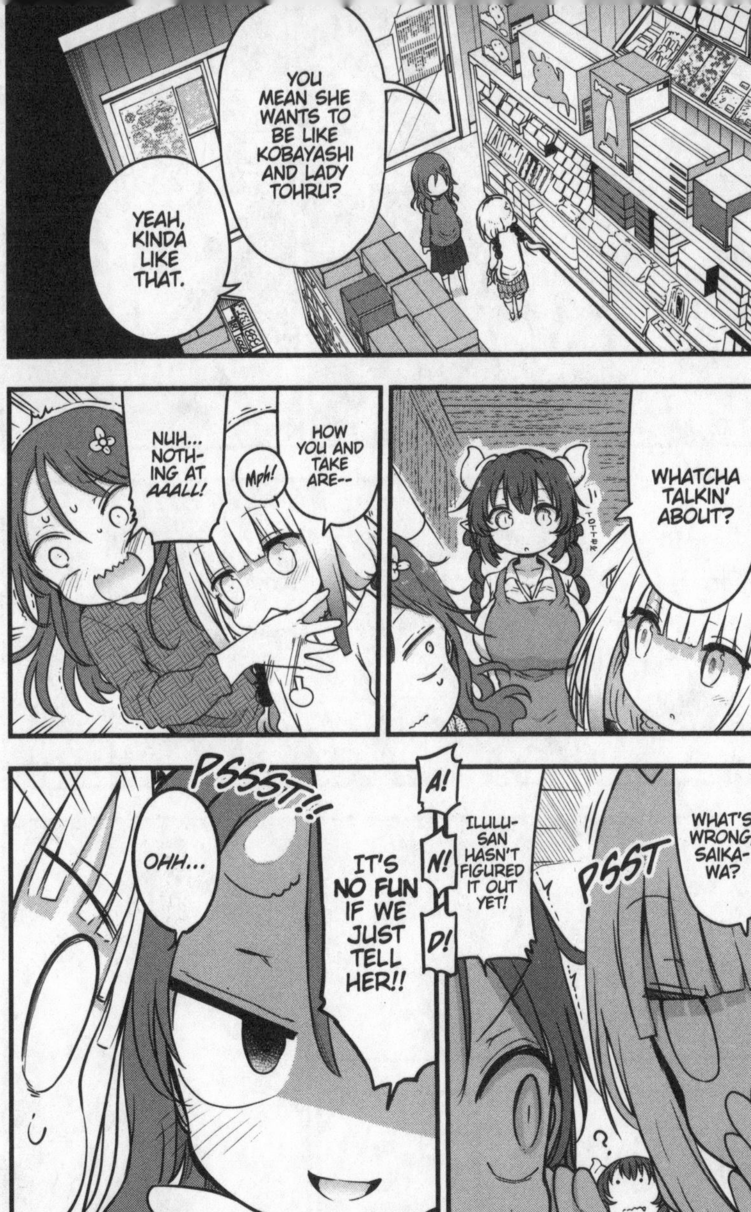
YOU MEAN SHE WANTS TO BE LIKE KOBAYASHI AND LADY TOHRU?
YEAH, KINDA LIKE THAT.
WHATCHA TALKIN' ABOUT?
TOTTER
HOW YOU AND TAKE ARE--
Mph!
NUH... NOTHING AT AAALL!
WHAT'S WRONG, SAIKAWA?
PSST
ILULU-SAN HASN'T FIGURED IT OUT YET!
A! N! D!
IT'S NO FUN IF WE JUST TELL HER!!
PSSST!!!
OHH...
PSST

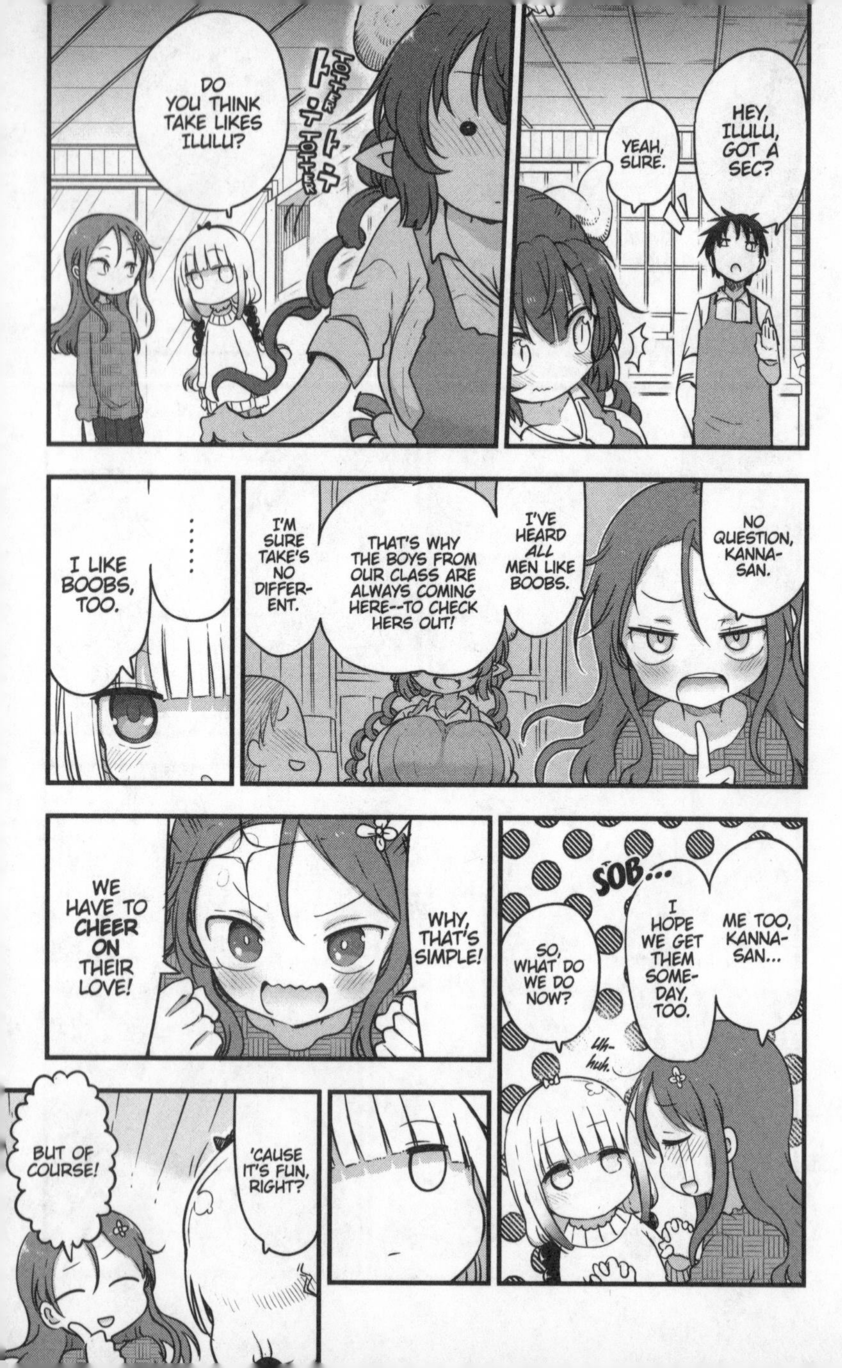
HEY, ILULU, GOT A SEC?
YEAH, SURE.
TOTTER TOTTER
DO YOU THINK TAKE LIKES ILULU?
NO QUESTION, KANNA-SAN.
I'VE HEARD *ALL* MEN LIKE BOOBS.
THAT'S WHY THE BOYS FROM OUR CLASS ARE ALWAYS COMING HERE--TO CHECK HERS OUT!
I'M SURE TAKE'S NO DIFFERENT.
......
I LIKE BOOBS, TOO.
SOB...
ME TOO, KANNA-SAN...
I HOPE WE GET THEM SOMEDAY, TOO.
Uh-huh.
SO, WHAT DO WE DO NOW?
WHY, THAT'S SIMPLE!
WE HAVE TO **CHEER ON** THEIR LOVE!
'CAUSE IT'S FUN, RIGHT?
BUT OF COURSE!

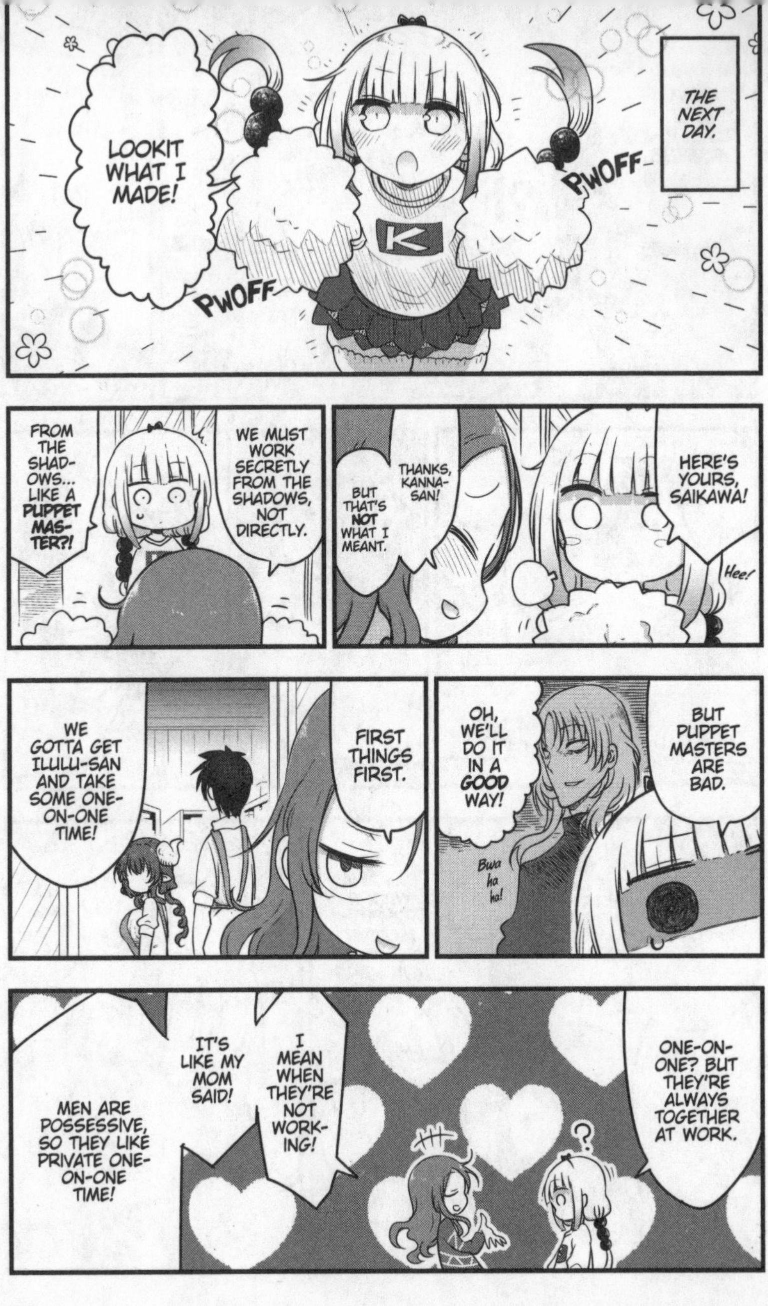
THE NEXT DAY.
PWOFF
LOOKIT WHAT I MADE!
PWOFF
HERE'S YOURS, SAIKAWA!
Hee!
THANKS, KANNA-SAN!
BUT THAT'S NOT WHAT I MEANT.
WE MUST WORK SECRETLY FROM THE SHADOWS, NOT DIRECTLY.
FROM THE SHADOWS... LIKE A PUPPET MASTER?!
BUT PUPPET MASTERS ARE BAD.
OH, WE'LL DO IT IN A GOOD WAY!
Bwa ha ha!
FIRST THINGS FIRST.
WE GOTTA GET ILULU-SAN AND TAKE SOME ONE-ON-ONE TIME!
ONE-ON-ONE? BUT THEY'RE ALWAYS TOGETHER AT WORK.
I MEAN WHEN THEY'RE NOT WORKING!
IT'S LIKE MY MOM SAID!
MEN ARE POSSESSIVE, SO THEY LIKE PRIVATE ONE-ON-ONE TIME!

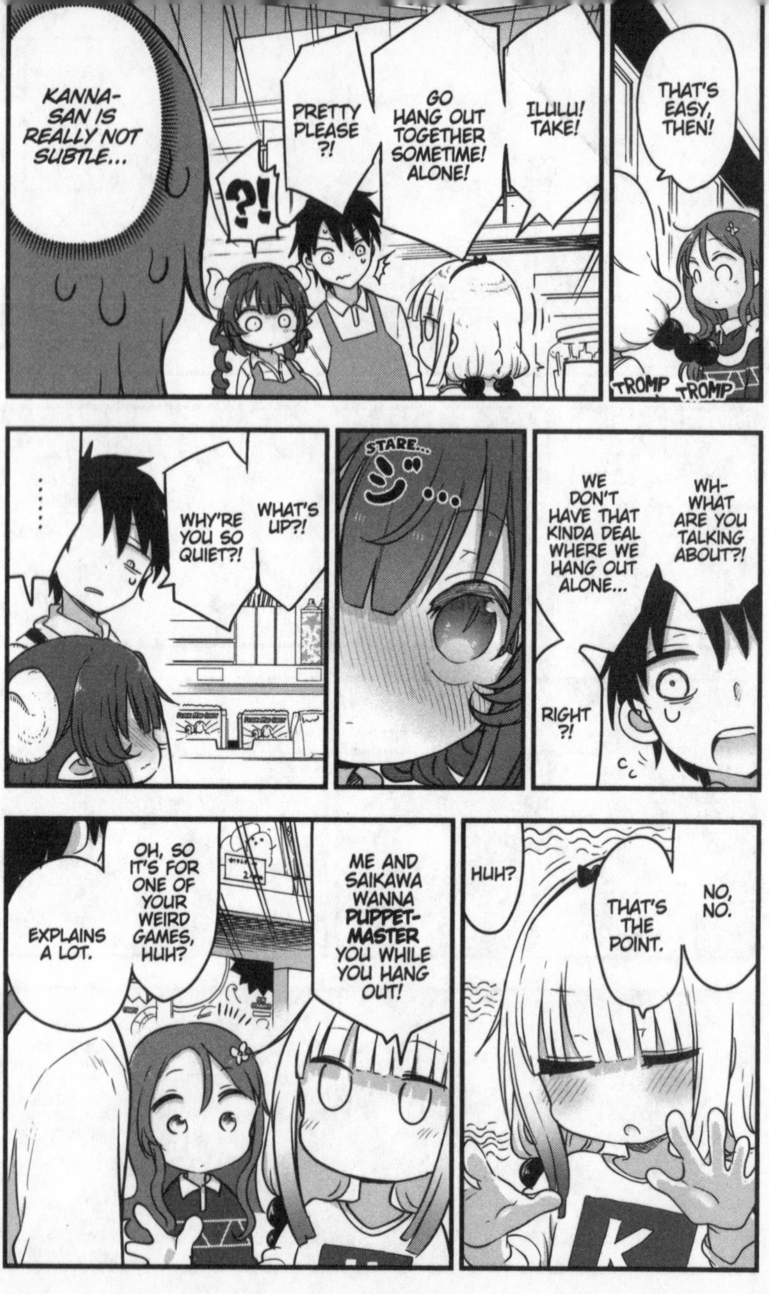
THAT'S EASY, THEN!
TROMP TROMP
ILULU! TAKE!
GO HANG OUT TOGETHER SOMETIME! ALONE!
PRETTY PLEASE ?!
?!
KANNA-SAN IS REALLY NOT SUBTLE...
WH- WHAT ARE YOU TALKING ABOUT?!
WE DON'T HAVE THAT KINDA DEAL WHERE WE HANG OUT ALONE...
RIGHT ?!
STARE...
...
WHAT'S UP?!
WHY'RE YOU SO QUIET?!
......
NO, NO.
THAT'S THE POINT.
HUH?
ME AND SAIKAWA WANNA PUPPET-MASTER YOU WHILE YOU HANG OUT!
OH, SO IT'S FOR ONE OF YOUR WEIRD GAMES, HUH?
EXPLAINS A LOT.

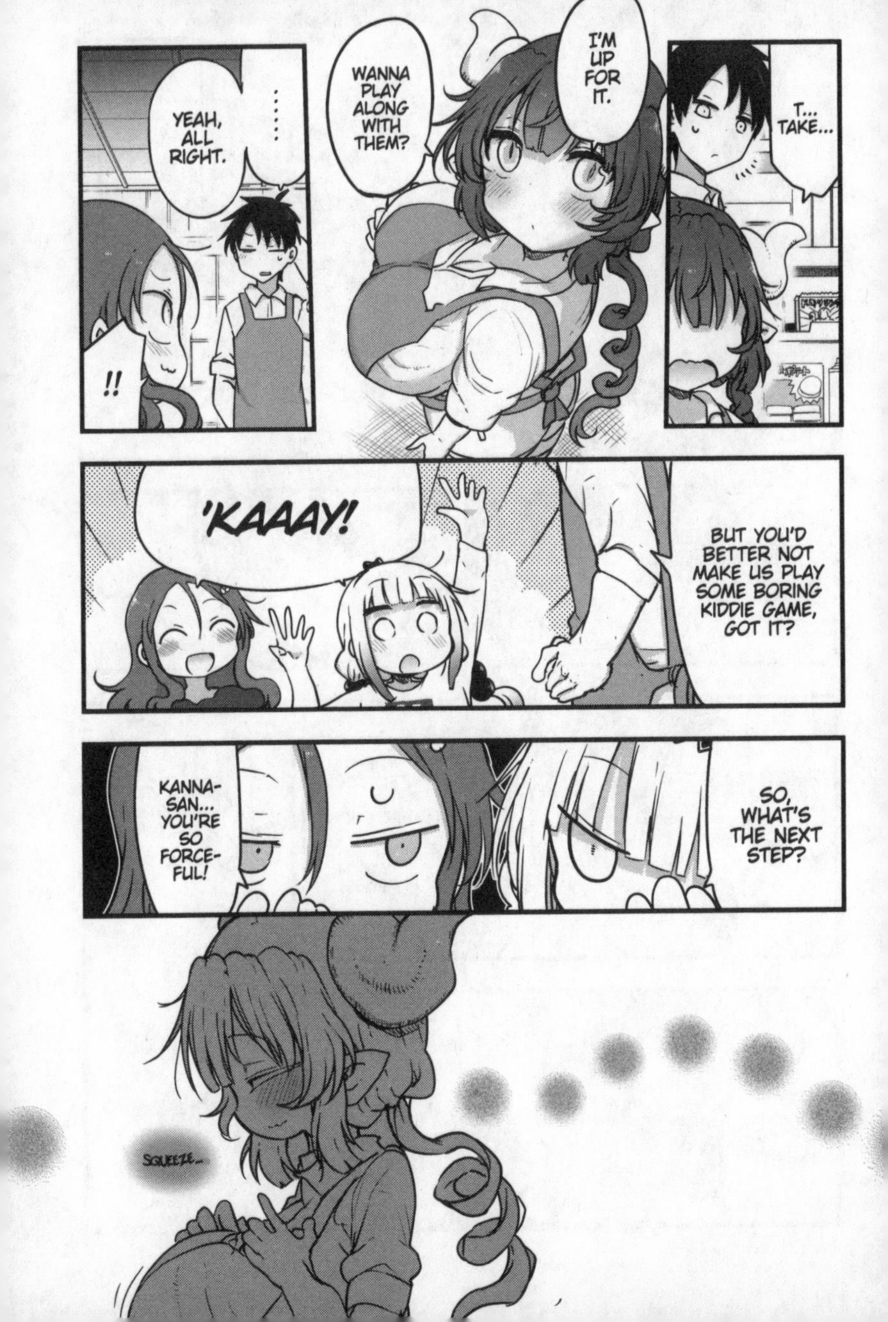
T... TAKE...
I'M UP FOR IT.
WANNA PLAY ALONG WITH THEM?
......
YEAH, ALL RIGHT.
!!
BUT YOU'D BETTER NOT MAKE US PLAY SOME BORING KIDDIE GAME, GOT IT?
'KAAAY!
SO, WHAT'S THE NEXT STEP?
KANNA-SAN... YOU'RE SO FORCE-FUL!
SQUEEZE...

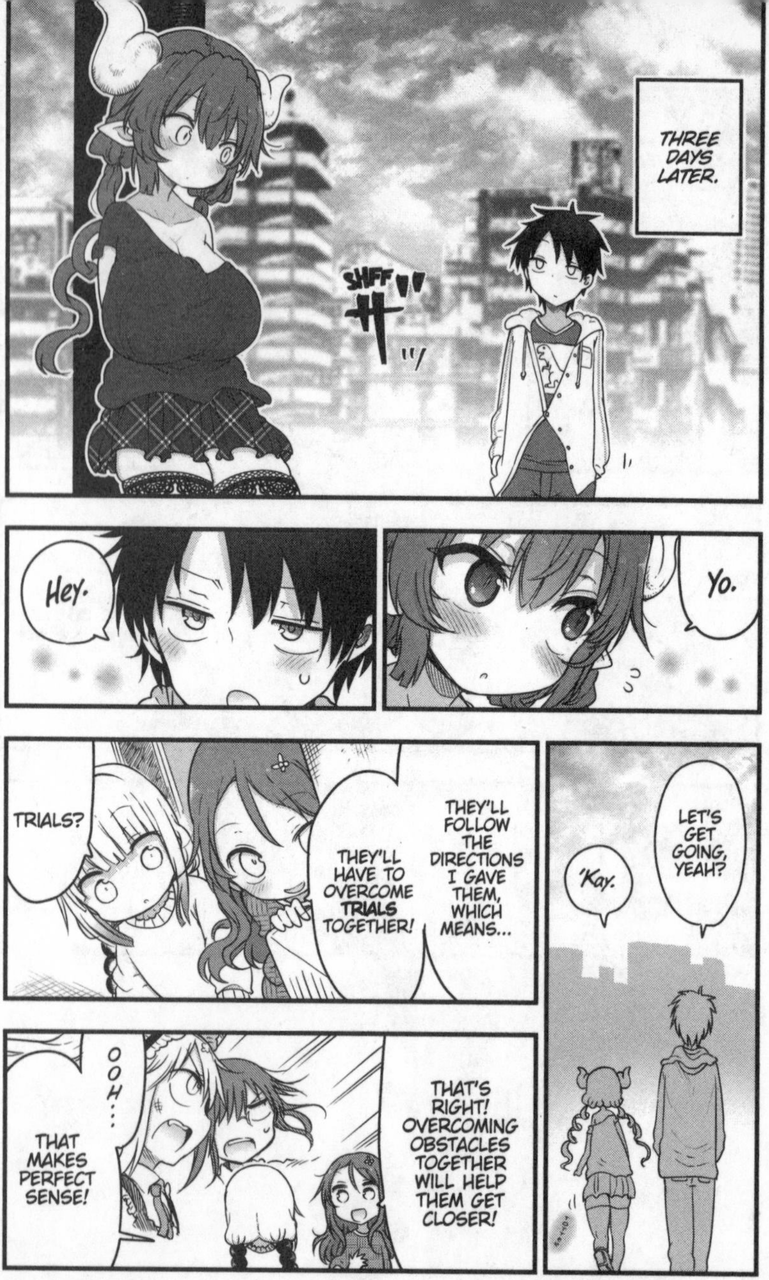
THREE DAYS LATER.
SHFF
Yo.
Hey.
LET'S GET GOING, YEAH?
'Kay.
THEY'LL FOLLOW THE DIRECTIONS I GAVE THEM, WHICH MEANS...
THEY'LL HAVE TO OVERCOME TRIALS TOGETHER!
TRIALS?
THAT'S RIGHT! OVERCOMING OBSTACLES TOGETHER WILL HELP THEM GET CLOSER!
OOH...
THAT MAKES PERFECT SENSE!

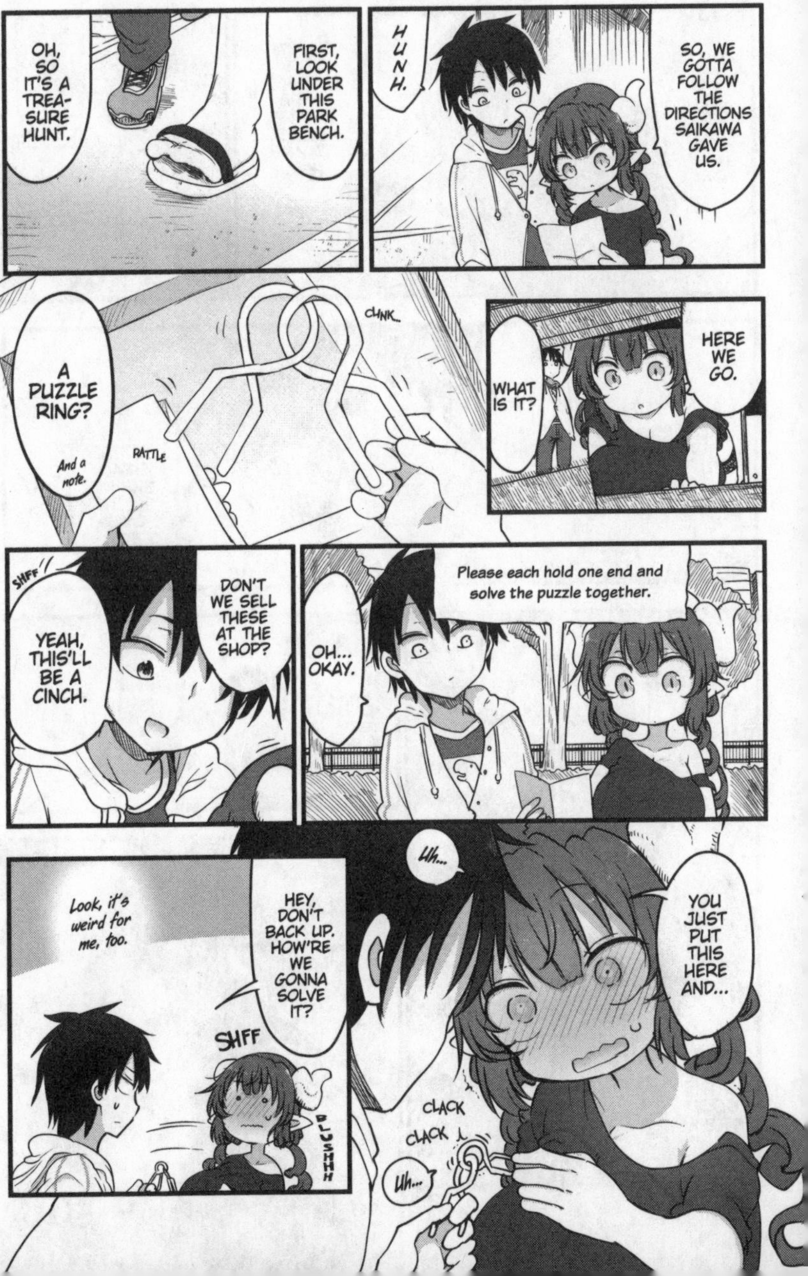
SO, WE GOTTA FOLLOW THE DIRECTIONS SAIKAWA GAVE US.
HUNH.
FIRST, LOOK UNDER THIS PARK BENCH.
OH, SO IT'S A TREA-SURE HUNT.
HERE WE GO.
WHAT IS IT?
CLINK...
A PUZZLE RING?
RATTLE
And a note.
Please each hold one end and solve the puzzle together.
OH... OKAY.
DON'T WE SELL THESE AT THE SHOP?
SHFF
YEAH, THIS'LL BE A CINCH.
Uh...
YOU JUST PUT THIS HERE AND...
CLACK
CLACK
Uh...
HEY, DON'T BACK UP. HOW'RE WE GONNA SOLVE IT?
SHFF
BLUSHHH
Look, it's weird for me, too.

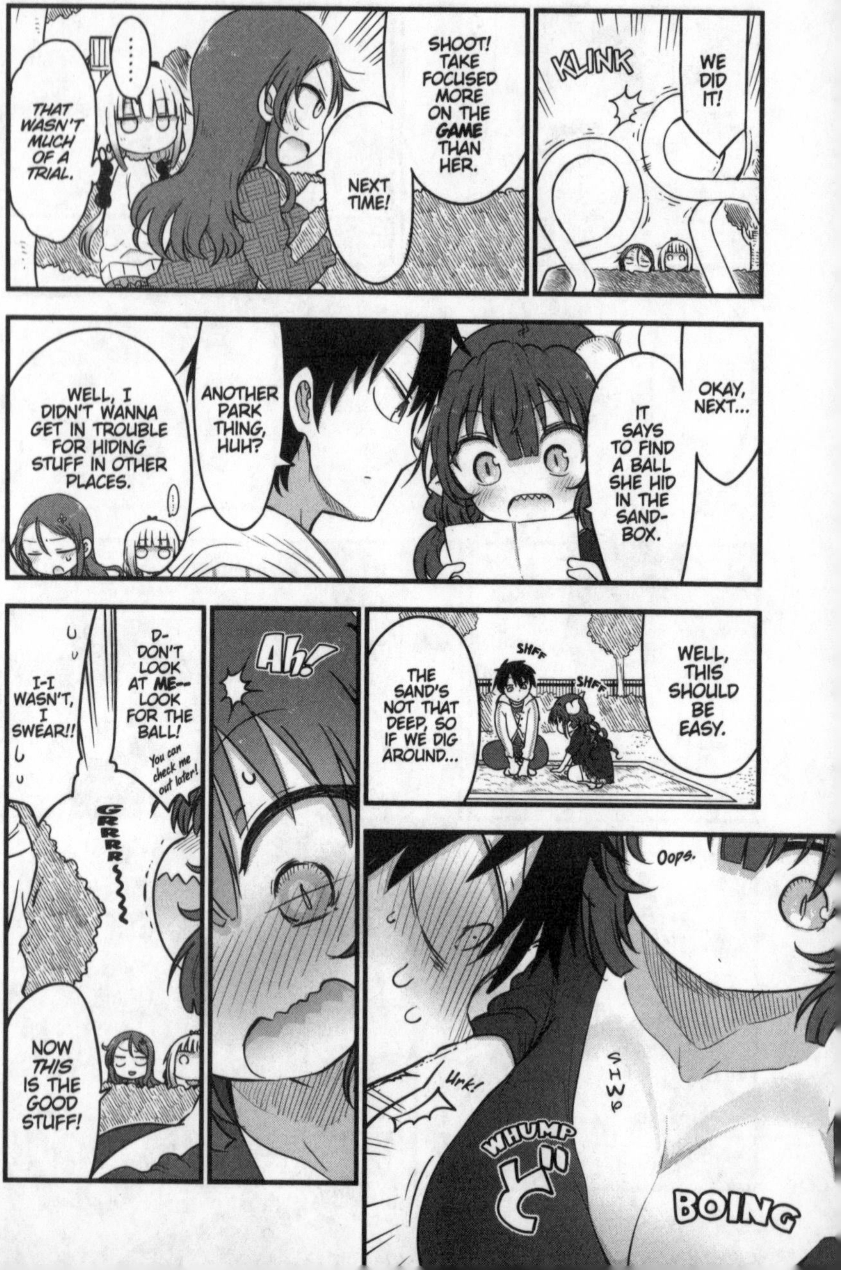
KLINK
WE DID IT!
SHOOT! TAKE FOCUSED MORE ON THE GAME THAN HER.
NEXT TIME!
......
THAT WASN'T MUCH OF A TRIAL.
OKAY, NEXT...
IT SAYS TO FIND A BALL SHE HID IN THE SAND-BOX.
ANOTHER PARK THING, HUH?
WELL, I DIDN'T WANNA GET IN TROUBLE FOR HIDING STUFF IN OTHER PLACES.
...
WELL, THIS SHOULD BE EASY.
SHFF
SHFF
THE SAND'S NOT THAT DEEP, SO IF WE DIG AROUND...
Oops.
SHWP
Urk!
WHUMP
BOING
Ah!
D-DON'T LOOK AT ME-- LOOK FOR THE BALL!
You can check me out later!
I-I WASN'T, I SWEAR!!
GRRRR
NOW THIS IS THE GOOD STUFF!

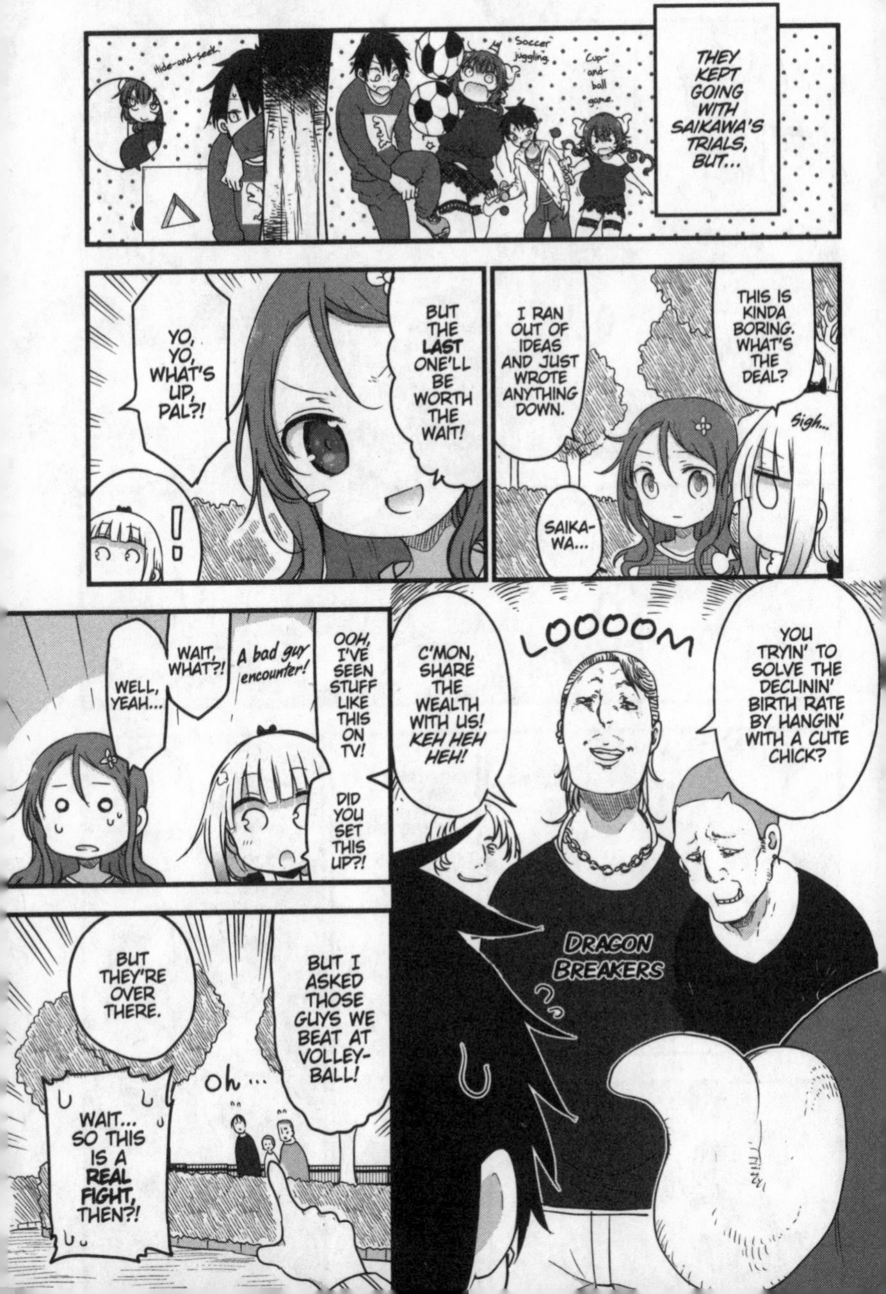
THEY KEPT GOING WITH SAIKAWA'S TRIALS, BUT...
Cup-and-ball game.
Soccer juggling.
Hide-and-seek
THIS IS KINDA BORING. WHAT'S THE DEAL?
Sigh...
I RAN OUT OF IDEAS AND JUST WROTE ANYTHING DOWN.
SAIKA-WA...
BUT THE LAST ONE'LL BE WORTH THE WAIT!
YO, YO, WHAT'S UP, PAL?!
!
YOU TRYIN' TO SOLVE THE DECLININ' BIRTH RATE BY HANGIN' WITH A CUTE CHICK?
LOOOOM
C'MON, SHARE THE WEALTH WITH US! KEH HEH HEH!
DRAGON BREAKERS
OOH, I'VE SEEN STUFF LIKE THIS ON TV!
A bad guy encounter!
WAIT, WHAT?!
DID YOU SET THIS UP?!
WELL, YEAH...
BUT I ASKED THOSE GUYS WE BEAT AT VOLLEY-BALL!
BUT THEY'RE OVER THERE.
oh...
WAIT... SO THIS IS A REAL FIGHT, THEN?!

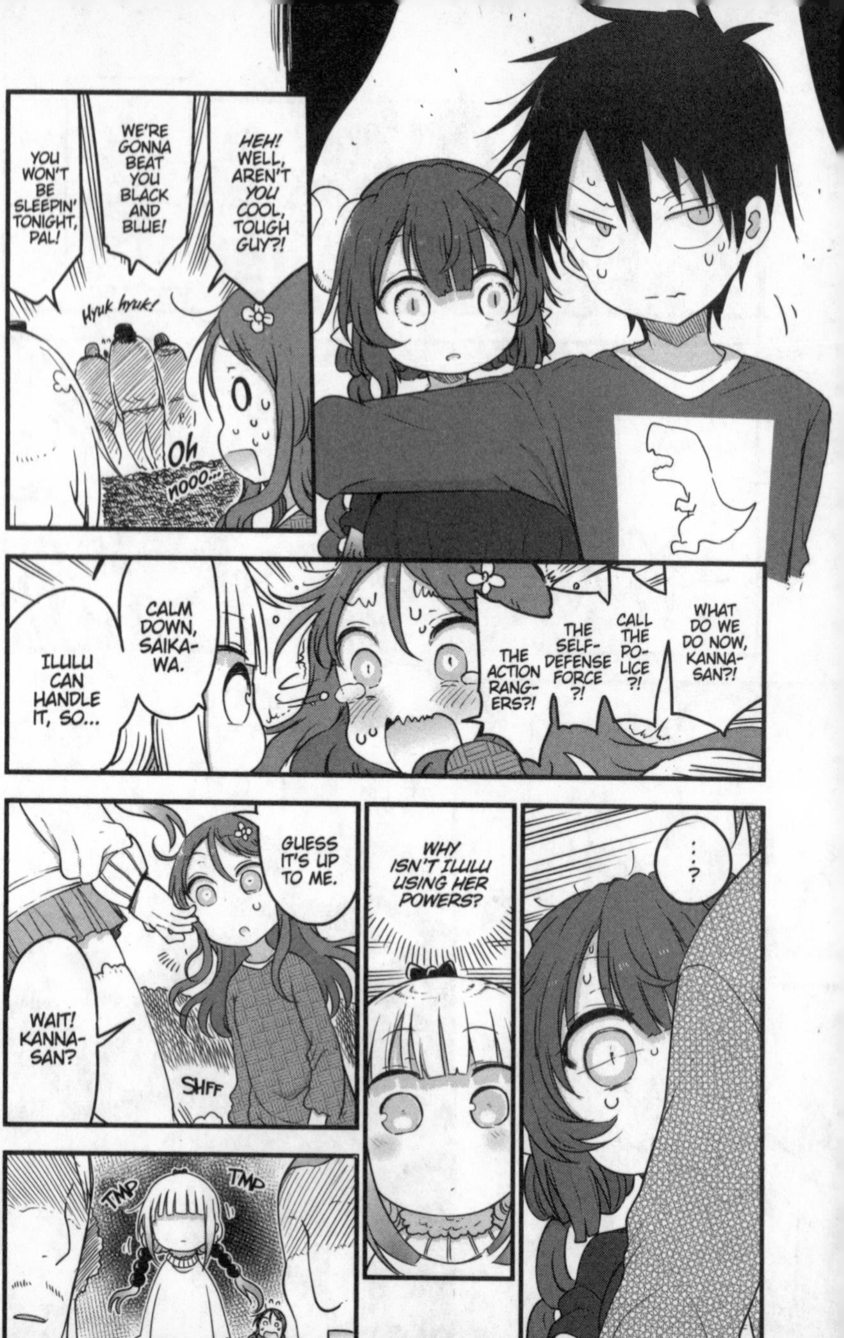
HEH! WELL, AREN'T YOU COOL, TOUGH GUY?!
WE'RE GONNA BEAT YOU BLACK AND BLUE!
YOU WON'T BE SLEEPIN' TONIGHT, PAL!
Hyuk hyuk!
Oh nooo...
WHAT DO WE DO NOW, KANNA-SAN?!
CALL THE POLICE?!
THE SELF-DEFENSE FORCE?!
THE ACTION RANGERS?!
CALM DOWN, SAIKAWA.
ILULU CAN HANDLE IT, SO...
...?
WHY ISN'T ILULU USING HER POWERS?
GUESS IT'S UP TO ME.
WAIT! KANNA-SAN?
SHFF
TMP
TMP

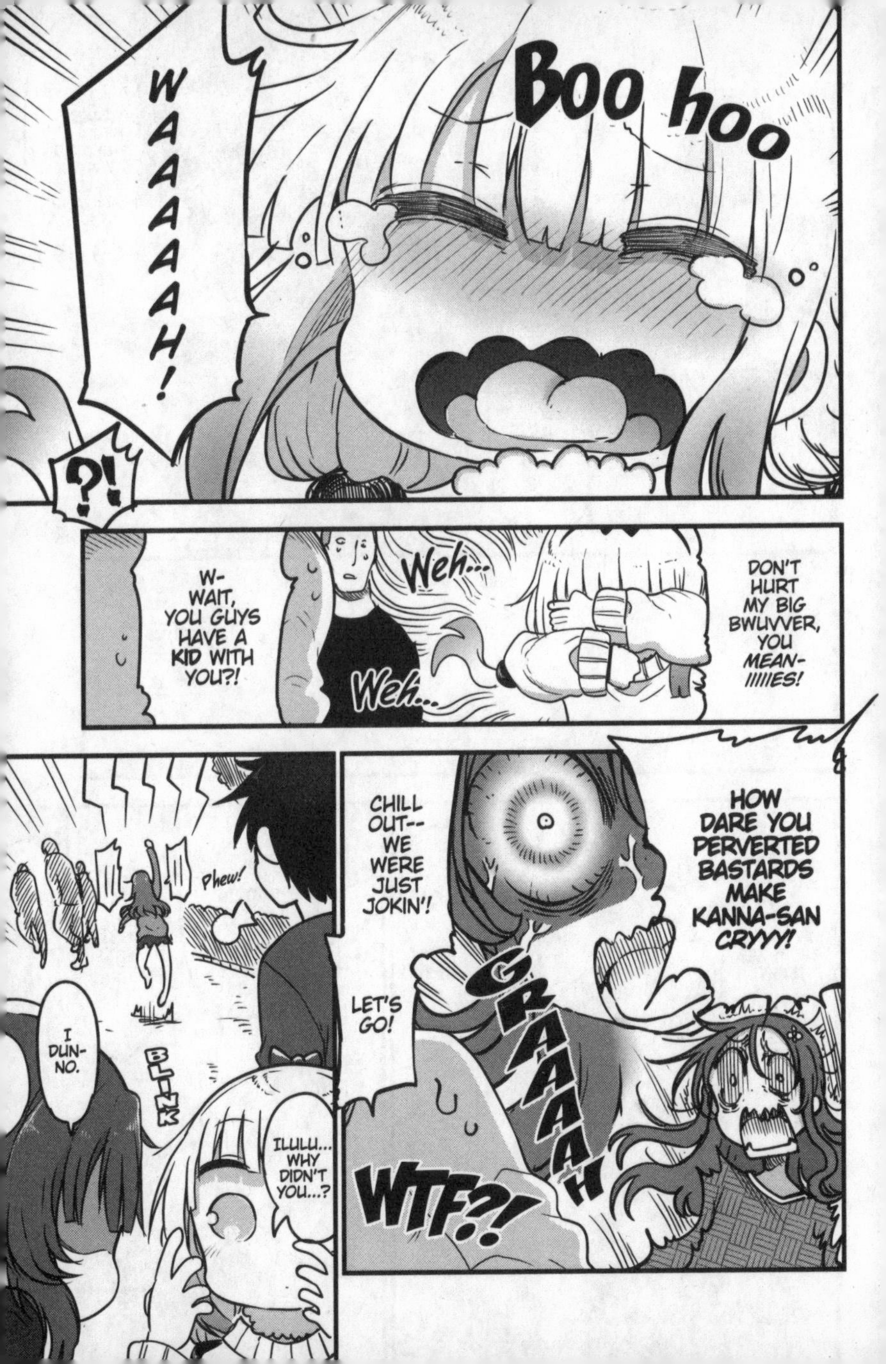

Boo hoo
WAAAAAAH!
?!
DON'T HURT MY BIG BWUVVER, YOU MEAN-IIIIIES!
Weh...
Weh...
W-WAIT, YOU GUYS HAVE A KID WITH YOU?!
HOW DARE YOU PERVERTED BASTARDS MAKE KANNA-SAN CRYYY!
CHILL OUT-- WE WERE JUST JOKIN'!
GRAAAAH
LET'S GO!
WTF?!
Phew!
BLINK
ILULU... WHY DIDN'T YOU...?
I DUN-NO.

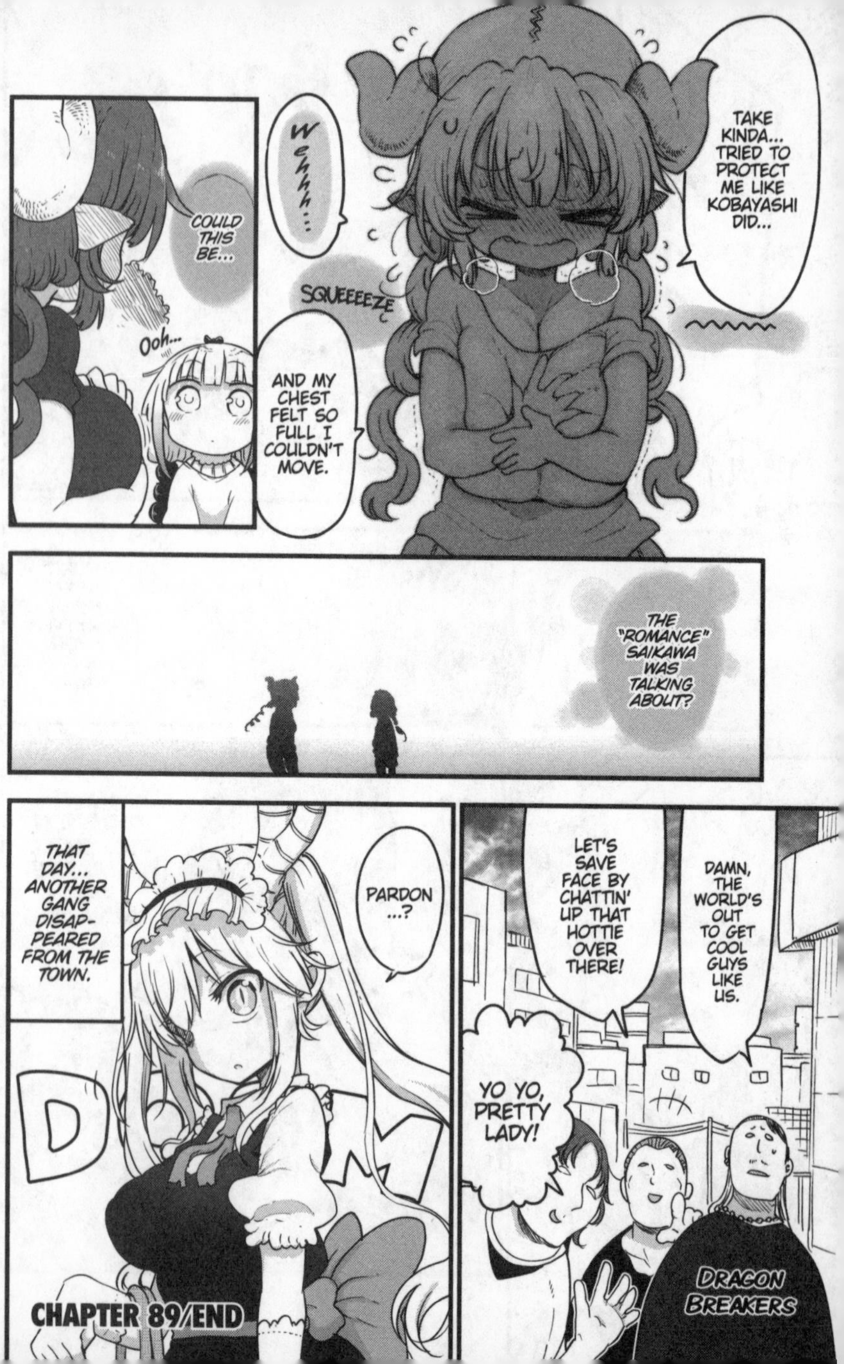
TAKE KINDA... TRIED TO PROTECT ME LIKE KOBAYASHI DID...
Wehhh...
SQUEEEEZE
AND MY CHEST FELT SO FULL I COULDN'T MOVE.
COULD THIS BE...
Ooh...
THE "ROMANCE" SAIKAWA WAS TALKING ABOUT?
DAMN, THE WORLD'S OUT TO GET COOL GUYS LIKE US.
LET'S SAVE FACE BY CHATTIN' UP THAT HOTTIE OVER THERE!
YO YO, PRETTY LADY!
DRAGON BREAKERS
PARDON ...?
THAT DAY... ANOTHER GANG DISAP-PEARED FROM THE TOWN.
CHAPTER 89/END

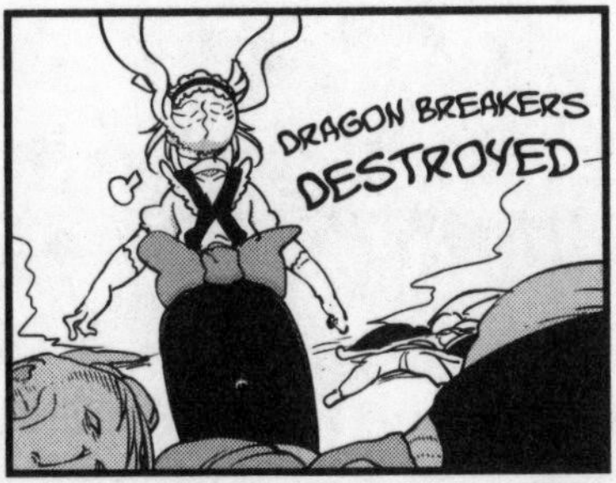
DRAGON BREAKERS
DESTROYED

Miss Kobayashi's
Dragon Maid

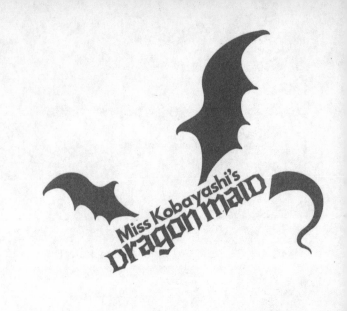

CHAPTER 90

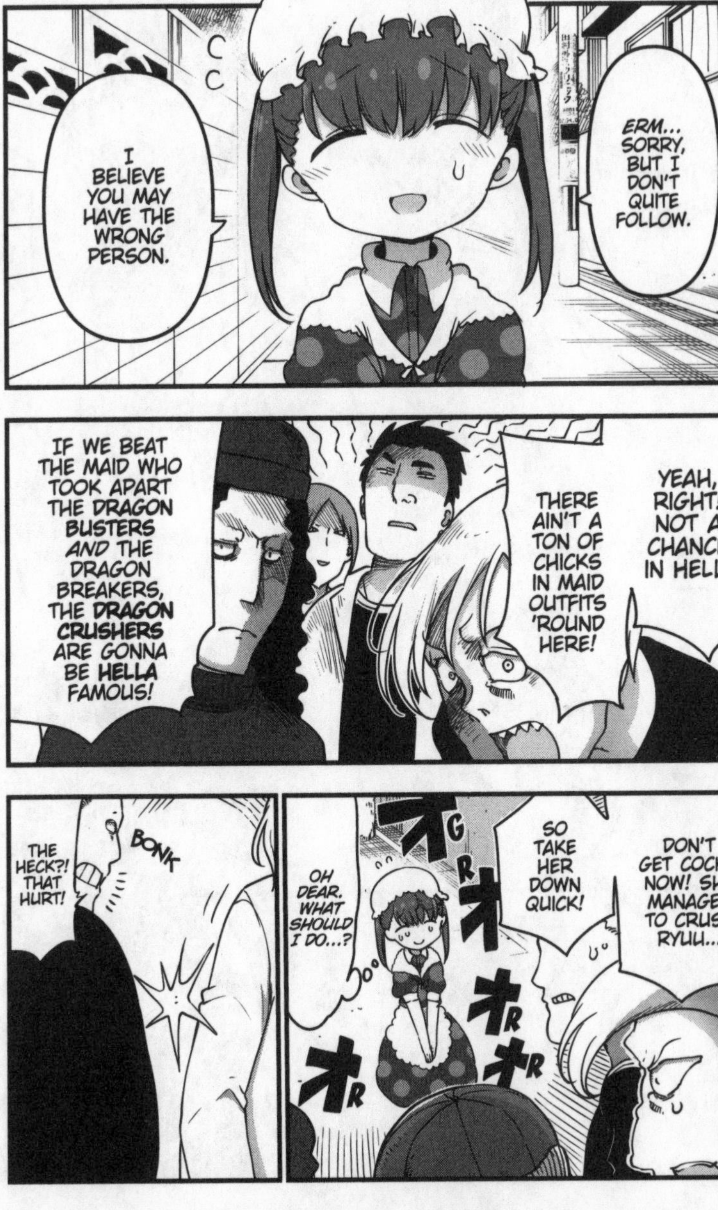
ERM... SORRY, BUT I DON'T QUITE FOLLOW.
I BELIEVE YOU MAY HAVE THE WRONG PERSON.
YEAH, RIGHT! NOT A CHANCE IN HELL!
THERE AIN'T A TON OF CHICKS IN MAID OUTFITS 'ROUND HERE!
IF WE BEAT THE MAID WHO TOOK APART THE DRAGON BUSTERS AND THE DRAGON BREAKERS, THE DRAGON CRUSHERS ARE GONNA BE HELLA FAMOUS!
DON'T GET COCKY, NOW! SHE MANAGED TO CRUSH RYUU...
SO TAKE HER DOWN QUICK!
OH DEAR. WHAT SHOULD I DO...?
BONK
THE HECK?! THAT HURT!

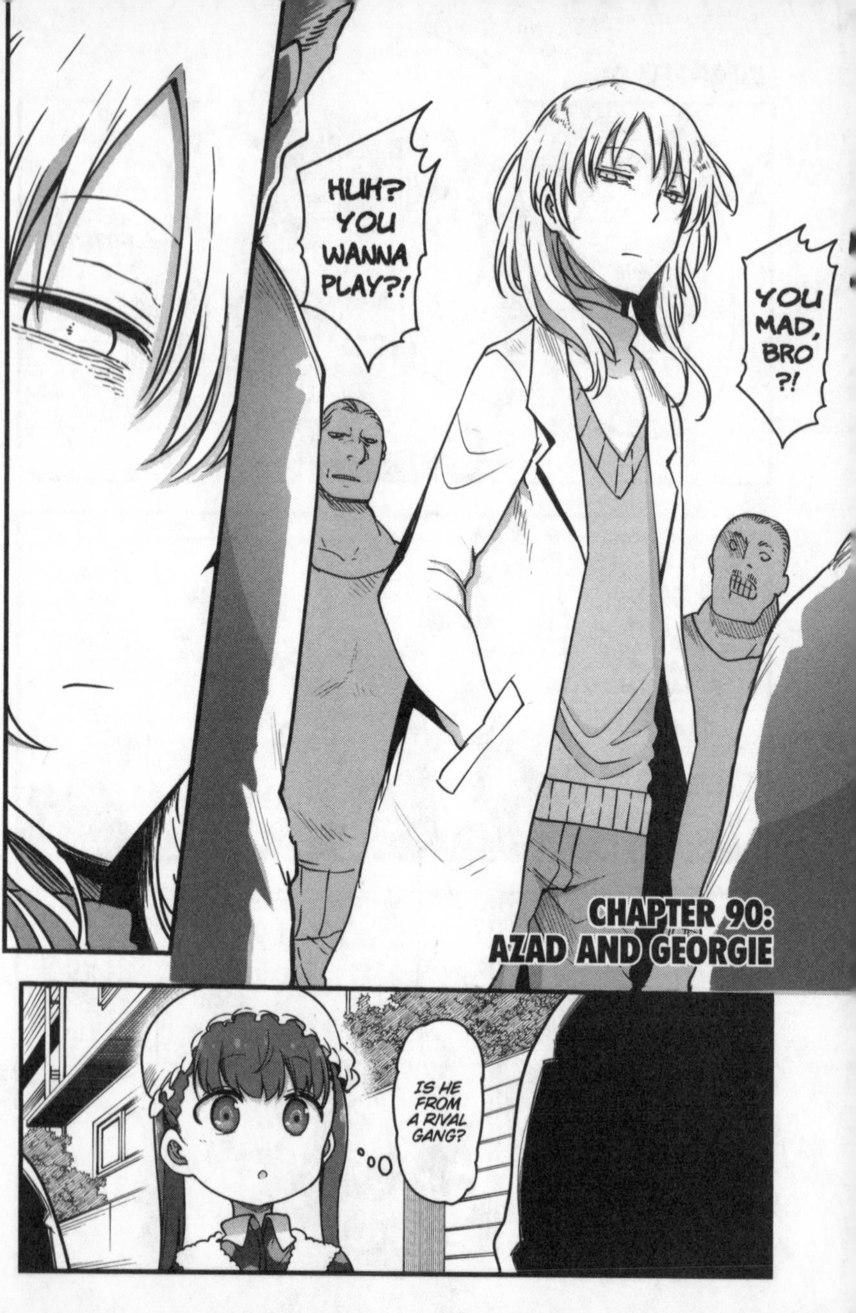
YOU MAD, BRO ?!
HUH? YOU WANNA PLAY?!
CHAPTER 90: AZAD AND GEORGIE
IS HE FROM A RIVAL GANG?

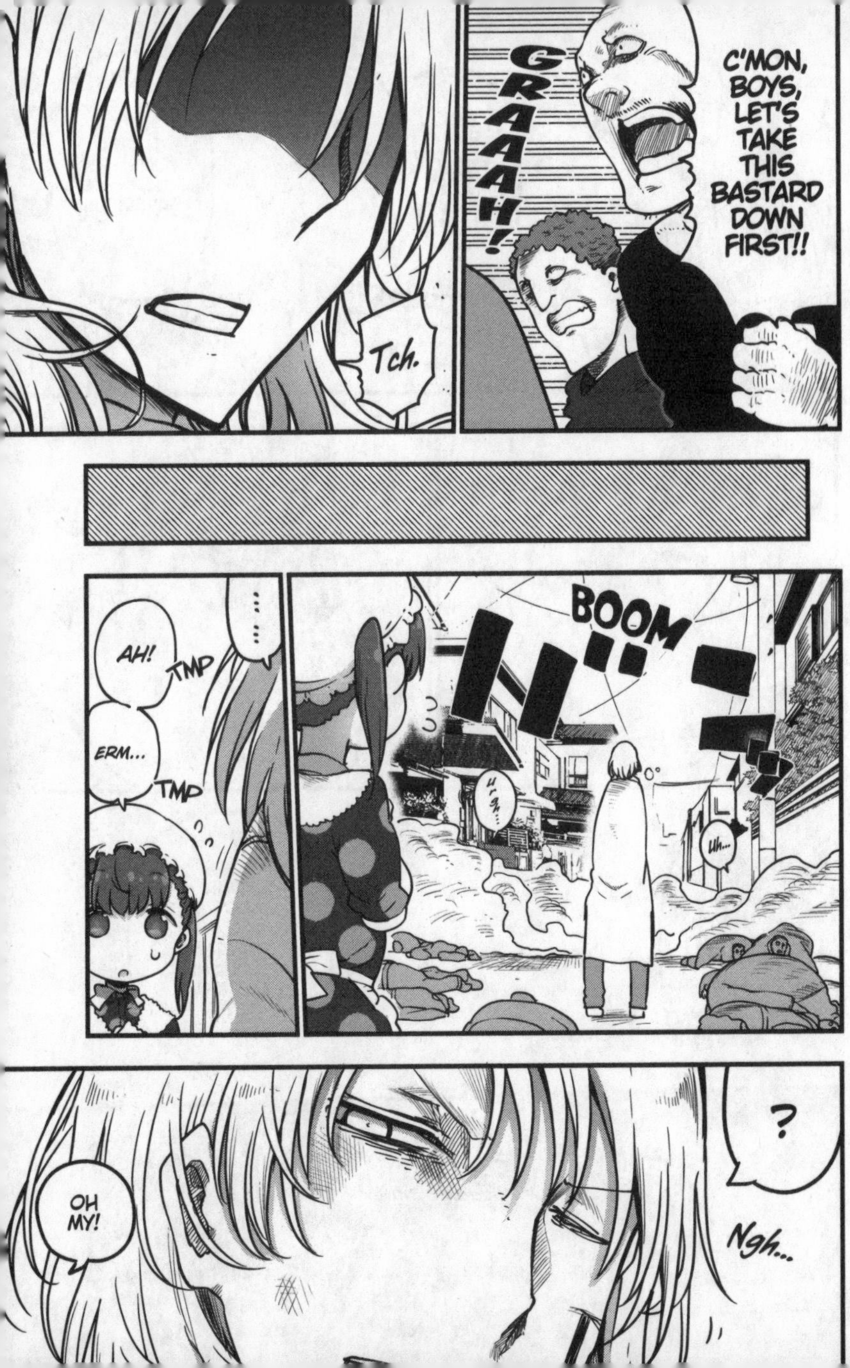
GRAAAAH!
C'MON, BOYS, LET'S TAKE THIS BASTARD DOWN FIRST!!
Tch.
BOOM
Uh...
...
AH!
TMP
ERM...
TMP
?
Ngh...
OH MY!

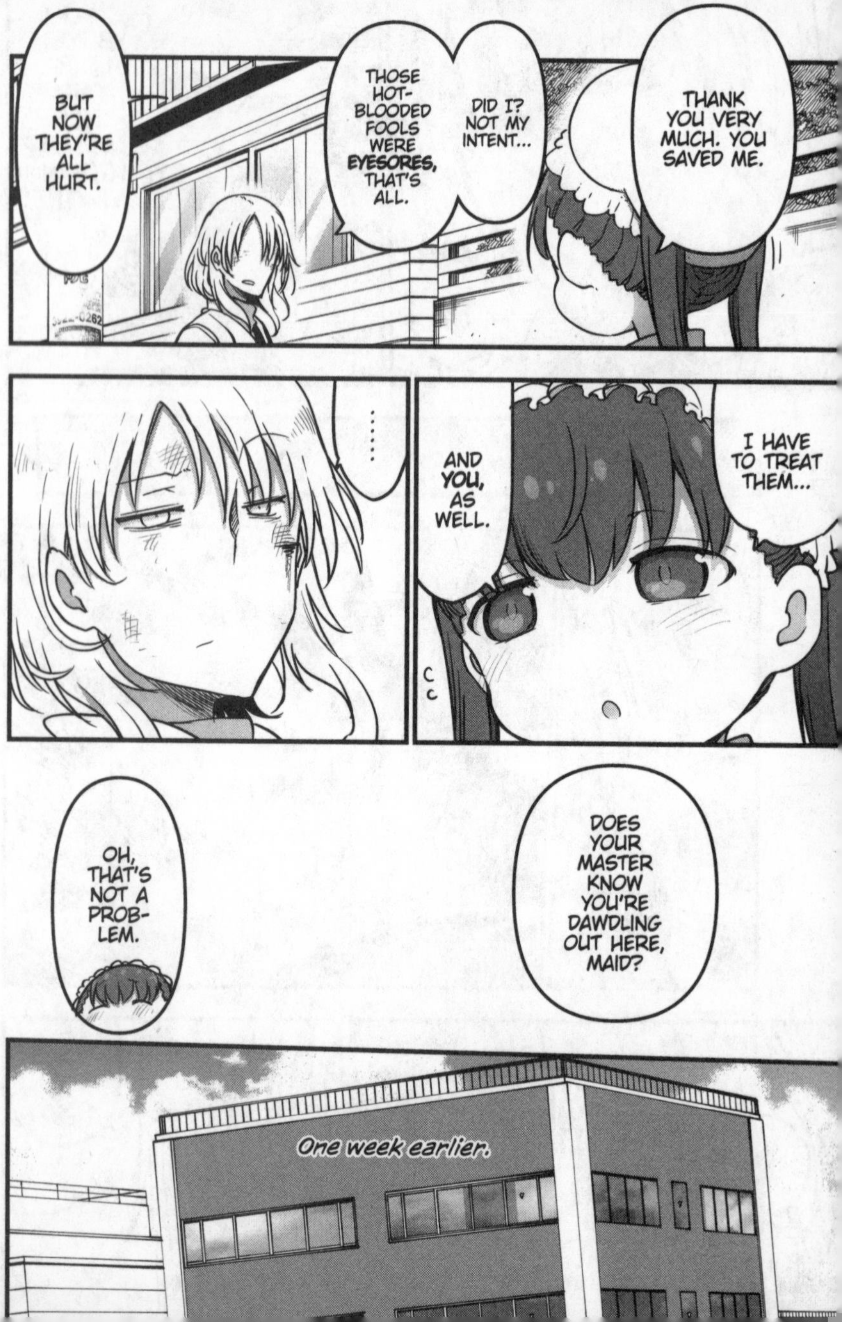
THANK YOU VERY MUCH. YOU SAVED ME.
DID I? NOT MY INTENT...
THOSE HOT-BLOODED FOOLS WERE **EYESORES,** THAT'S ALL.
BUT NOW THEY'RE ALL HURT.
I HAVE TO TREAT THEM...
AND **YOU,** AS WELL.
......
DOES YOUR MASTER KNOW YOU'RE DAWDLING OUT HERE, MAID?
OH, THAT'S NOT A PROBLEM.
One week earlier.

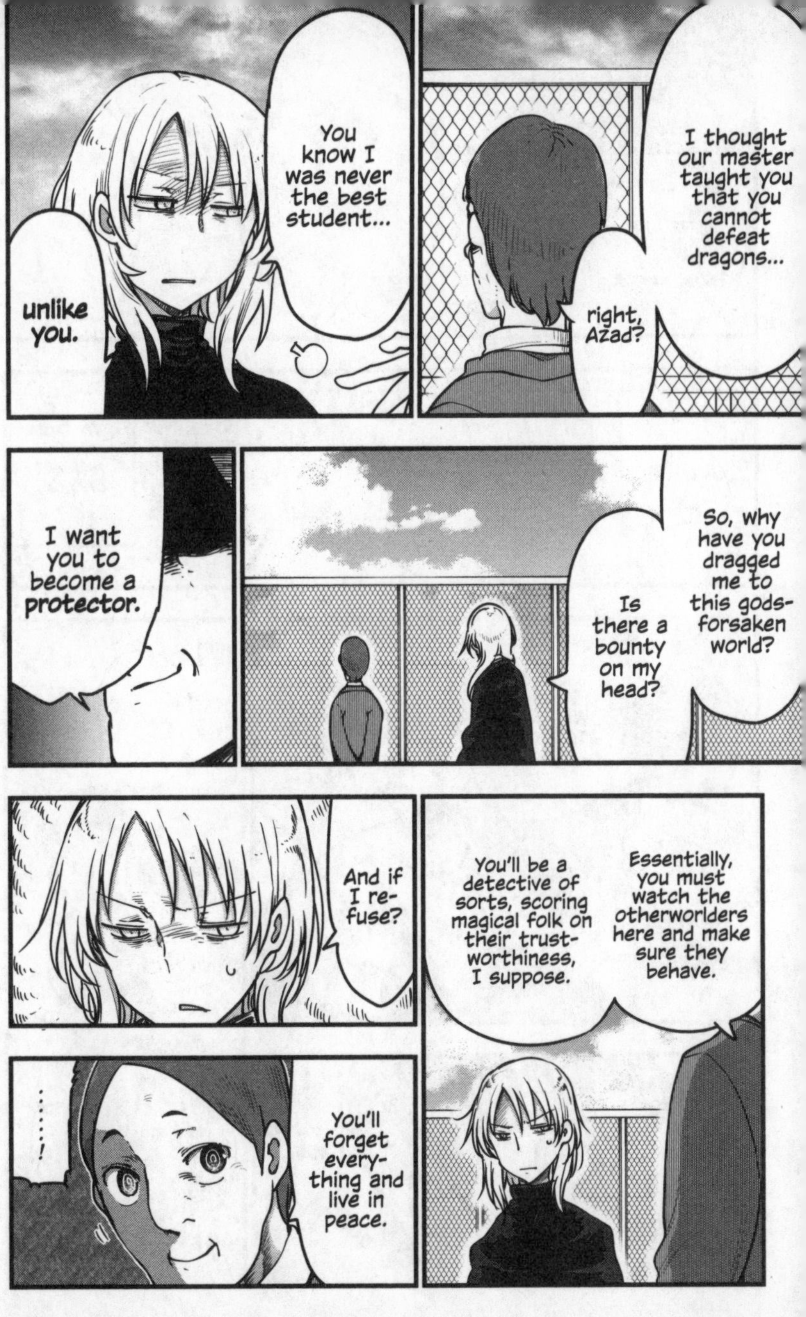

I thought our master taught you that you cannot defeat dragons...
right, Azad?
You know I was never the best student...
unlike you.
So, why have you dragged me to this gods-forsaken world?
Is there a bounty on my head?
I want you to become a protector.
Essentially, you must watch the otherworlders here and make sure they behave.
You'll be a detective of sorts, scoring magical folk on their trust-worthiness, I suppose.
And if I re-fuse?
You'll forget every-thing and live in peace.
......!

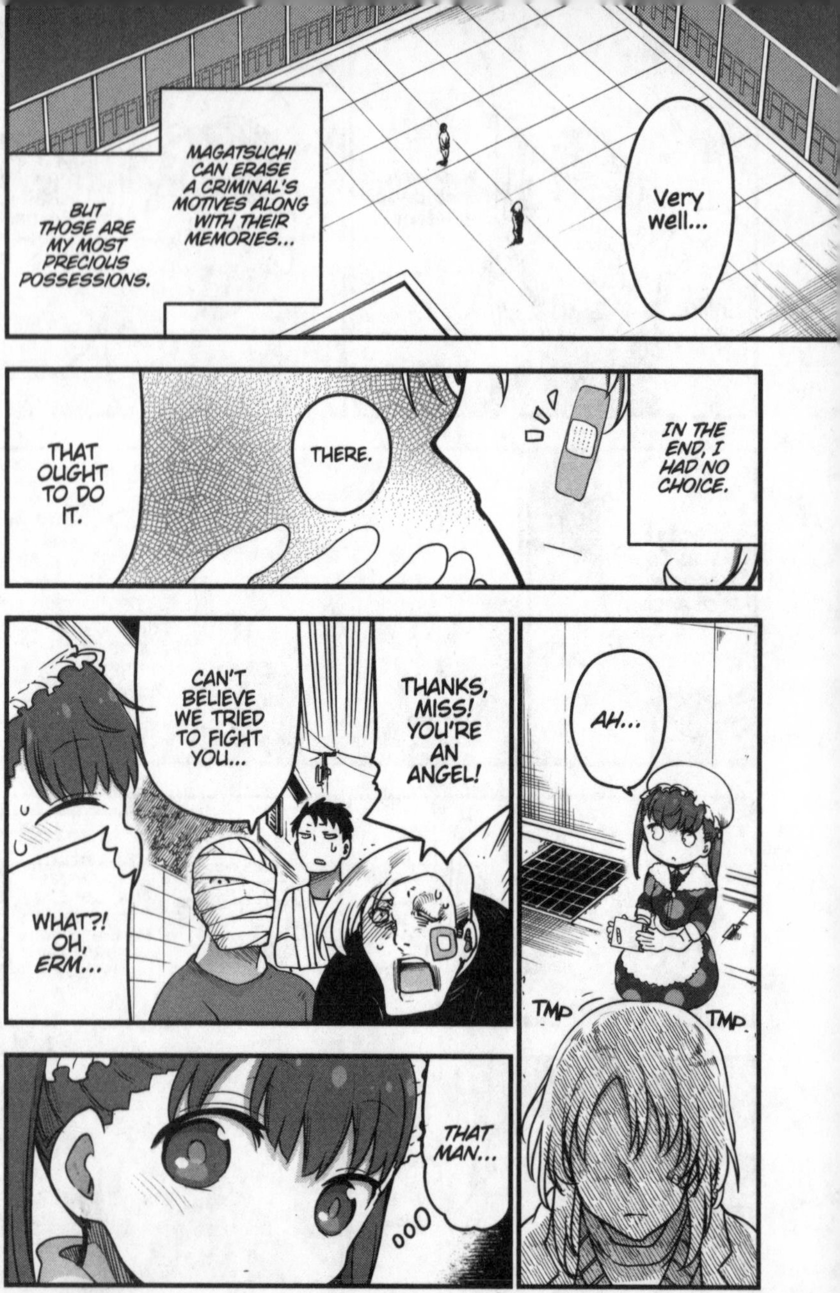
Very well...
MAGATSUCHI CAN ERASE A CRIMINAL'S MOTIVES ALONG WITH THEIR MEMORIES...
BUT THOSE ARE MY MOST PRECIOUS POSSESSIONS.
IN THE END, I HAD NO CHOICE.
THERE.
THAT OUGHT TO DO IT.
AH...
TMP
TMP
THANKS, MISS! YOU'RE AN ANGEL!
CAN'T BELIEVE WE TRIED TO FIGHT YOU...
WHAT?! OH, ERM...
THAT MAN...

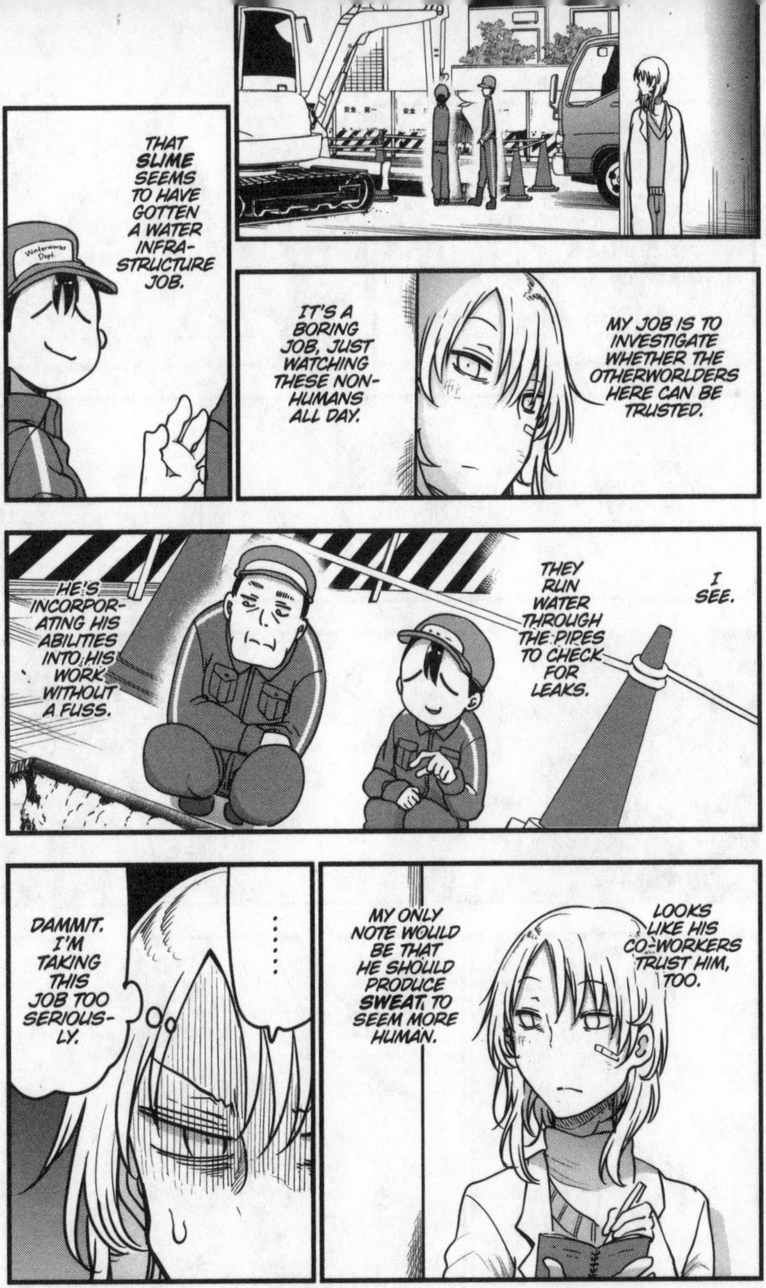
MY JOB IS TO INVESTIGATE WHETHER THE OTHERWORLDERS HERE CAN BE TRUSTED.
IT'S A BORING JOB, JUST WATCHING THESE NON-HUMANS ALL DAY.
THAT SLIME SEEMS TO HAVE GOTTEN A WATER INFRA-STRUCTURE JOB.
Waterworks Dept.
I SEE.
THEY RUN WATER THROUGH THE PIPES TO CHECK FOR LEAKS.
HE'S INCORPOR-ATING HIS ABILITIES INTO HIS WORK WITHOUT A FUSS.
LOOKS LIKE HIS CO-WORKERS TRUST HIM, TOO.
MY ONLY NOTE WOULD BE THAT HE SHOULD PRODUCE SWEAT, TO SEEM MORE HUMAN.
......
DAMMIT. I'M TAKING THIS JOB TOO SERIOUS-LY.

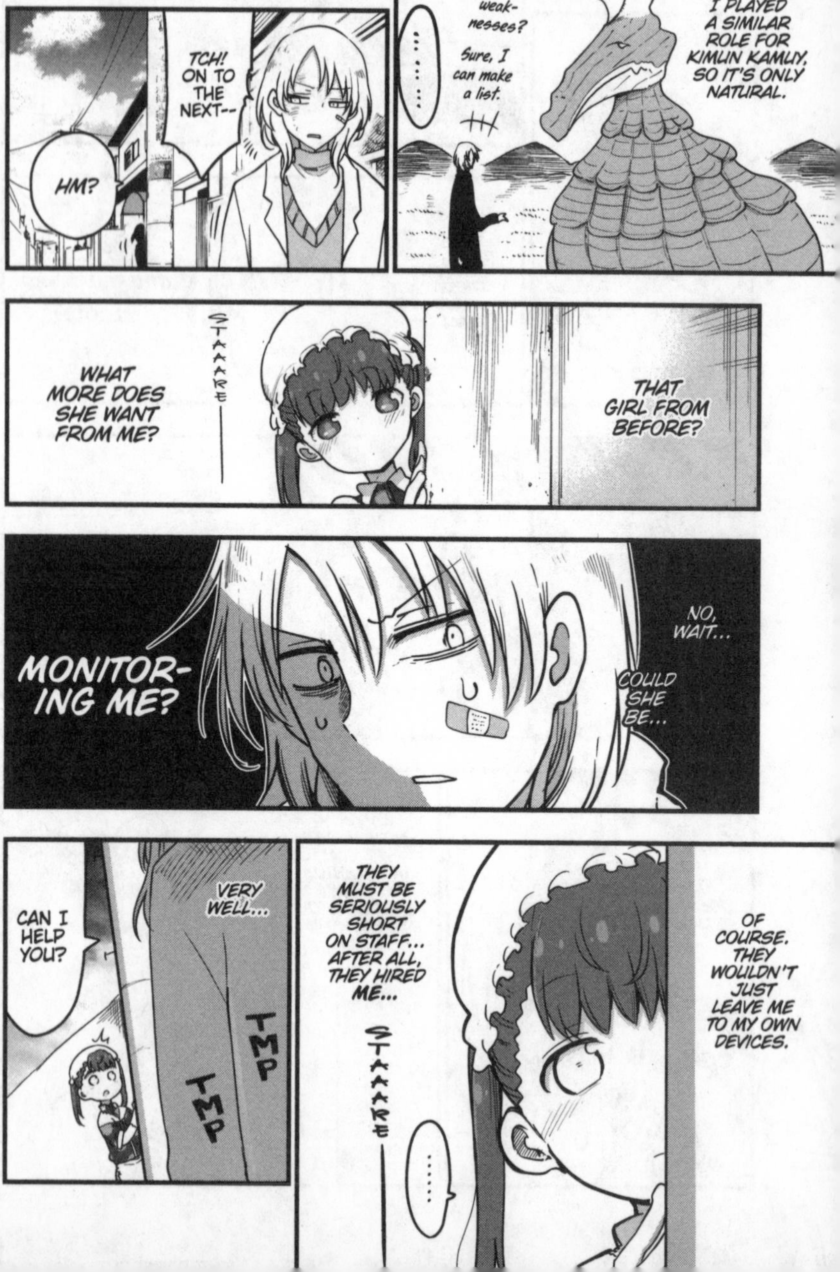
I PLAYED A SIMILAR ROLE FOR KIMUN KAMUY, SO IT'S ONLY NATURAL.
Your weak-nesses? Sure, I can make a list.
......
TCH! ON TO THE NEXT--
HM?
THAT GIRL FROM BEFORE?
STAAARE
WHAT MORE DOES SHE WANT FROM ME?
NO, WAIT...
COULD SHE BE...
MONITOR-ING ME?
OF COURSE. THEY WOULDN'T JUST LEAVE ME TO MY OWN DEVICES.
THEY MUST BE SERIOUSLY SHORT ON STAFF... AFTER ALL, THEY HIRED ME...
STAAAARE
......
VERY WELL...
CAN I HELP YOU?
TMP
TMP

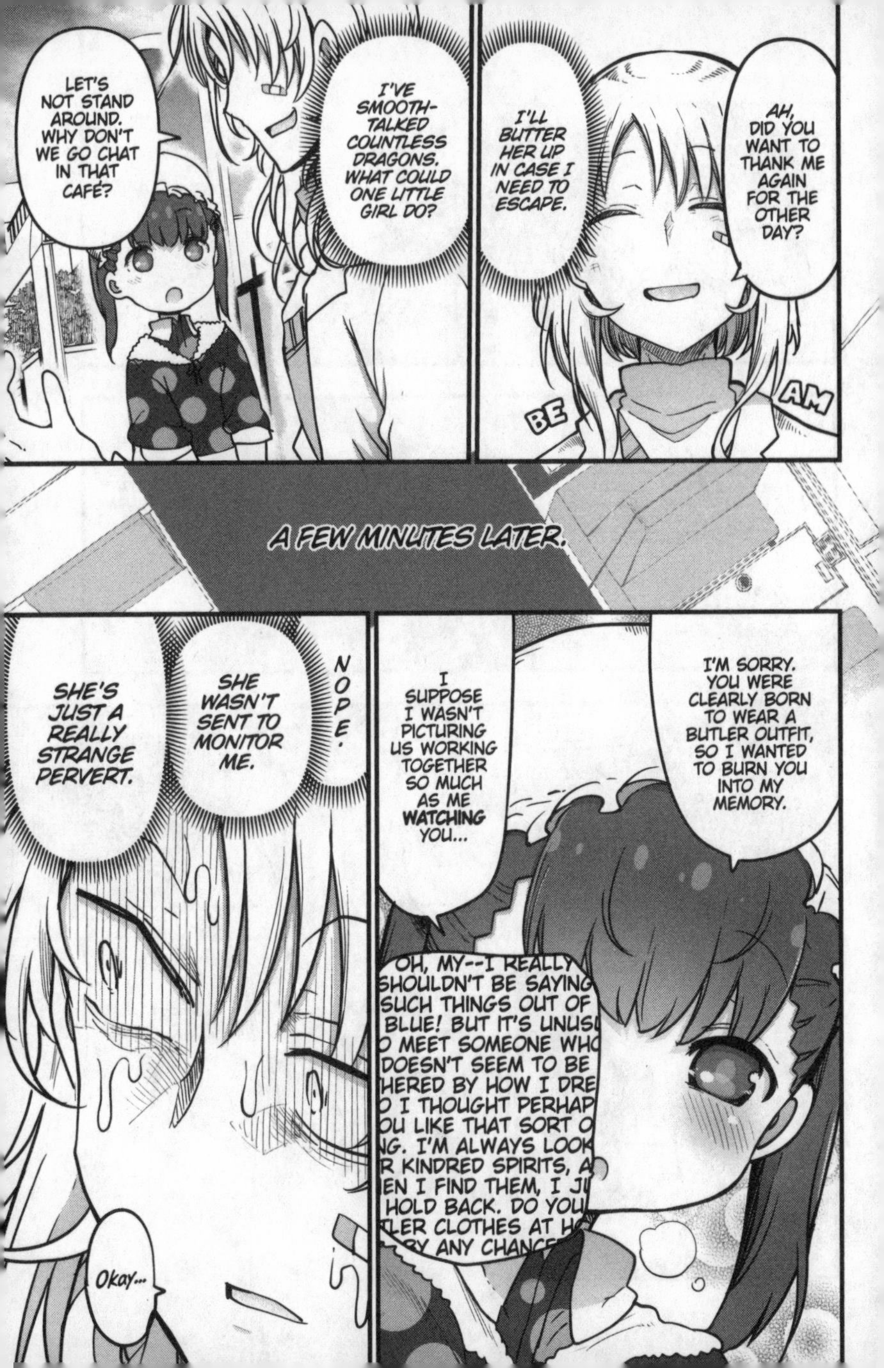
AH, DID YOU WANT TO THANK ME AGAIN FOR THE OTHER DAY?
I'LL BUTTER HER UP IN CASE I NEED TO ESCAPE.
AM
BE
I'VE SMOOTH-TALKED COUNTLESS DRAGONS. WHAT COULD ONE LITTLE GIRL DO?
LET'S NOT STAND AROUND. WHY DON'T WE GO CHAT IN THAT CAFÉ?
A FEW MINUTES LATER.
I'M SORRY. YOU WERE CLEARLY BORN TO WEAR A BUTLER OUTFIT, SO I WANTED TO BURN YOU INTO MY MEMORY.
I SUPPOSE I WASN'T PICTURING US WORKING TOGETHER SO MUCH AS ME **WATCHING** YOU...
OH, MY--I REALLY SHOULDN'T BE SAYING SUCH THINGS OUT OF BLUE! BUT IT'S UNUSU O MEET SOMEONE WHO DOESN'T SEEM TO BE HERED BY HOW I DRE O I THOUGHT PERHAP OU LIKE THAT SORT O NG. I'M ALWAYS LOOK R KINDRED SPIRITS, A EN I FIND THEM, I JU HOLD BACK. DO YOU TLER CLOTHES AT H RY ANY CHANC
NOPE.
SHE WASN'T SENT TO MONITOR ME.
SHE'S JUST A REALLY STRANGE PERVERT.
Okay...

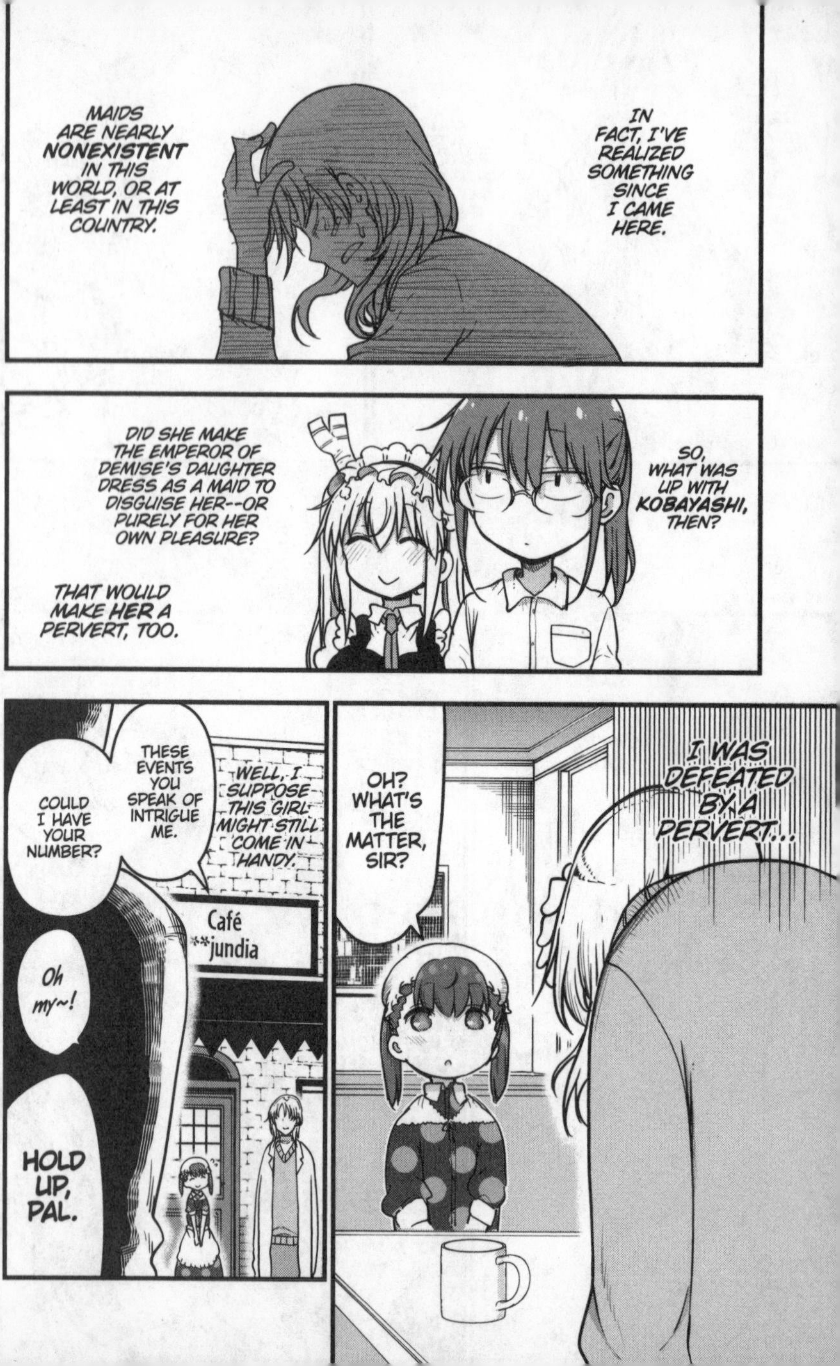
IN FACT, I'VE REALIZED SOMETHING SINCE I CAME HERE.
MAIDS ARE NEARLY NONEXISTENT IN THIS WORLD, OR AT LEAST IN THIS COUNTRY.
SO, WHAT WAS UP WITH KOBAYASHI, THEN?
DID SHE MAKE THE EMPEROR OF DEMISE'S DAUGHTER DRESS AS A MAID TO DISGUISE HER--OR PURELY FOR HER OWN PLEASURE?
THAT WOULD MAKE HER A PERVERT, TOO.
I WAS DEFEATED BY A PERVERT...
OH? WHAT'S THE MATTER, SIR?
WELL, I SUPPOSE THIS GIRL MIGHT STILL COME IN HANDY.
THESE EVENTS YOU SPEAK OF INTRIGUE ME.
COULD I HAVE YOUR NUMBER?
Café **jundia
Oh my~!
HOLD UP, PAL.

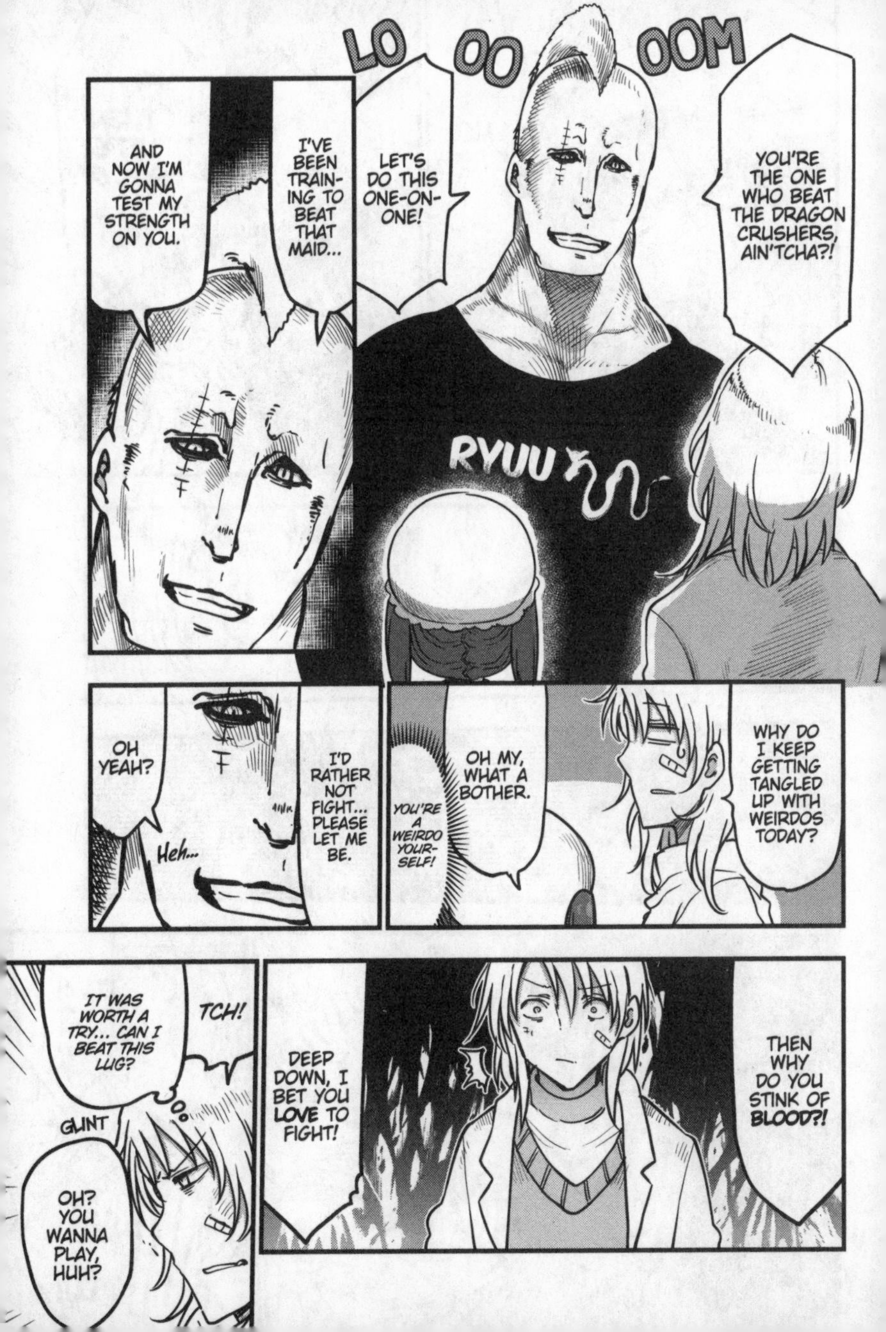
LO OO OOM
YOU'RE THE ONE WHO BEAT THE DRAGON CRUSHERS, AIN'TCHA?!
LET'S DO THIS ONE-ON-ONE!
RYUU
I'VE BEEN TRAIN-ING TO BEAT THAT MAID...
AND NOW I'M GONNA TEST MY STRENGTH ON YOU.
WHY DO I KEEP GETTING TANGLED UP WITH WEIRDOS TODAY?
OH MY, WHAT A BOTHER.
YOU'RE A WEIRDO YOUR-SELF!
I'D RATHER NOT FIGHT... PLEASE LET ME BE.
OH YEAH?
Heh...
THEN WHY DO YOU STINK OF BLOOD?!
DEEP DOWN, I BET YOU LOVE TO FIGHT!
TCH!
IT WAS WORTH A TRY... CAN I BEAT THIS LUG?
GLINT
OH? YOU WANNA PLAY, HUH?

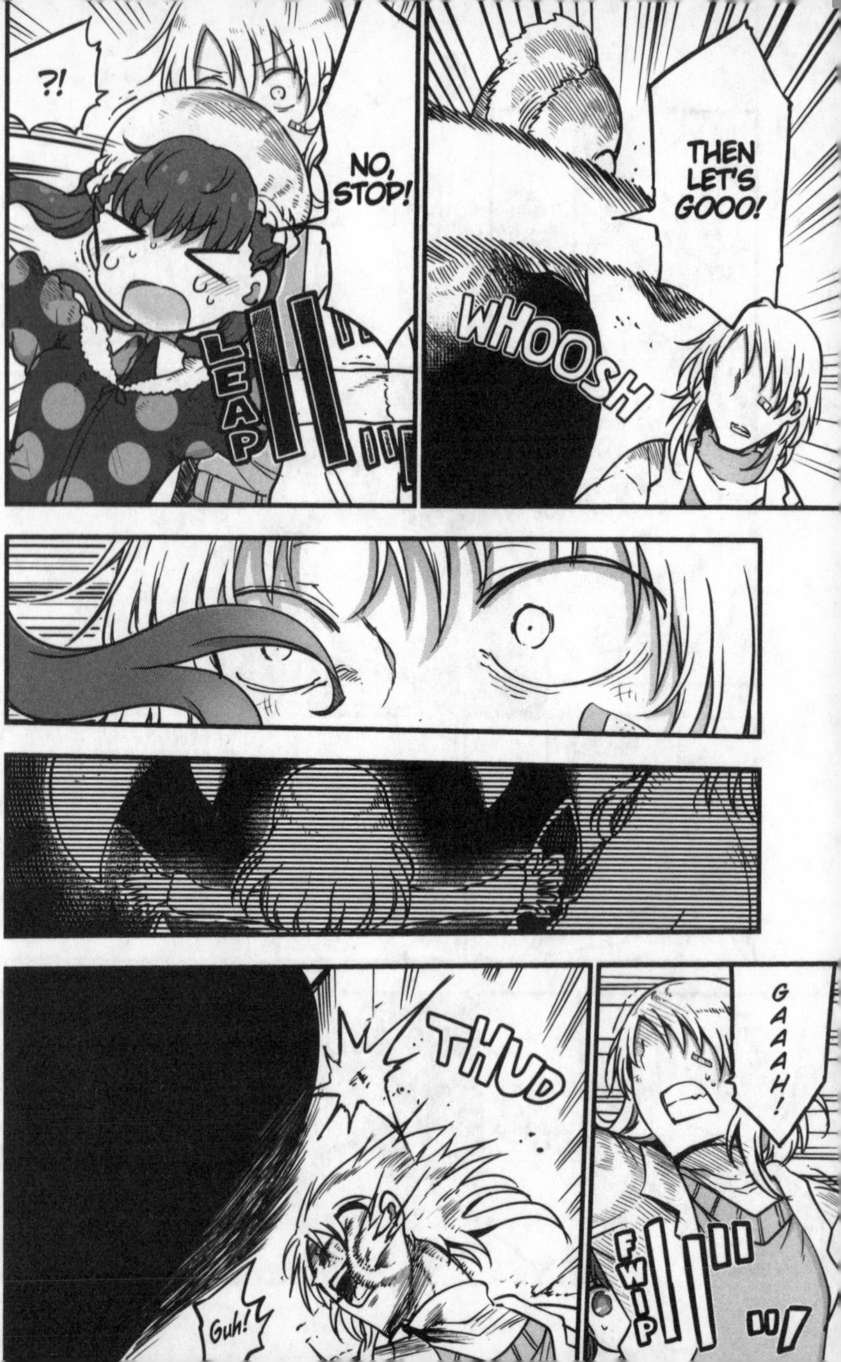
THEN LET'S GOOO!
WHOOSH
?!
NO, STOP!
LEAP
GAAAH!
FWIP
THUD
Guh!

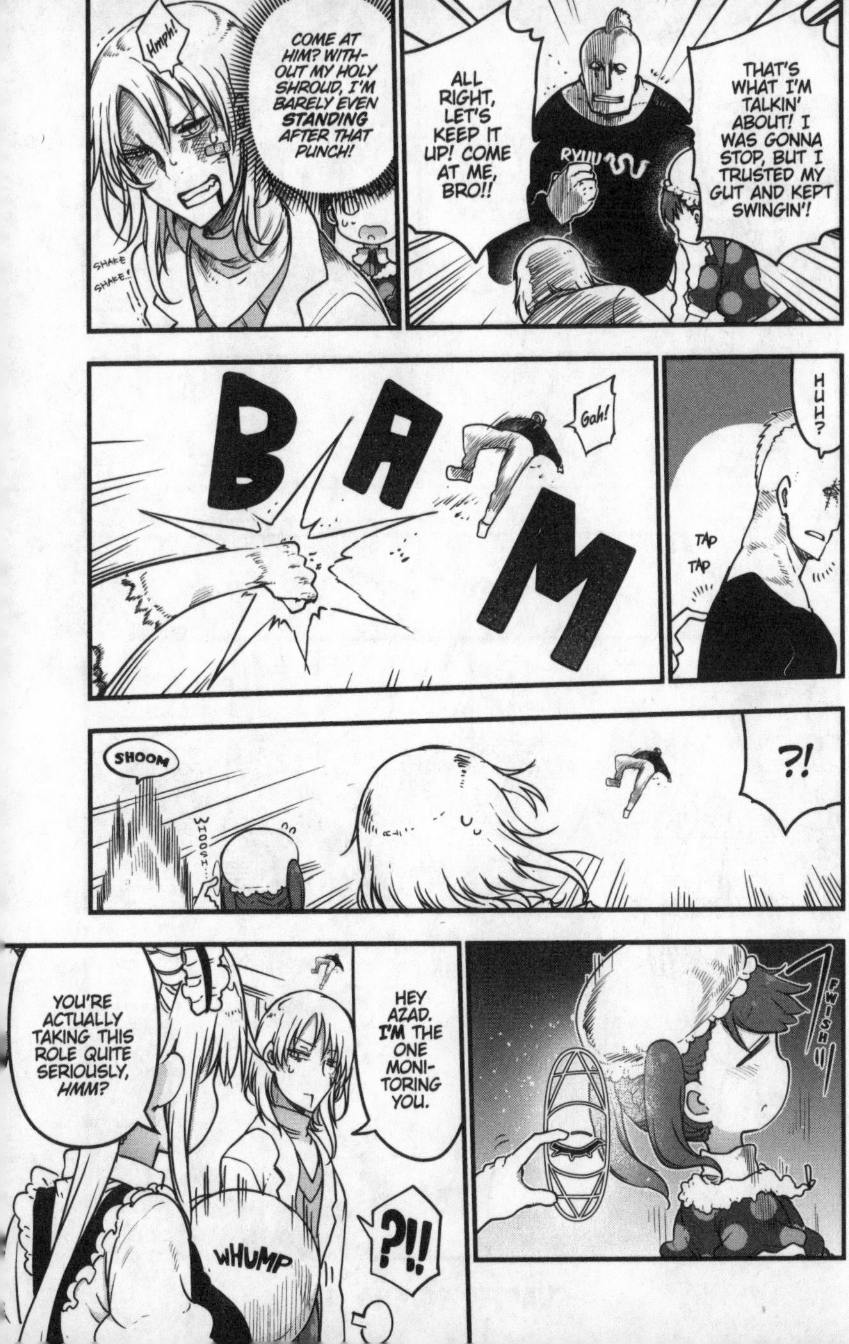
THAT'S WHAT I'M TALKIN' ABOUT! I WAS GONNA STOP, BUT I TRUSTED MY GUT AND KEPT SWINGIN'!
ALL RIGHT, LET'S KEEP IT UP! COME AT ME, BRO!!
RYUU
COME AT HIM? WITHOUT MY HOLY SHROUD, I'M BARELY EVEN STANDING AFTER THAT PUNCH!
Hmph!
SHAKE SHAKE...
HUH?
TAP TAP
Gah!
BAM
?!
SHOOM
WHOOSH...
FWISH!!
HEY AZAD. I'M THE ONE MONITORING YOU.
YOU'RE ACTUALLY TAKING THIS ROLE QUITE SERIOUSLY, HMM?
?!!
WHUMP

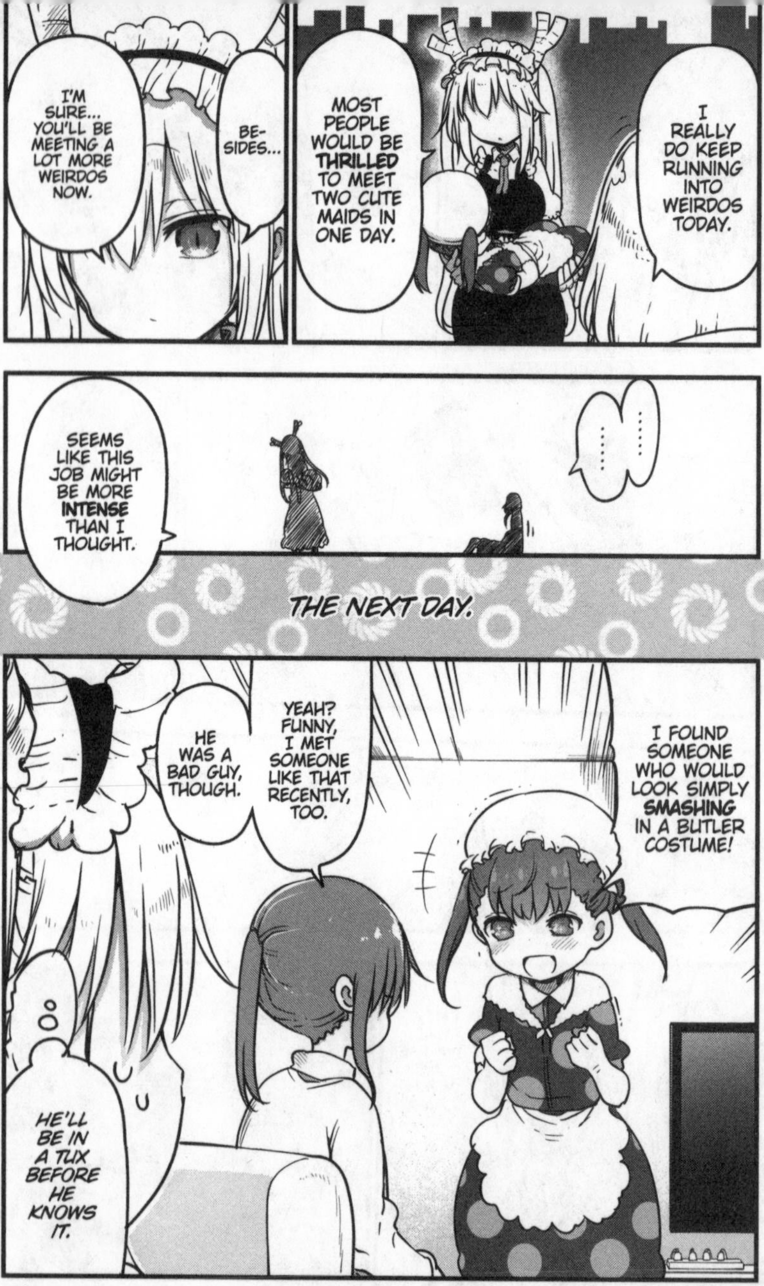
I REALLY DO KEEP RUNNING INTO WEIRDOS TODAY.
MOST PEOPLE WOULD BE THRILLED TO MEET TWO CUTE MAIDS IN ONE DAY.
BE-SIDES...
I'M SURE... YOU'LL BE MEETING A LOT MORE WEIRDOS NOW.
......
SEEMS LIKE THIS JOB MIGHT BE MORE INTENSE THAN I THOUGHT.
THE NEXT DAY.
I FOUND SOMEONE WHO WOULD LOOK SIMPLY SMASHING IN A BUTLER COSTUME!
YEAH? FUNNY, I MET SOMEONE LIKE THAT RECENTLY, TOO.
HE WAS A BAD GUY, THOUGH.
HE'LL BE IN A TUX BEFORE HE KNOWS IT.

CHAPTER 90/END

Miss Kobayashi's
Dragon Maid

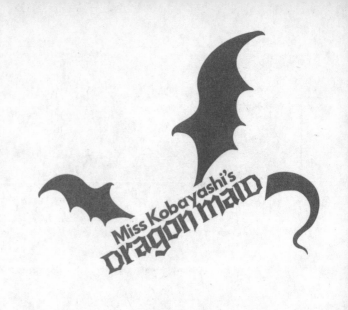

CHAPTER 91

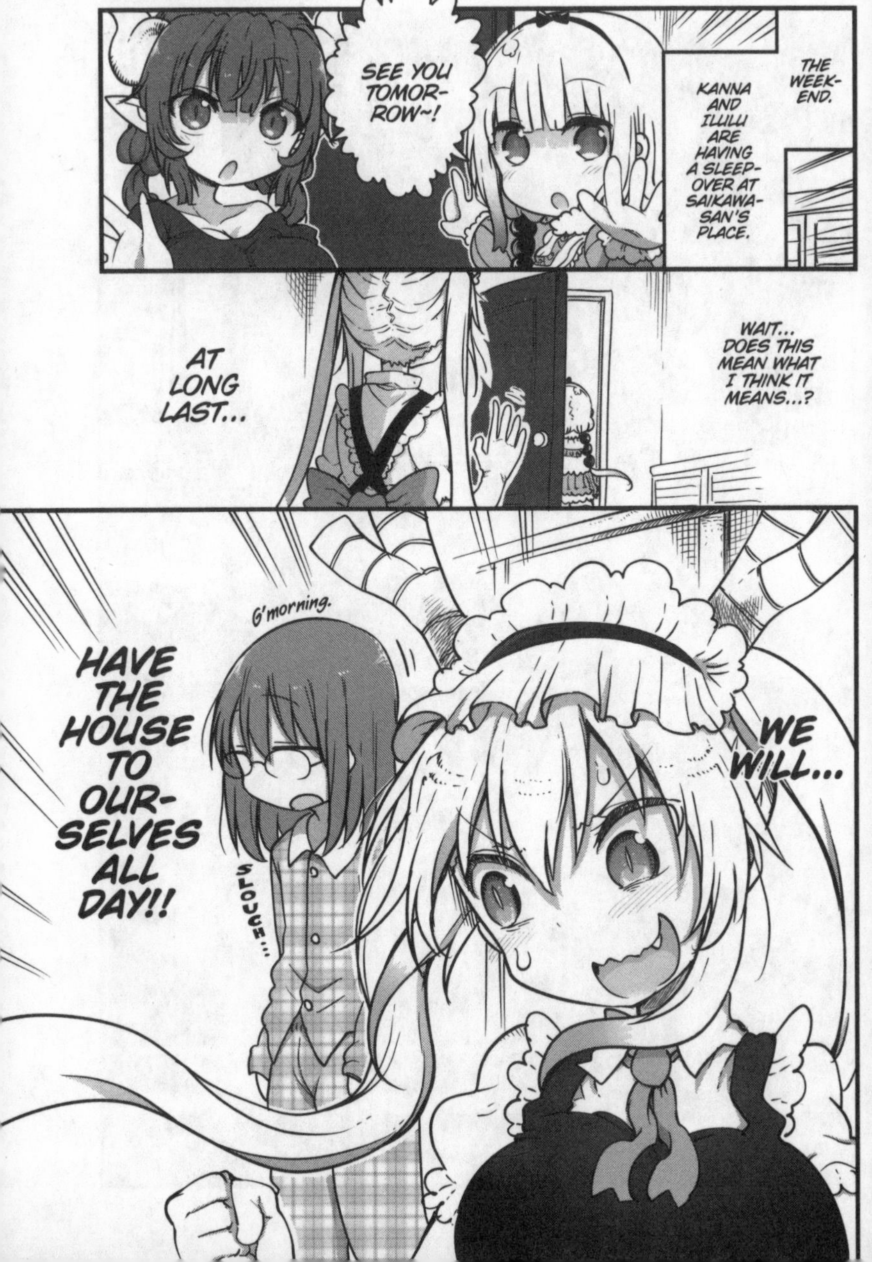
THE WEEKEND.
KANNA AND ILULU ARE HAVING A SLEEPOVER AT SAIKAWA-SAN'S PLACE.
SEE YOU TOMORROW~!
WAIT... DOES THIS MEAN WHAT I THINK IT MEANS...?
AT LONG LAST...
WE WILL...
G'morning.
HAVE THE HOUSE TO OURSELVES ALL DAY!!
SLOUCH...

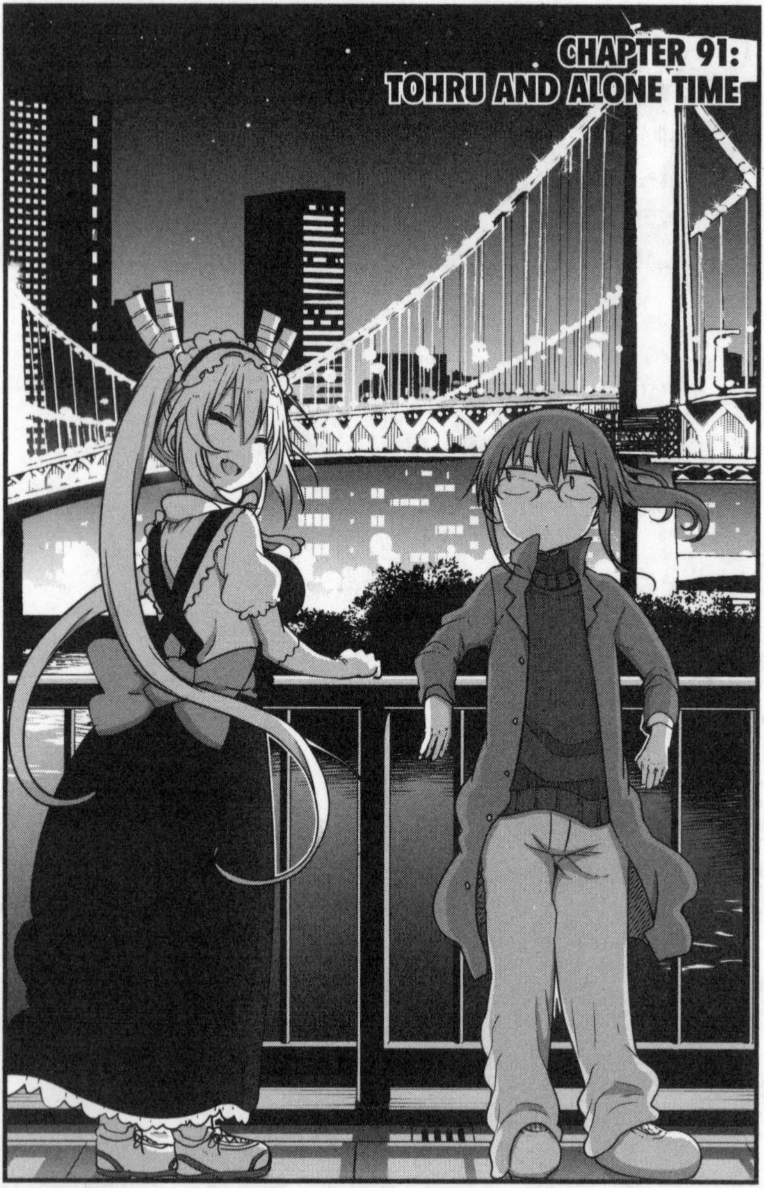
CHAPTER 91:
TOHRU AND ALONE TIME

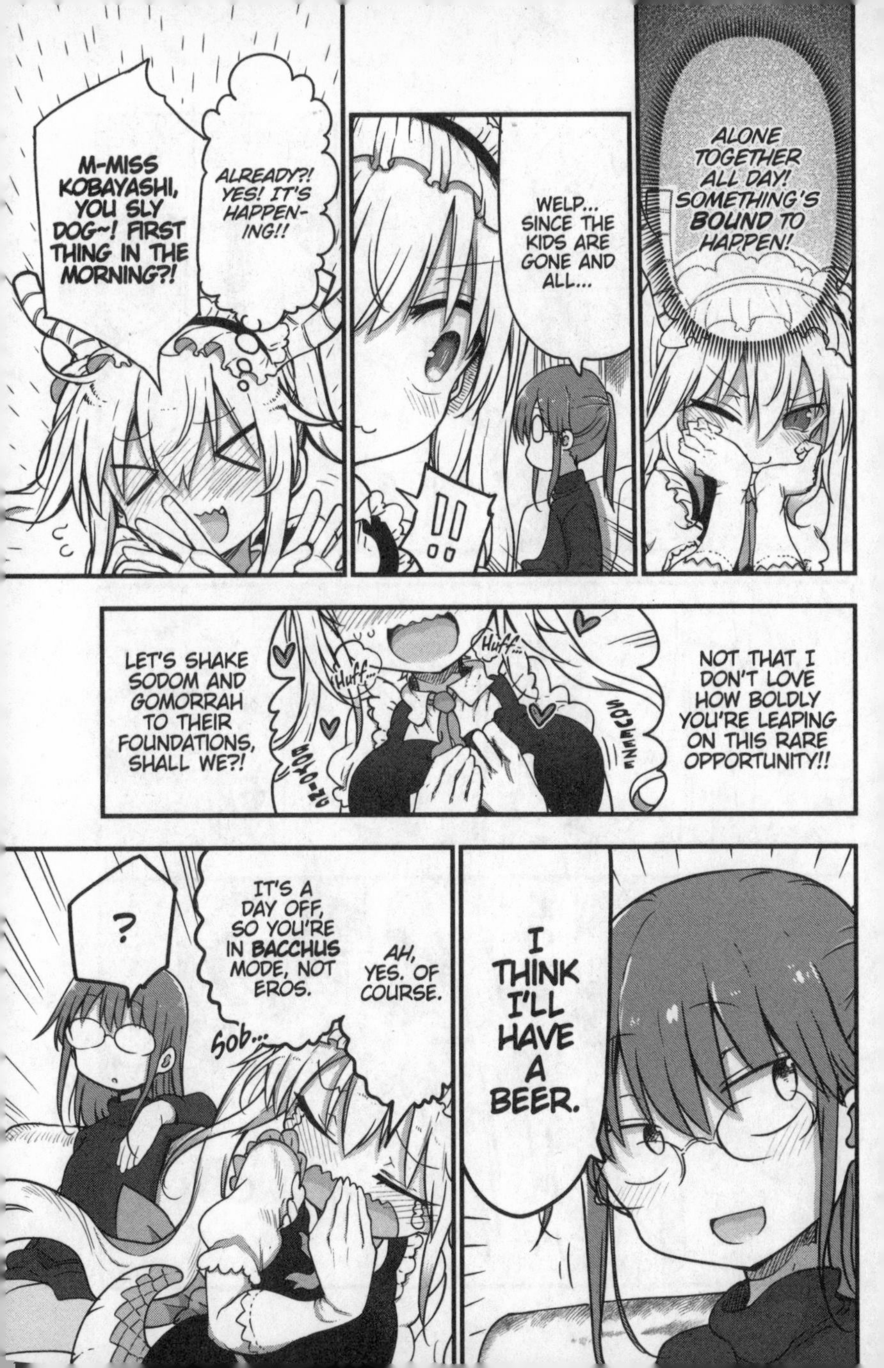
ALONE TOGETHER ALL DAY! SOMETHING'S BOUND TO HAPPEN!
WELP... SINCE THE KIDS ARE GONE AND ALL...
!!
ALREADY?! YES! IT'S HAPPEN-ING!!
M-MISS KOBAYASHI, YOU SLY DOG~! FIRST THING IN THE MORNING?!
NOT THAT I DON'T LOVE HOW BOLDLY YOU'RE LEAPING ON THIS RARE OPPORTUNITY!!
Huff...
Huff...
LET'S SHAKE SODOM AND GOMORRAH TO THEIR FOUNDATIONS, SHALL WE?!
I THINK I'LL HAVE A BEER.
AH, YES. OF COURSE.
IT'S A DAY OFF, SO YOU'RE IN BACCHUS MODE, NOT EROS.
?
Sob...

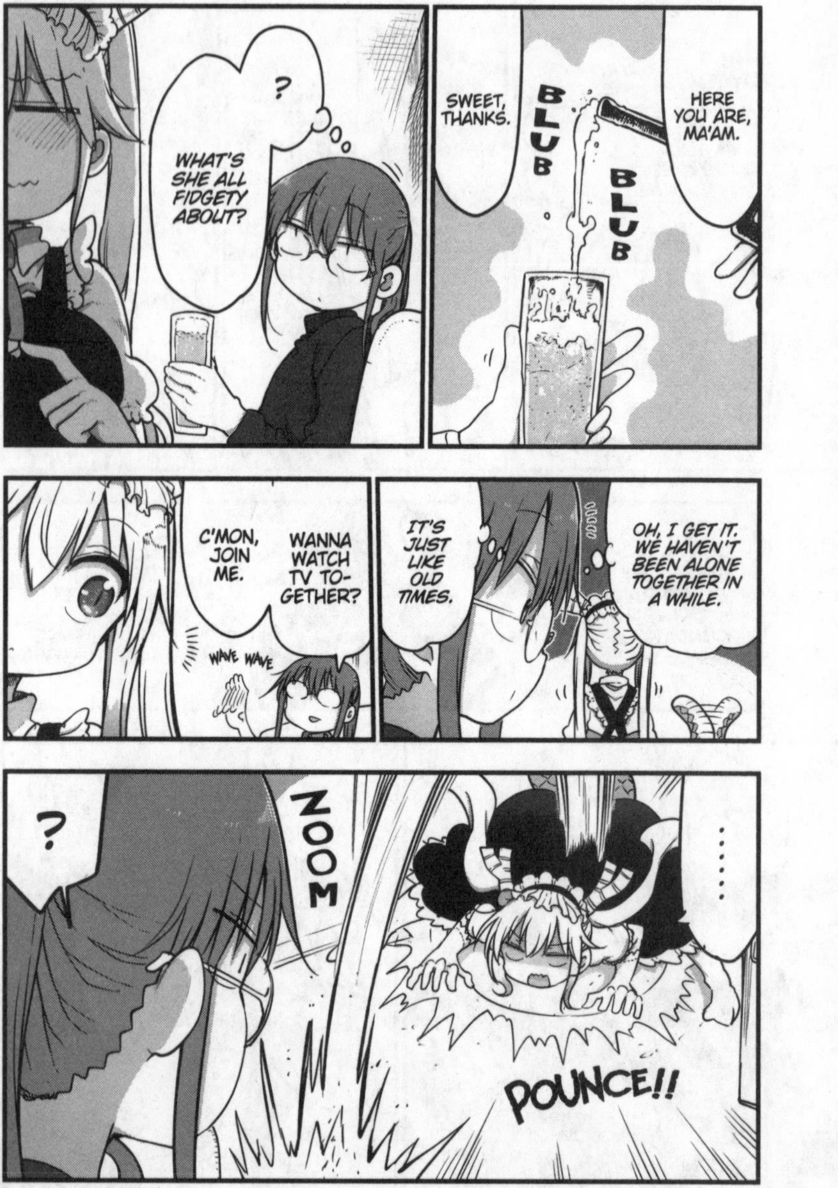
HERE YOU ARE, MA'AM.
BLUB
BLUB
SWEET, THANKS.
?
WHAT'S SHE ALL FIDGETY ABOUT?
OH, I GET IT. WE HAVEN'T BEEN ALONE TOGETHER IN A WHILE.
IT'S JUST LIKE OLD TIMES.
WANNA WATCH TV TO-GETHER?
C'MON, JOIN ME.
WAVE WAVE
......
ZOOM
?
POUNCE!!

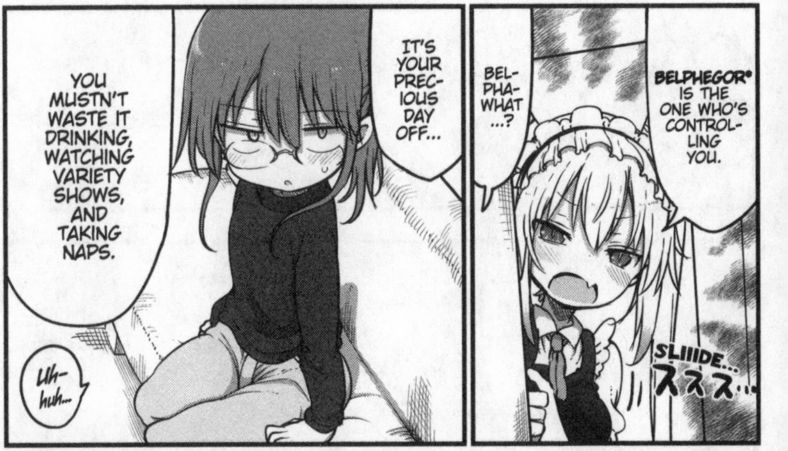
BELPHEGOR* IS THE ONE WHO'S CONTROL-LING YOU.
BEL-PHA-WHAT...?
SLIIIDE... ススス...
IT'S YOUR PREC-IOUS DAY OFF...
YOU MUSTN'T WASTE IT DRINKING, WATCHING VARIETY SHOWS, AND TAKING NAPS.
Uh-huh...

*Belphegor: The demon of Sloth

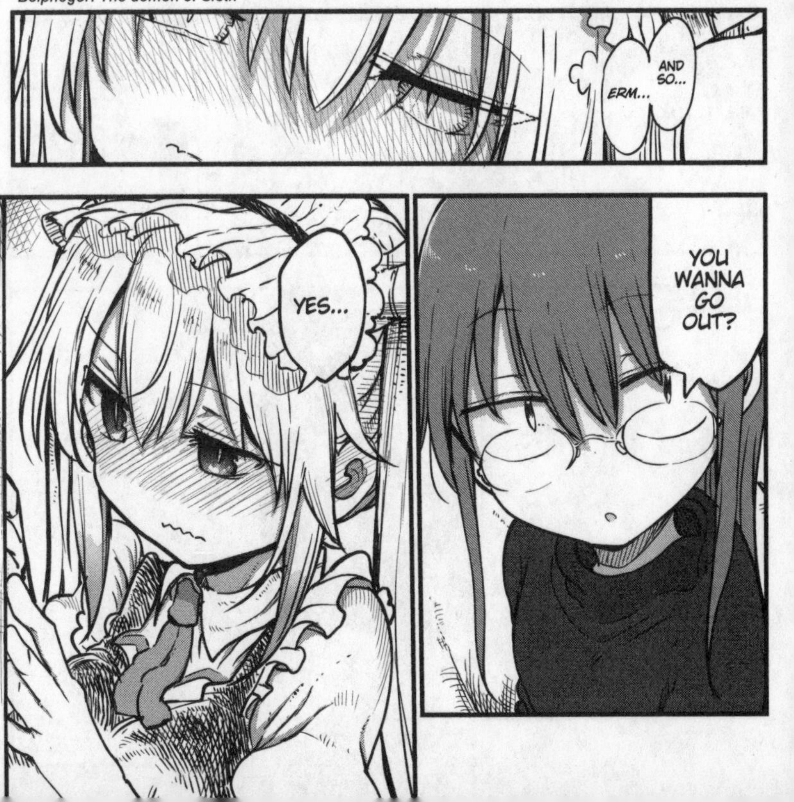
AND SO... ERM...
YOU WANNA GO OUT?
YES...

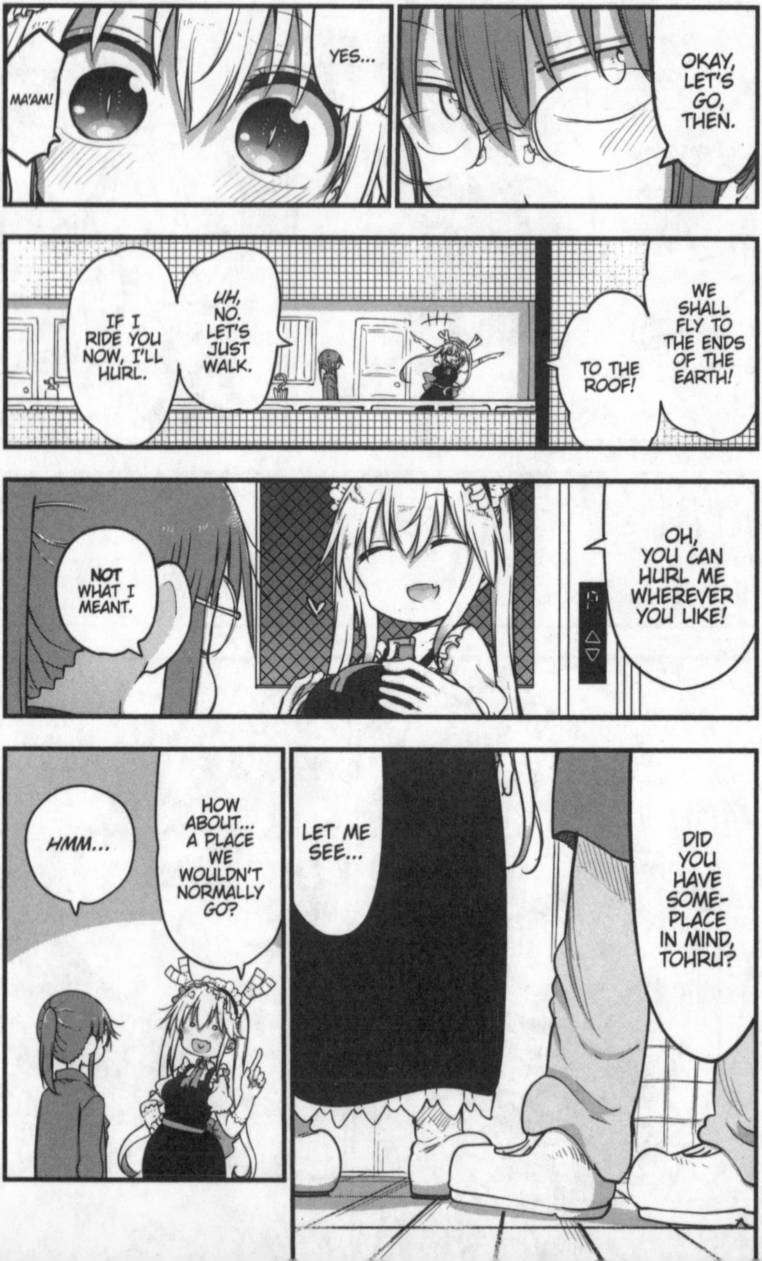
OKAY, LET'S GO, THEN.
YES...
MA'AM!
WE SHALL FLY TO THE ENDS OF THE EARTH!
TO THE ROOF!
UH, NO. LET'S JUST WALK.
IF I RIDE YOU NOW, I'LL HURL.
OH, YOU CAN HURL ME WHEREVER YOU LIKE!
NOT WHAT I MEANT.
DID YOU HAVE SOME-PLACE IN MIND, TOHRU?
LET ME SEE...
HOW ABOUT... A PLACE WE WOULDN'T NORMALLY GO?
HMM...

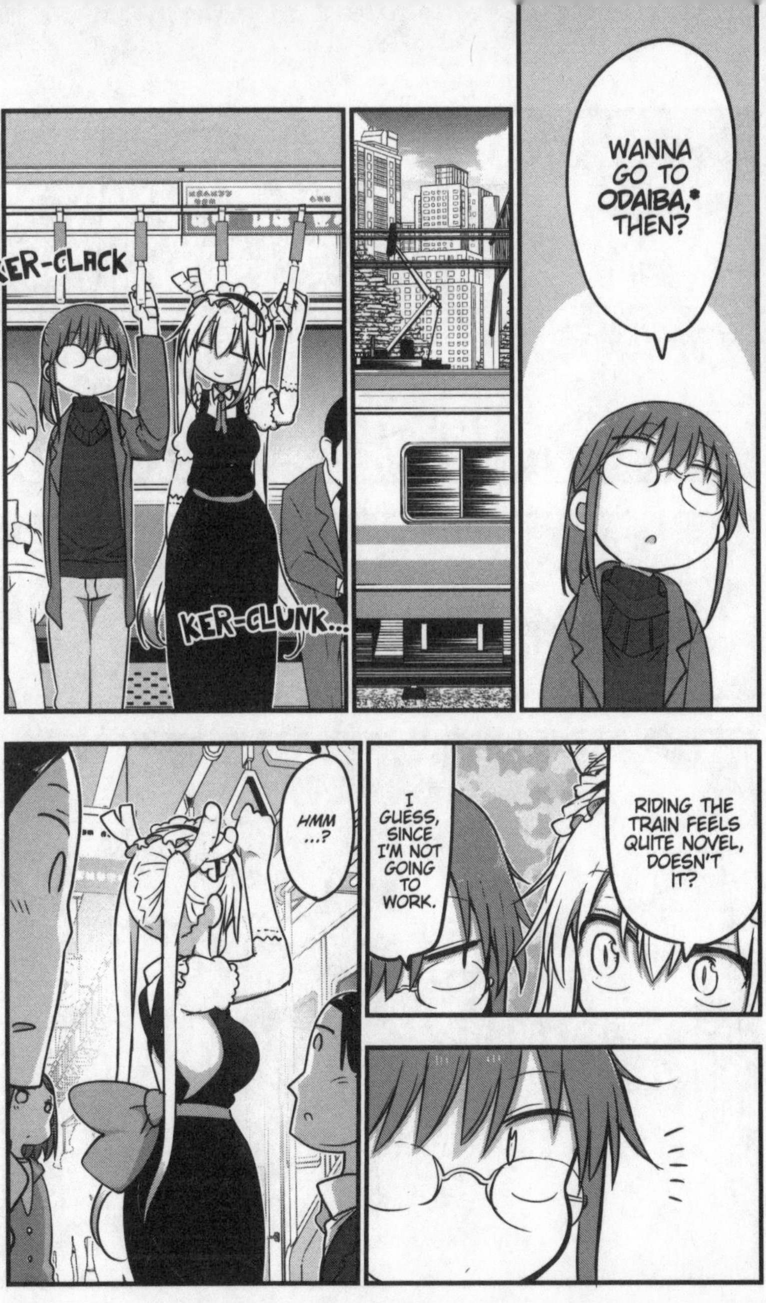
WANNA GO TO ODAIBA,* THEN?
KER-CLACK
KER-CLUNK...
RIDING THE TRAIN FEELS QUITE NOVEL, DOESN'T IT?
I GUESS, SINCE I'M NOT GOING TO WORK.
HMM ...?

*Odaiba is an artificial island in Tokyo Bay, a popular tourist attraction.

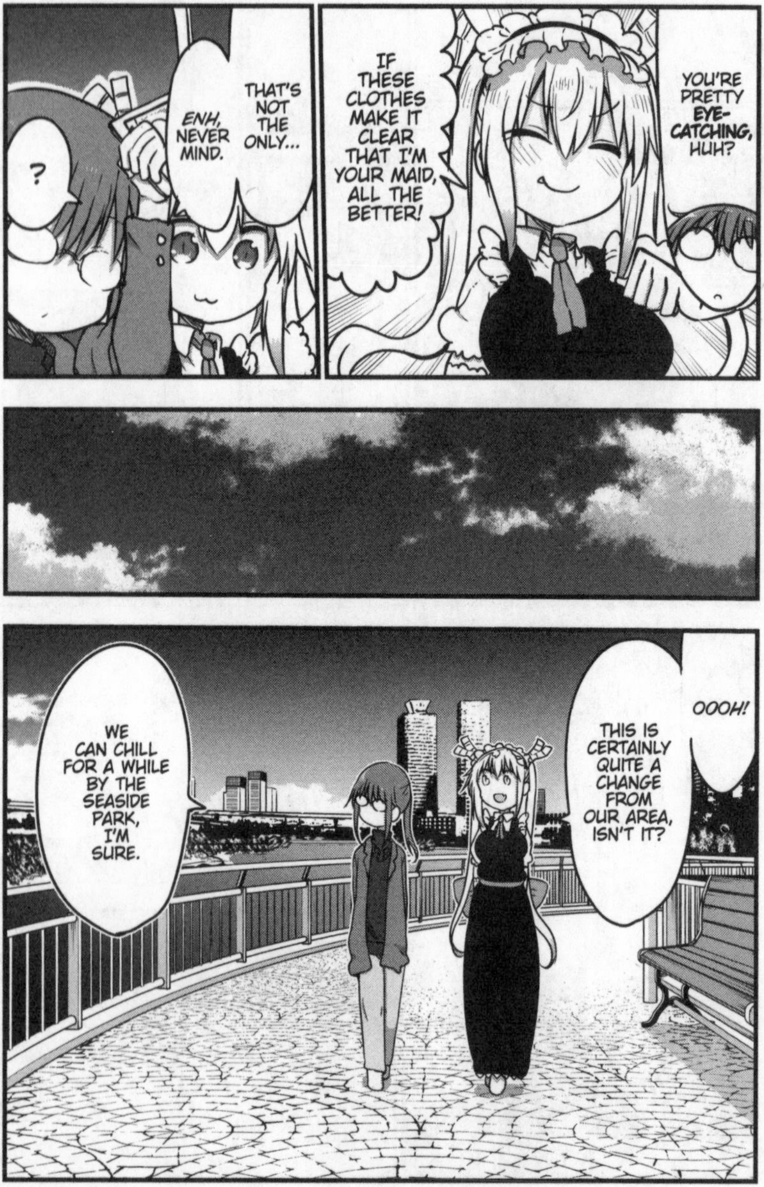
YOU'RE PRETTY EYE-CATCHING, HUH?
IF THESE CLOTHES MAKE IT CLEAR THAT I'M YOUR MAID, ALL THE BETTER!
THAT'S NOT THE ONLY...
ENH, NEVER MIND.
?
OOOH!
THIS IS CERTAINLY QUITE A CHANGE FROM OUR AREA, ISN'T IT?
WE CAN CHILL FOR A WHILE BY THE SEASIDE PARK, I'M SURE.

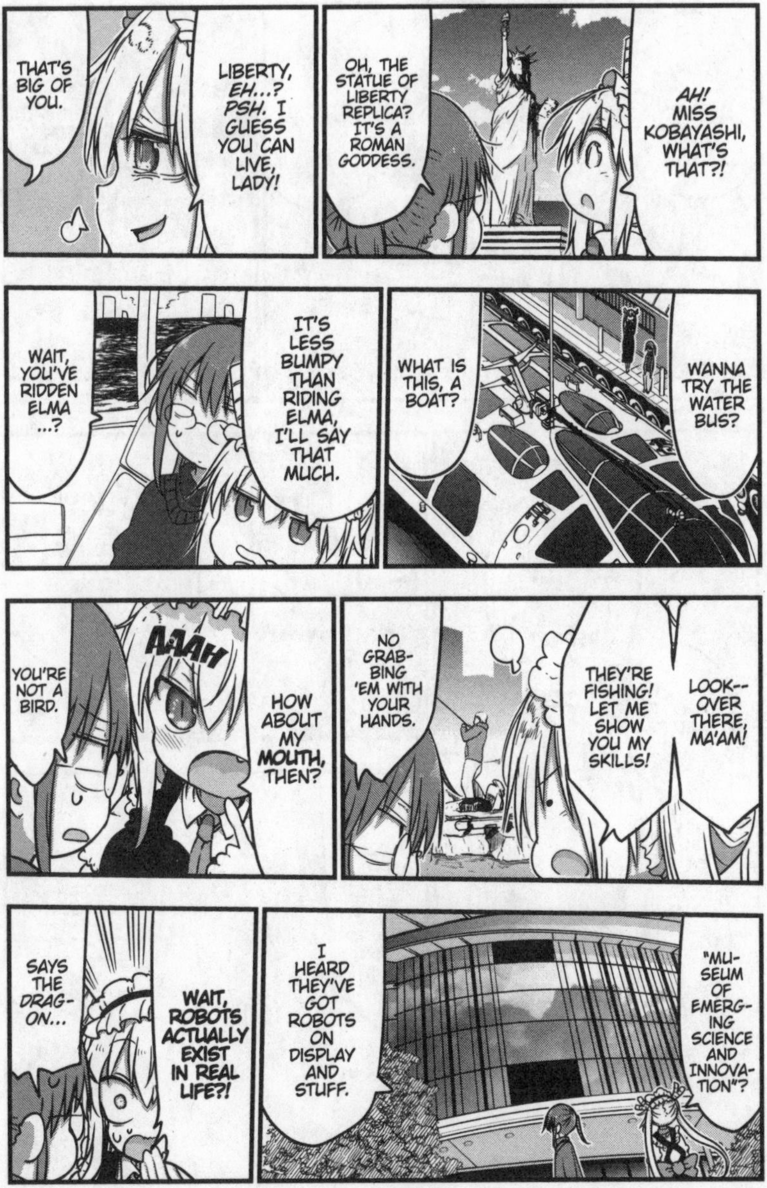
AH! MISS KOBAYASHI, WHAT'S THAT?!
OH, THE STATUE OF LIBERTY REPLICA? IT'S A ROMAN GODDESS.
LIBERTY, *EH...? PSH*. I GUESS YOU CAN LIVE, LADY!
THAT'S BIG OF YOU.
WANNA TRY THE WATER BUS?
WHAT IS THIS, A BOAT?
IT'S LESS BUMPY THAN RIDING ELMA, I'LL SAY THAT MUCH.
WAIT, YOU'VE RIDDEN ELMA ...?
LOOK-- OVER THERE, MA'AM!
THEY'RE FISHING! LET ME SHOW YOU MY SKILLS!
NO GRABBING 'EM WITH YOUR HANDS.
AAAH
HOW ABOUT MY **MOUTH**, THEN?
YOU'RE NOT A BIRD.
"MUSEUM OF EMERGING SCIENCE AND INNOVATION"?
I HEARD THEY'VE GOT ROBOTS ON DISPLAY AND STUFF.
WAIT, ROBOTS ACTUALLY EXIST IN REAL LIFE?!
SAYS THE *DRAGON...*

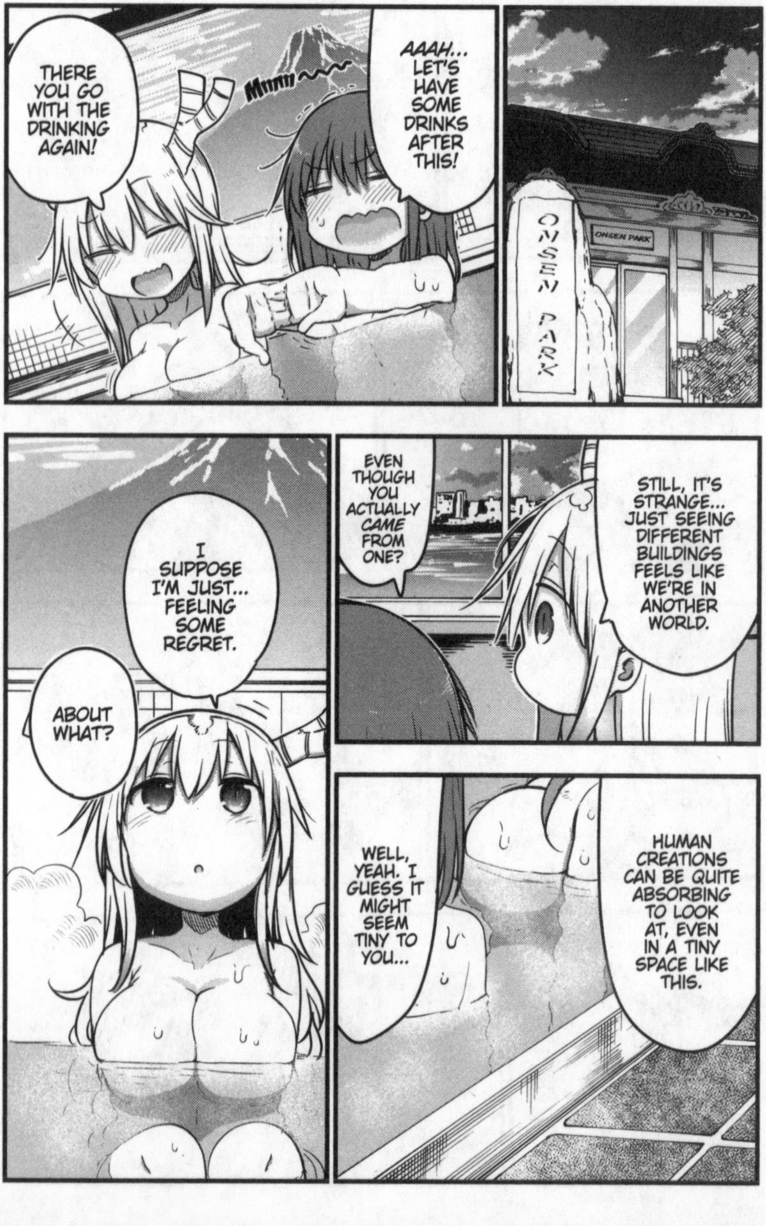
ONSEN PARK
ONSEN PARK
AAAH... LET'S HAVE SOME DRINKS AFTER THIS!
Mmm~~
THERE YOU GO WITH THE DRINKING AGAIN!
STILL, IT'S STRANGE... JUST SEEING DIFFERENT BUILDINGS FEELS LIKE WE'RE IN ANOTHER WORLD.
EVEN THOUGH YOU ACTUALLY CAME FROM ONE?
HUMAN CREATIONS CAN BE QUITE ABSORBING TO LOOK AT, EVEN IN A TINY SPACE LIKE THIS.
WELL, YEAH. I GUESS IT MIGHT SEEM TINY TO YOU...
I SUPPOSE I'M JUST... FEELING SOME REGRET.
ABOUT WHAT?

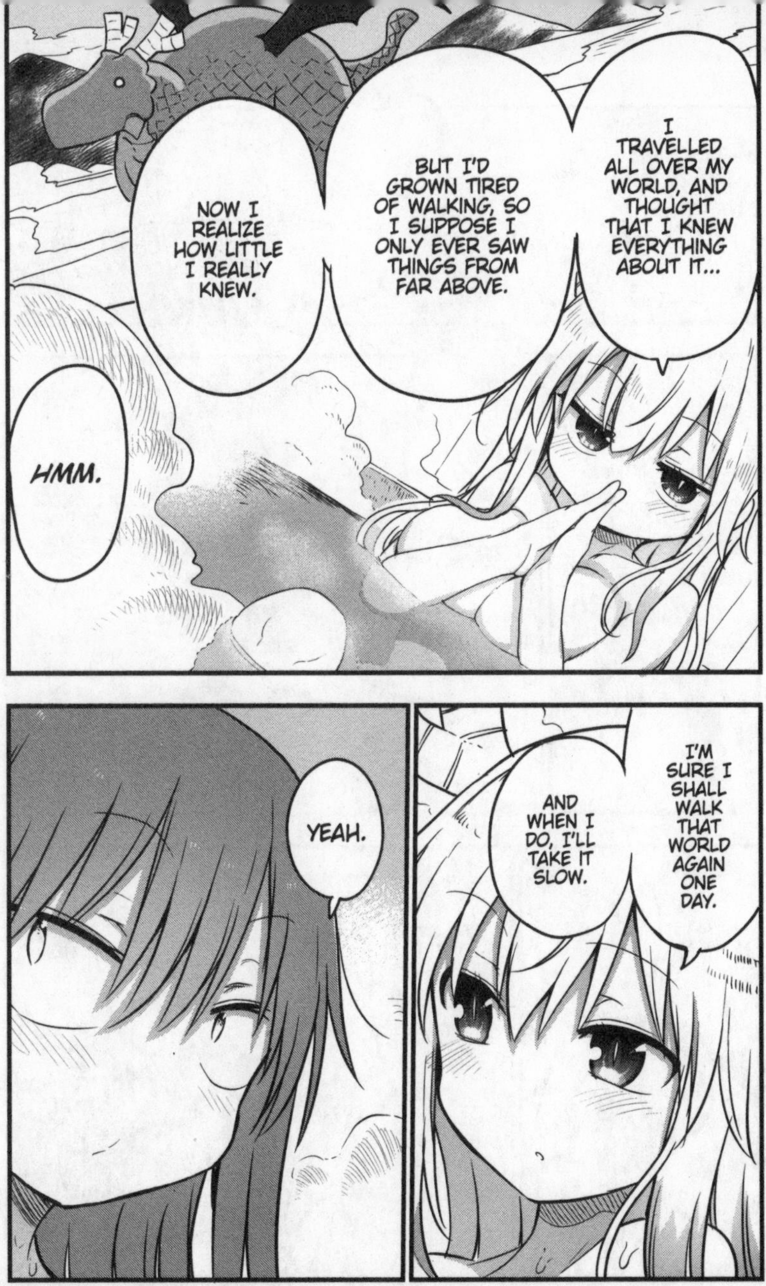
I TRAVELLED ALL OVER MY WORLD, AND THOUGHT THAT I KNEW EVERYTHING ABOUT IT...
BUT I'D GROWN TIRED OF WALKING, SO I SUPPOSE I ONLY EVER SAW THINGS FROM FAR ABOVE.
NOW I REALIZE HOW LITTLE I REALLY KNEW.
HMM.
I'M SURE I SHALL WALK THAT WORLD AGAIN ONE DAY.
AND WHEN I DO, I'LL TAKE IT SLOW.
YEAH.

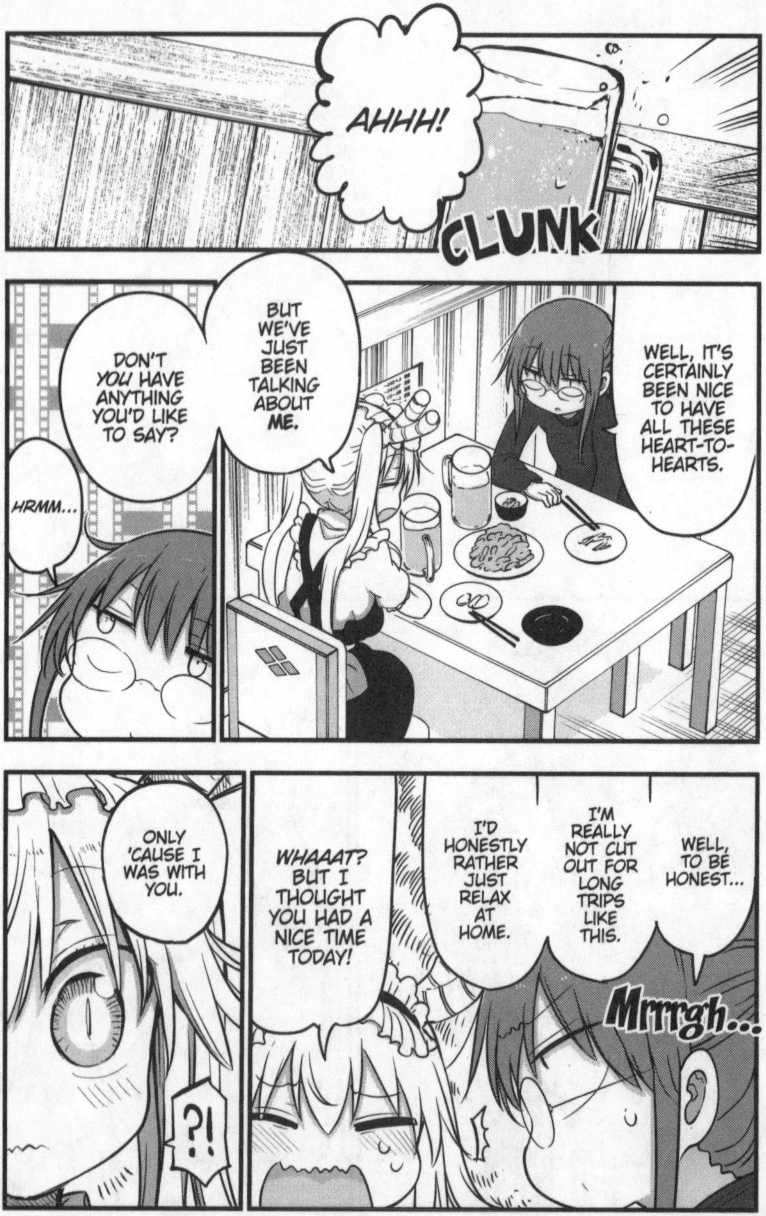
AHHH!
CLUNK
WELL, IT'S CERTAINLY BEEN NICE TO HAVE ALL THESE HEART-TO-HEARTS.
BUT WE'VE JUST BEEN TALKING ABOUT ME.
DON'T YOU HAVE ANYTHING YOU'D LIKE TO SAY?
HRMM...
WELL, TO BE HONEST...
I'M REALLY NOT CUT OUT FOR LONG TRIPS LIKE THIS.
I'D HONESTLY RATHER JUST RELAX AT HOME.
Mrrrgh...
WHAAAT? BUT I THOUGHT YOU HAD A NICE TIME TODAY!
ONLY 'CAUSE I WAS WITH YOU.
?!

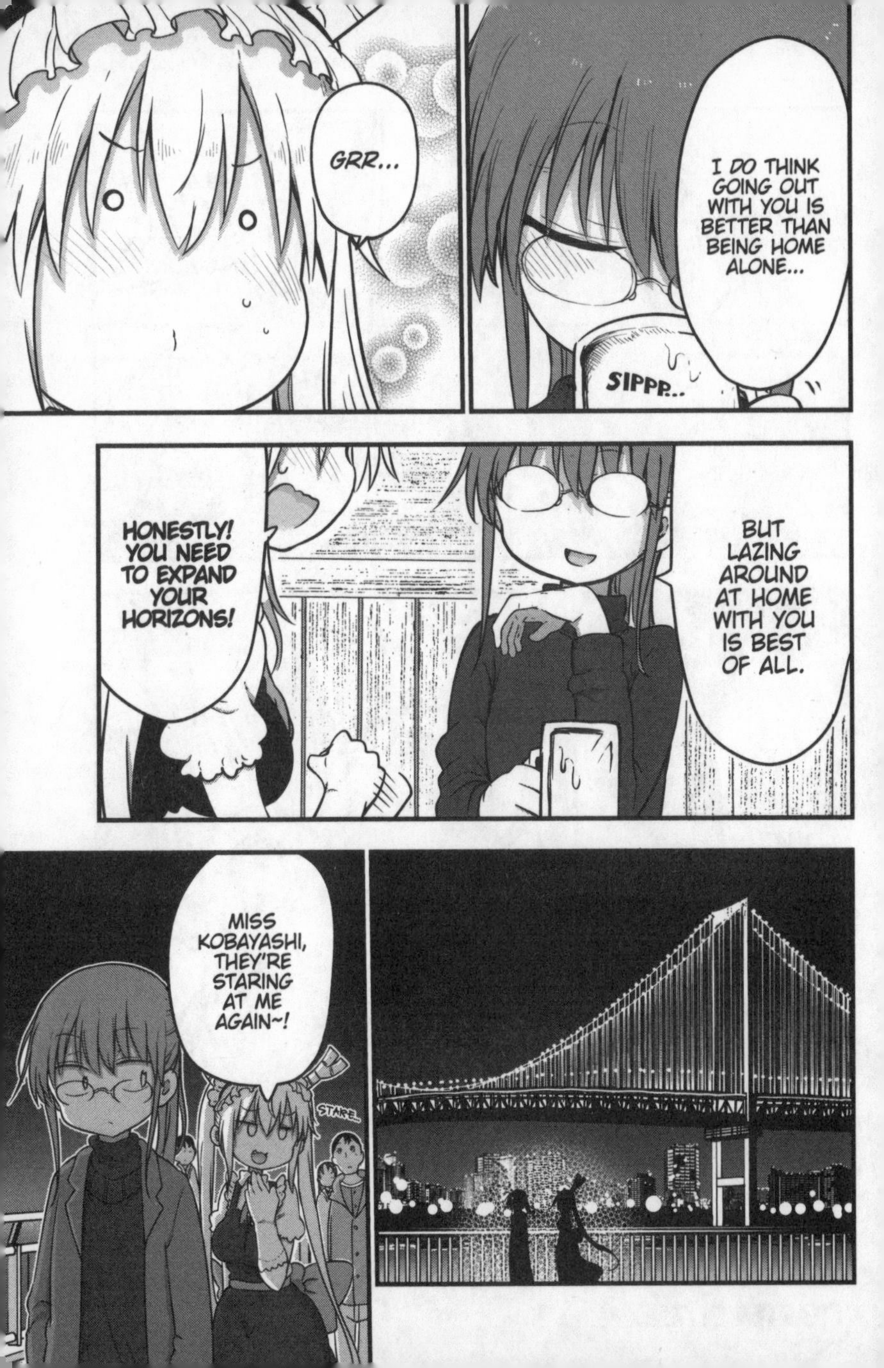
I DO THINK GOING OUT WITH YOU IS BETTER THAN BEING HOME ALONE...
SIPPP...
GRR...
BUT LAZING AROUND AT HOME WITH YOU IS BEST OF ALL.
HONESTLY! YOU NEED TO EXPAND YOUR HORIZONS!
MISS KOBAYASHI, THEY'RE STARING AT ME AGAIN~!
STARE...

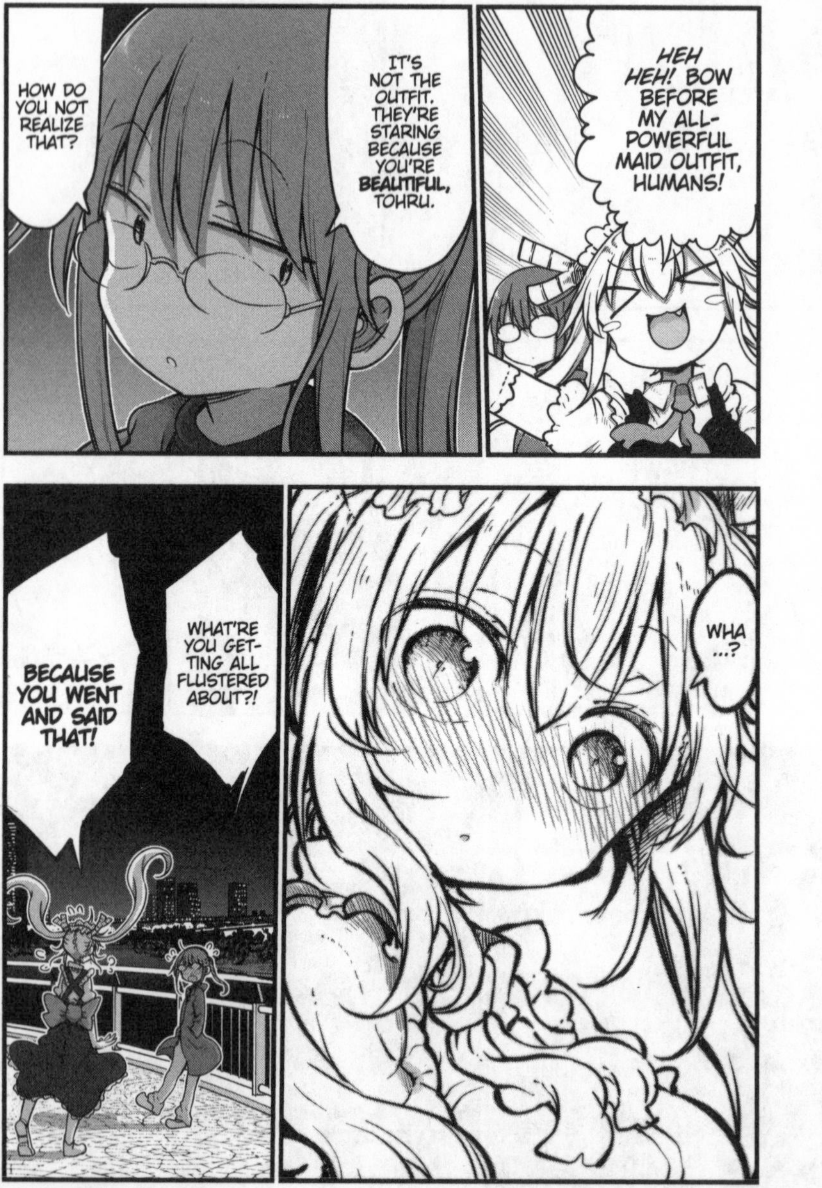
HEH HEH! BOW BEFORE MY ALL-POWERFUL MAID OUTFIT, HUMANS!
IT'S NOT THE OUTFIT. THEY'RE STARING BECAUSE YOU'RE BEAUTIFUL, TOHRU.
HOW DO YOU NOT REALIZE THAT?
WHA ...?
WHAT'RE YOU GET-TING ALL FLUSTERED ABOUT?!
BECAUSE YOU WENT AND SAID THAT!

CHAPTER 91/END

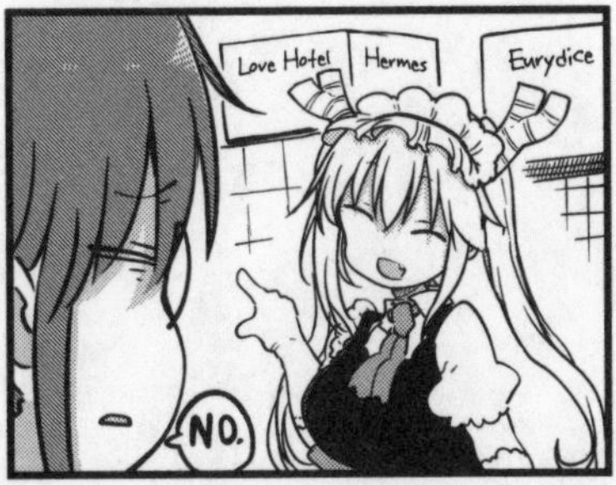
Love Hotel
Hermes
Eurydice
NO.

Miss Kobayashi's
DRAGON MAID

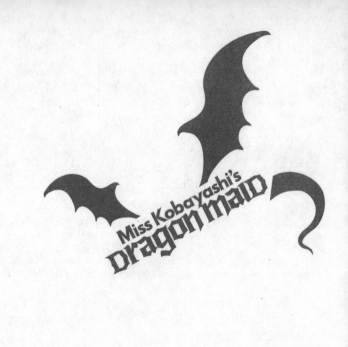

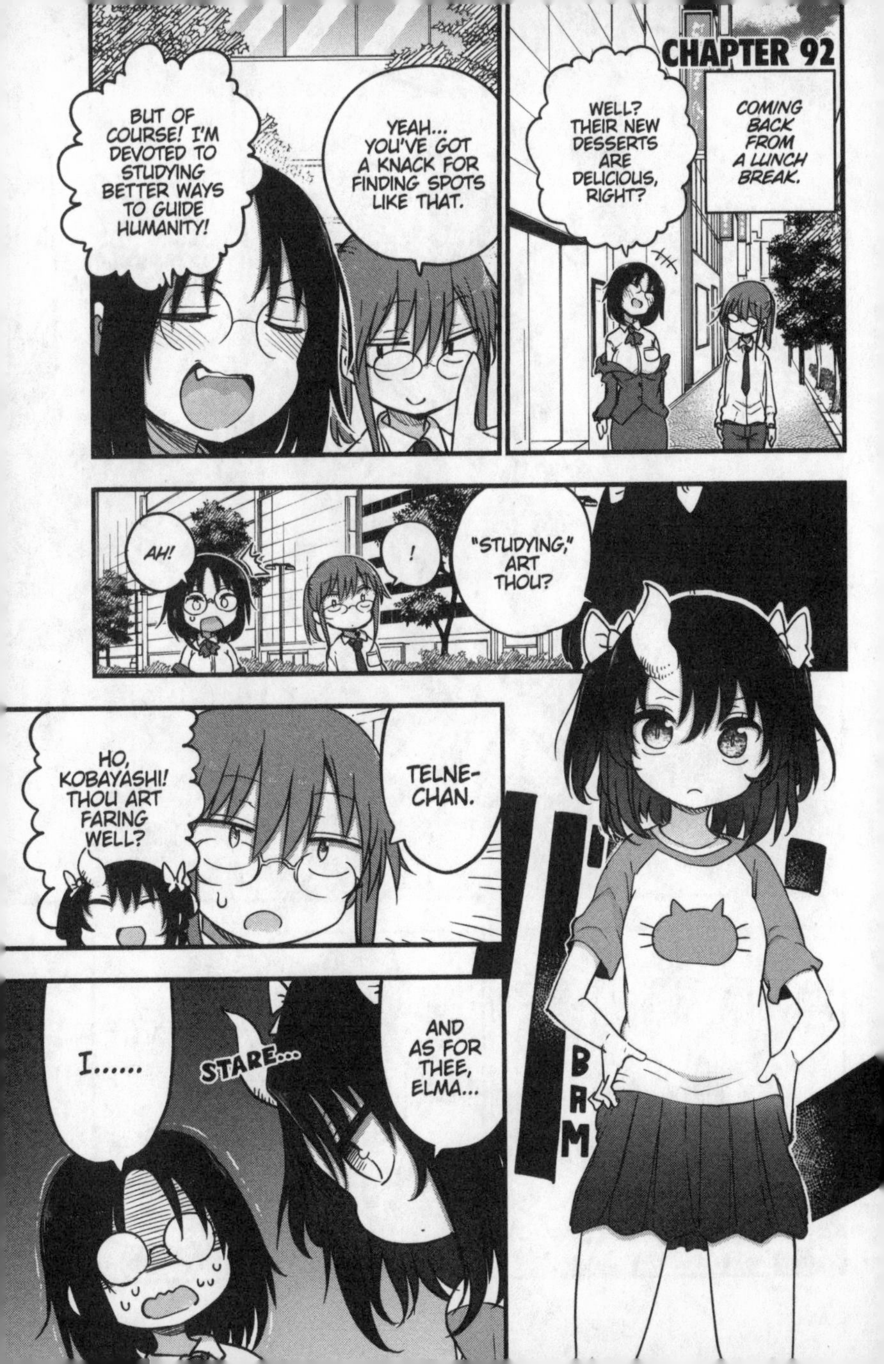
CHAPTER 92
COMING BACK FROM A LUNCH BREAK.
WELL? THEIR NEW DESSERTS ARE DELICIOUS, RIGHT?
YEAH... YOU'VE GOT A KNACK FOR FINDING SPOTS LIKE THAT.
BUT OF COURSE! I'M DEVOTED TO STUDYING BETTER WAYS TO GUIDE HUMANITY!
"STUDYING," ART THOU?
BRM
!
AH!
TELNE-CHAN.
HO, KOBAYASHI! THOU ART FARING WELL?
AND AS FOR THEE, ELMA...
STARE...
I......

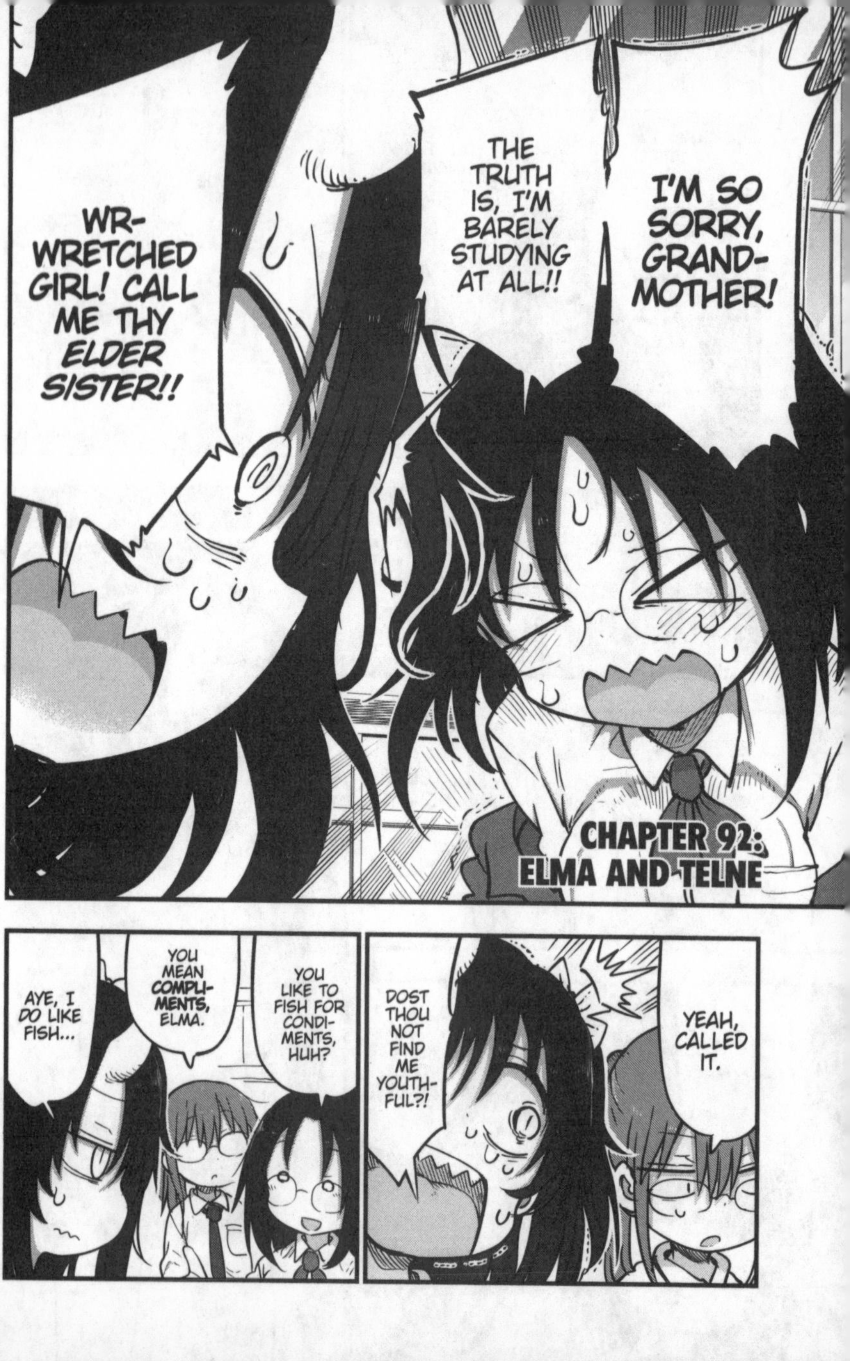
I'M SO SORRY, GRANDMOTHER!
THE TRUTH IS, I'M BARELY STUDYING AT ALL!!
WR-WRETCHED GIRL! CALL ME THY ELDER SISTER!!
CHAPTER 92: ELMA AND TELNE
YEAH, CALLED IT.
DOST THOU NOT FIND ME YOUTHFUL?!
YOU LIKE TO FISH FOR CONDIMENTS, HUH?
YOU MEAN COMPLIMENTS, ELMA.
AYE, I DO LIKE FISH...

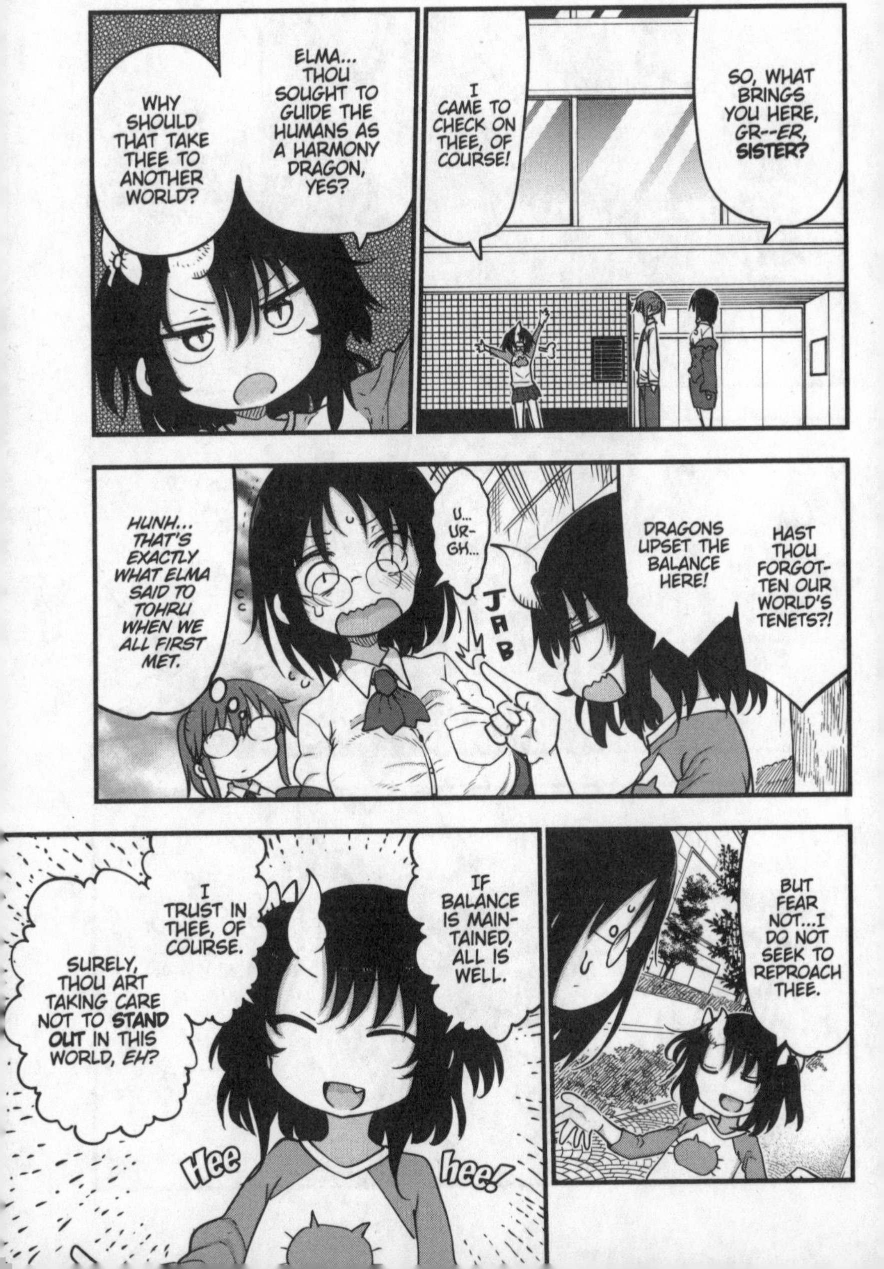
SO, WHAT BRINGS YOU HERE, GR--ER, SISTER?
I CAME TO CHECK ON THEE, OF COURSE!
ELMA... THOU SOUGHT TO GUIDE THE HUMANS AS A HARMONY DRAGON, YES?
WHY SHOULD THAT TAKE THEE TO ANOTHER WORLD?
HAST THOU FORGOTTEN OUR WORLD'S TENETS?!
DRAGONS UPSET THE BALANCE HERE!
U... URGH...
JAB
HUNH... THAT'S EXACTLY WHAT ELMA SAID TO TOHRU WHEN WE ALL FIRST MET.
BUT FEAR NOT...I DO NOT SEEK TO REPROACH THEE.
IF BALANCE IS MAINTAINED, ALL IS WELL.
I TRUST IN THEE, OF COURSE.
SURELY, THOU ART TAKING CARE NOT TO STAND OUT IN THIS WORLD, EH?
Hee hee!

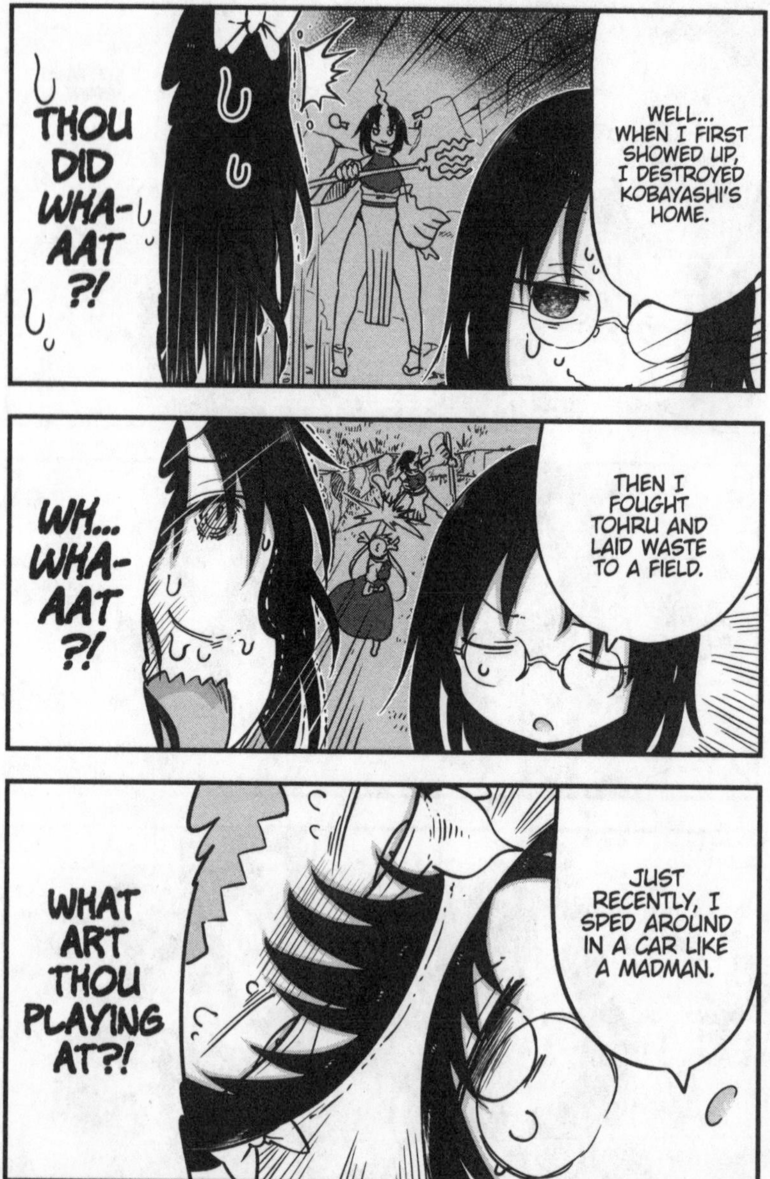
WELL... WHEN I FIRST SHOWED UP, I DESTROYED KOBAYASHI'S HOME.
THOU DID WHA-AAT?!
THEN I FOUGHT TOHRU AND LAID WASTE TO A FIELD.
WH... WHA-AAT?!
JUST RECENTLY, I SPED AROUND IN A CAR LIKE A MADMAN.
WHAT ART THOU PLAYING AT?!

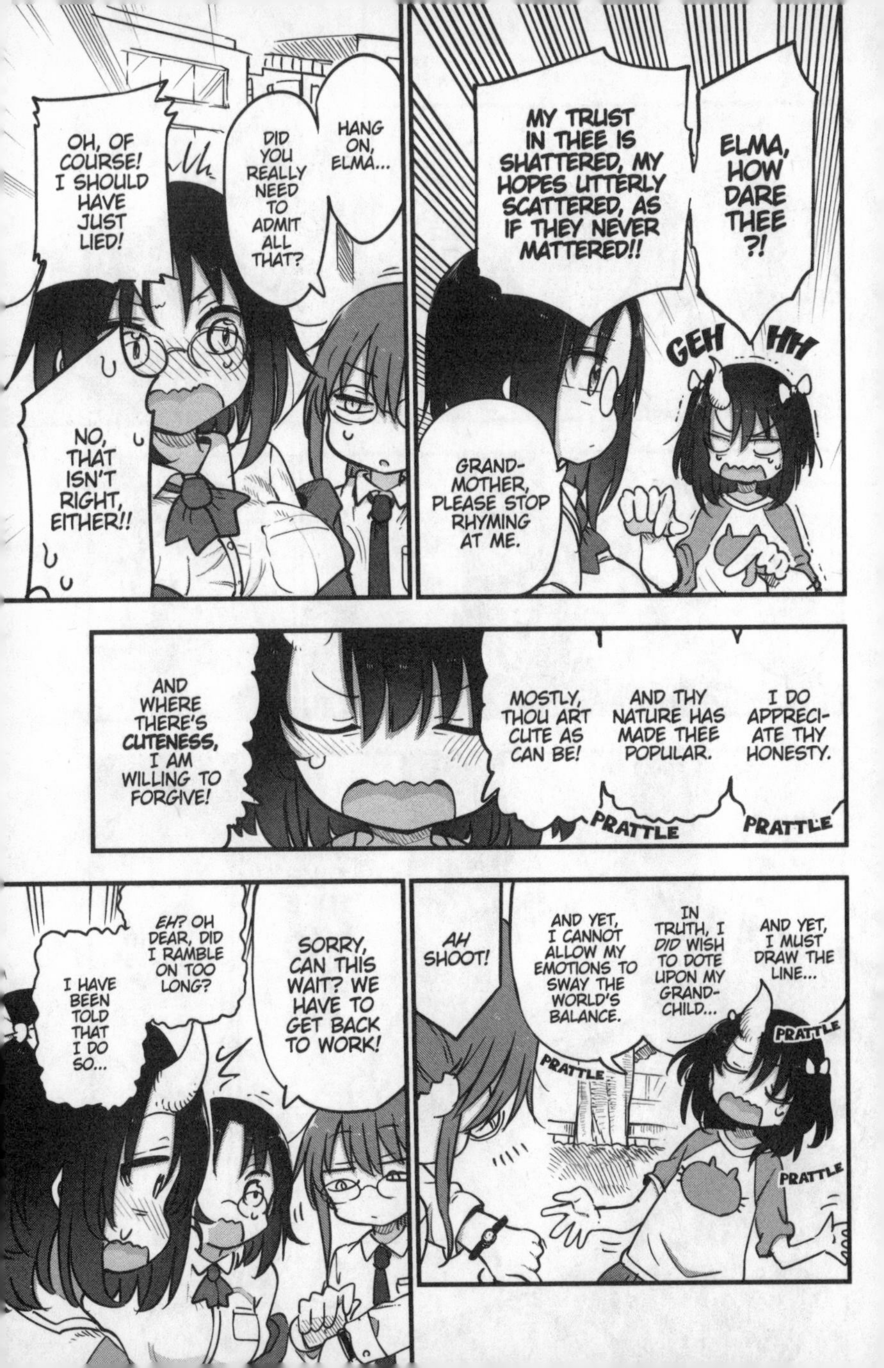
ELMA, HOW DARE THEE ?!
MY TRUST IN THEE IS SHATTERED, MY HOPES UTTERLY SCATTERED, AS IF THEY NEVER MATTERED!!
GEH HH
GRAND-MOTHER, PLEASE STOP RHYMING AT ME.
HANG ON, ELMA...
DID YOU REALLY NEED TO ADMIT ALL THAT?
OH, OF COURSE! I SHOULD HAVE JUST LIED!
NO, THAT ISN'T RIGHT, EITHER!!
I DO APPRECI-ATE THY HONESTY.
AND THY NATURE HAS MADE THEE POPULAR.
MOSTLY, THOU ART CUTE AS CAN BE!
PRATTLE
PRATTLE
AND WHERE THERE'S **CUTENESS,** I AM WILLING TO FORGIVE!
AND YET, I MUST DRAW THE LINE...
IN TRUTH, I *DID* WISH TO DOTE UPON MY GRAND-CHILD...
PRATTLE
AND YET, I CANNOT ALLOW MY EMOTIONS TO SWAY THE WORLD'S BALANCE.
PRATTLE
PRATTLE
AH SHOOT!
SORRY, CAN THIS WAIT? WE HAVE TO GET BACK TO WORK!
EH? OH DEAR, DID I RAMBLE ON TOO LONG?
I HAVE BEEN TOLD THAT I DO SO...

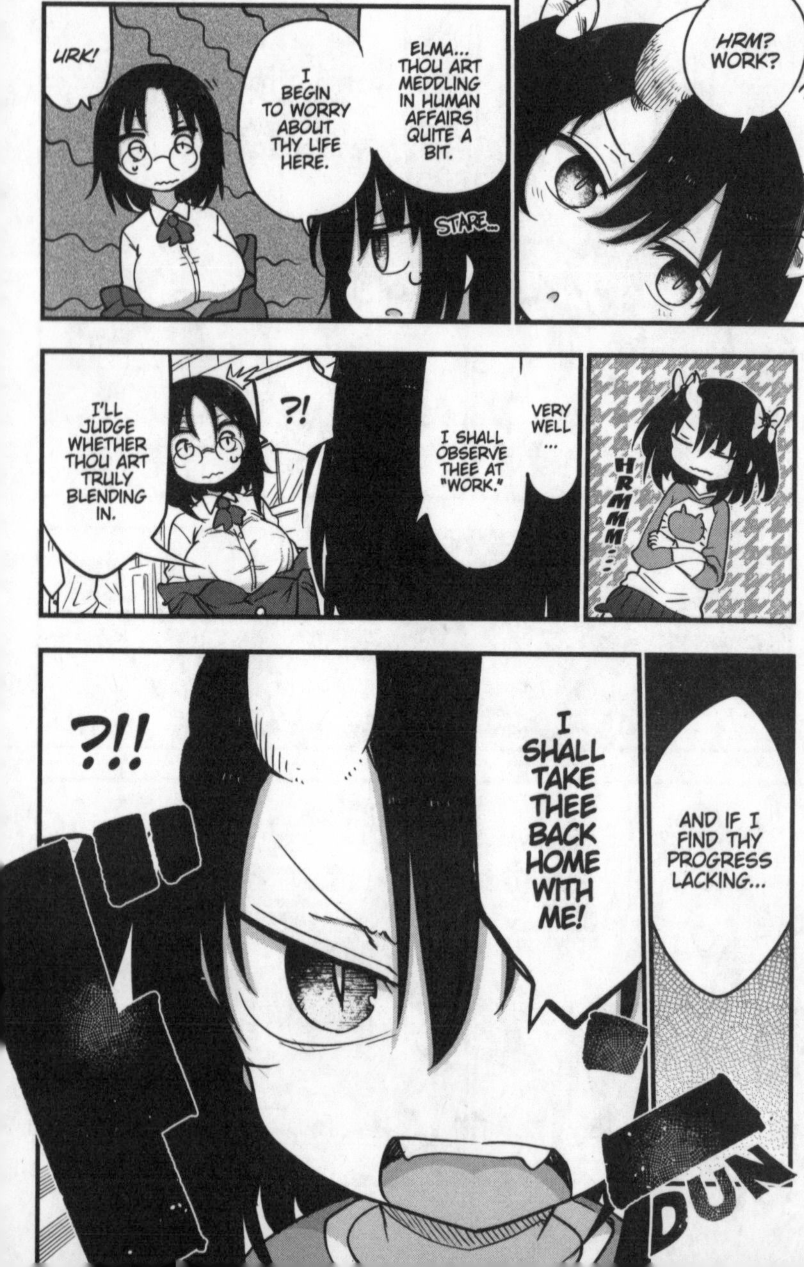
HRM? WORK?
ELMA... THOU ART MEDDLING IN HUMAN AFFAIRS QUITE A BIT.
STARE...
I BEGIN TO WORRY ABOUT THY LIFE HERE.
URK!
HRMMM...
VERY WELL...
I SHALL OBSERVE THEE AT "WORK."
?!
I'LL JUDGE WHETHER THOU ART TRULY BLENDING IN.
AND IF I FIND THY PROGRESS LACKING...
I SHALL TAKE THEE BACK HOME WITH ME!
?!!
DUN

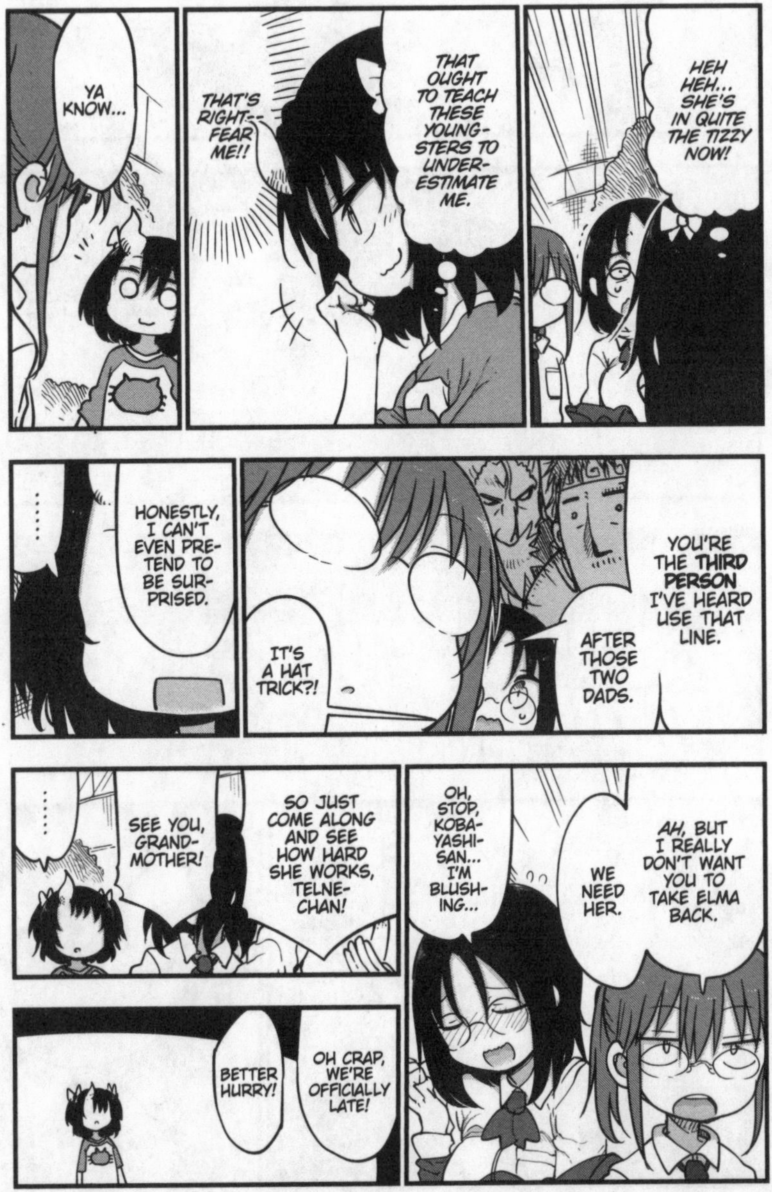
HEH HEH... SHE'S IN QUITE THE TIZZY NOW!
THAT OUGHT TO TEACH THESE YOUNGSTERS TO UNDERESTIMATE ME.
THAT'S RIGHT--FEAR ME!!
YA KNOW...
YOU'RE THE **THIRD PERSON** I'VE HEARD USE THAT LINE.
AFTER THOSE TWO DADS.
IT'S A HAT TRICK?!
HONESTLY, I CAN'T EVEN PRETEND TO BE SURPRISED.
......
AH, BUT I REALLY DON'T WANT YOU TO TAKE ELMA BACK.
WE NEED HER.
OH, STOP, KOBAYASHI-SAN... I'M BLUSHING...
SO JUST COME ALONG AND SEE HOW HARD SHE WORKS, TELNE-CHAN!
SEE YOU, GRANDMOTHER!
......
OH CRAP, WE'RE OFFICIALLY LATE!
BETTER HURRY!

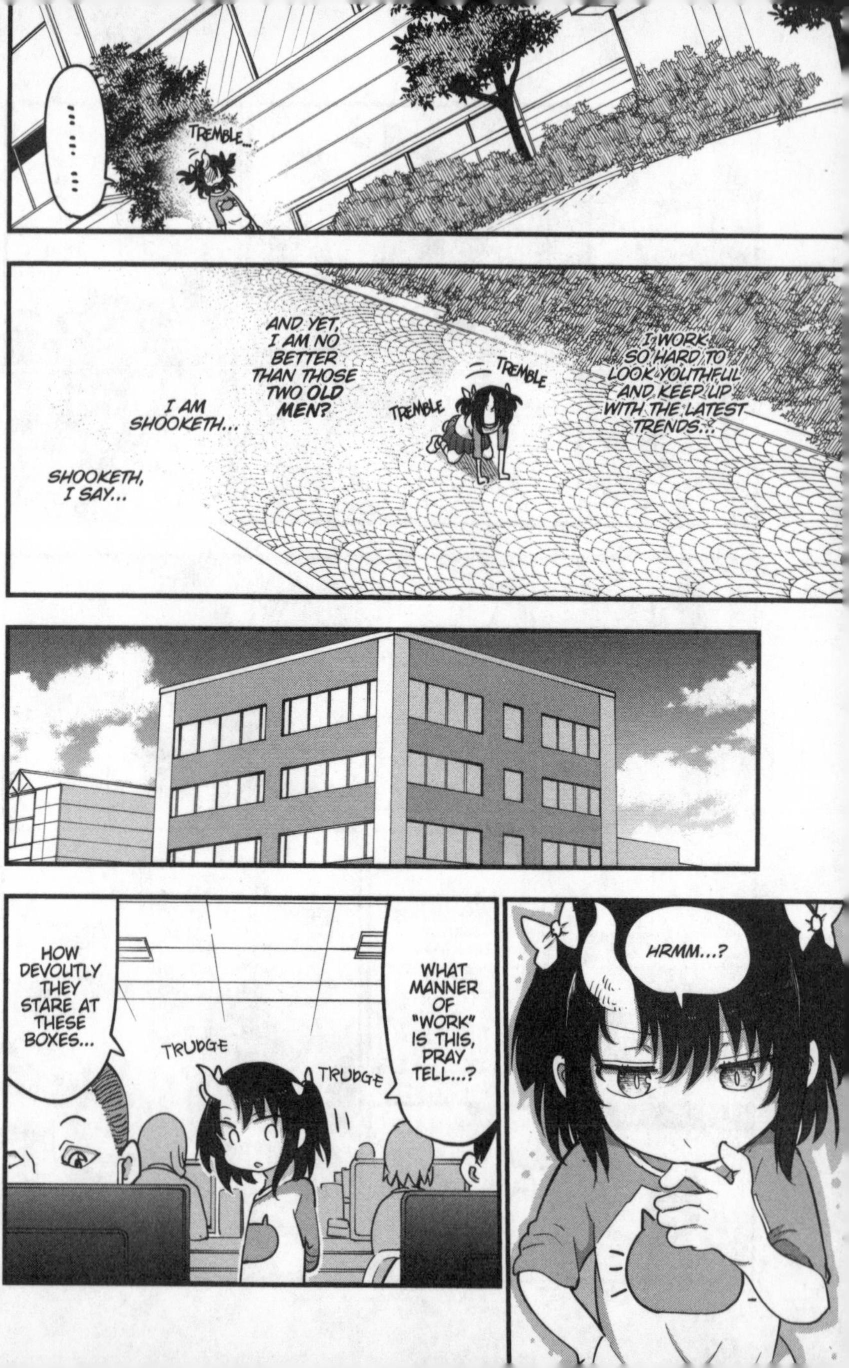
......
TREMBLE...
I WORK SO HARD TO LOOK YOUTHFUL AND KEEP UP WITH THE LATEST TRENDS...
TREMBLE
TREMBLE
AND YET, I AM NO BETTER THAN THOSE TWO OLD MEN?
I AM SHOOKETH...
SHOOKETH, I SAY...
HRMM...?
WHAT MANNER OF "WORK" IS THIS, PRAY TELL...?
TRUDGE
TRUDGE
HOW DEVOUTLY THEY STARE AT THESE BOXES...

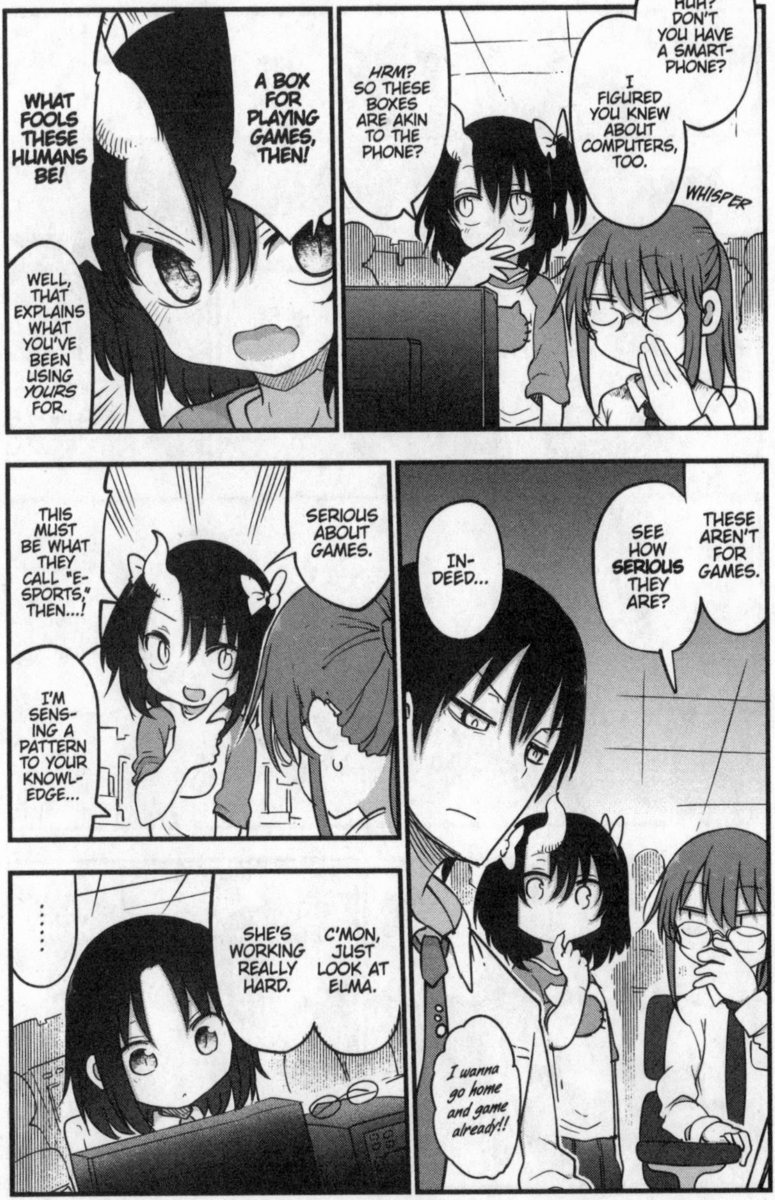
HUH? DON'T YOU HAVE A SMART-PHONE?
I FIGURED YOU KNEW ABOUT COMPUTERS, TOO.
WHISPER
HRM? SO THESE BOXES ARE AKIN TO THE PHONE?
A BOX FOR PLAYING GAMES, THEN!
WHAT FOOLS THESE HUMANS BE!
WELL, THAT EXPLAINS WHAT YOU'VE BEEN USING YOURS FOR.
THESE AREN'T FOR GAMES.
SEE HOW SERIOUS THEY ARE?
IN-DEED...
I wanna go home and game already!!
SERIOUS ABOUT GAMES.
THIS MUST BE WHAT THEY CALL "E-SPORTS," THEN...!
I'M SENSING A PATTERN TO YOUR KNOWL-EDGE...
C'MON, JUST LOOK AT ELMA.
SHE'S WORKING REALLY HARD.
......

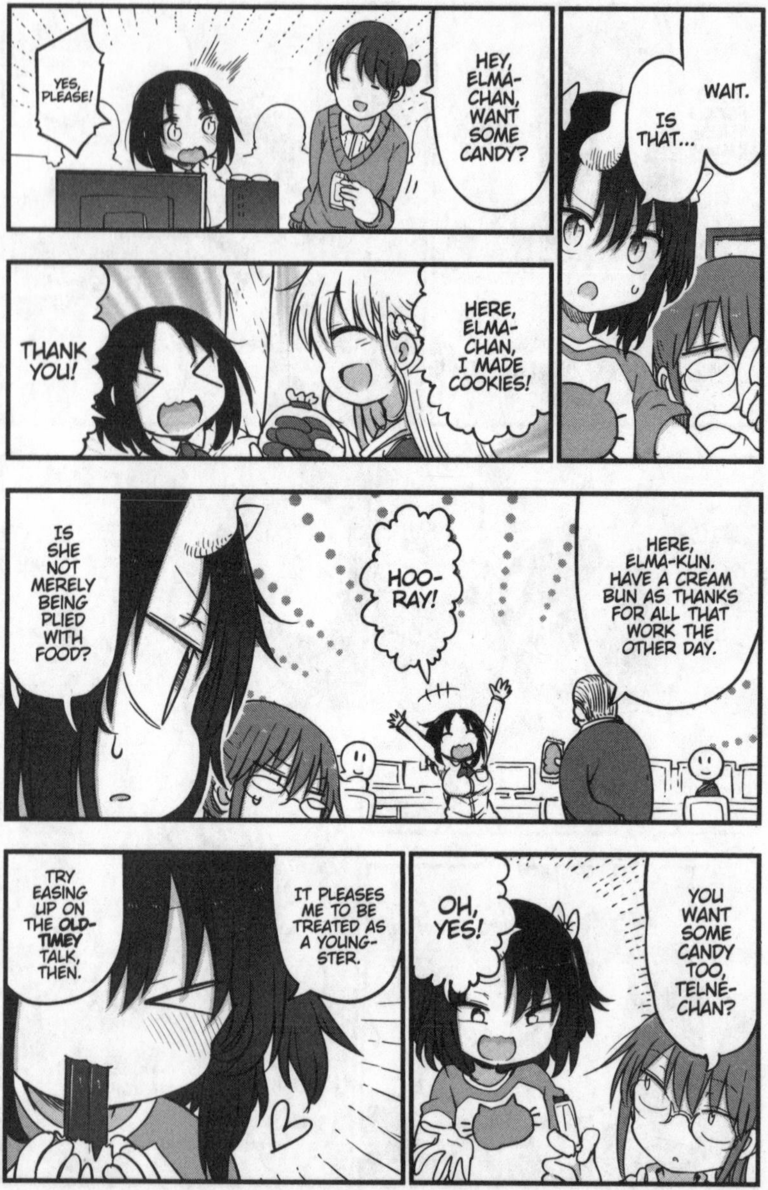
WAIT.
IS THAT...
HEY, ELMA-CHAN, WANT SOME CANDY?
YES, PLEASE!
HERE, ELMA-CHAN, I MADE COOKIES!
THANK YOU!
HERE, ELMA-KUN. HAVE A CREAM BUN AS THANKS FOR ALL THAT WORK THE OTHER DAY.
HOO-RAY!
IS SHE NOT MERELY BEING PLIED WITH FOOD?
YOU WANT SOME CANDY TOO, TELNÉ-CHAN?
OH, YES!
IT PLEASES ME TO BE TREATED AS A YOUNGSTER.
TRY EASING UP ON THE OLD-TIMEY TALK, THEN.

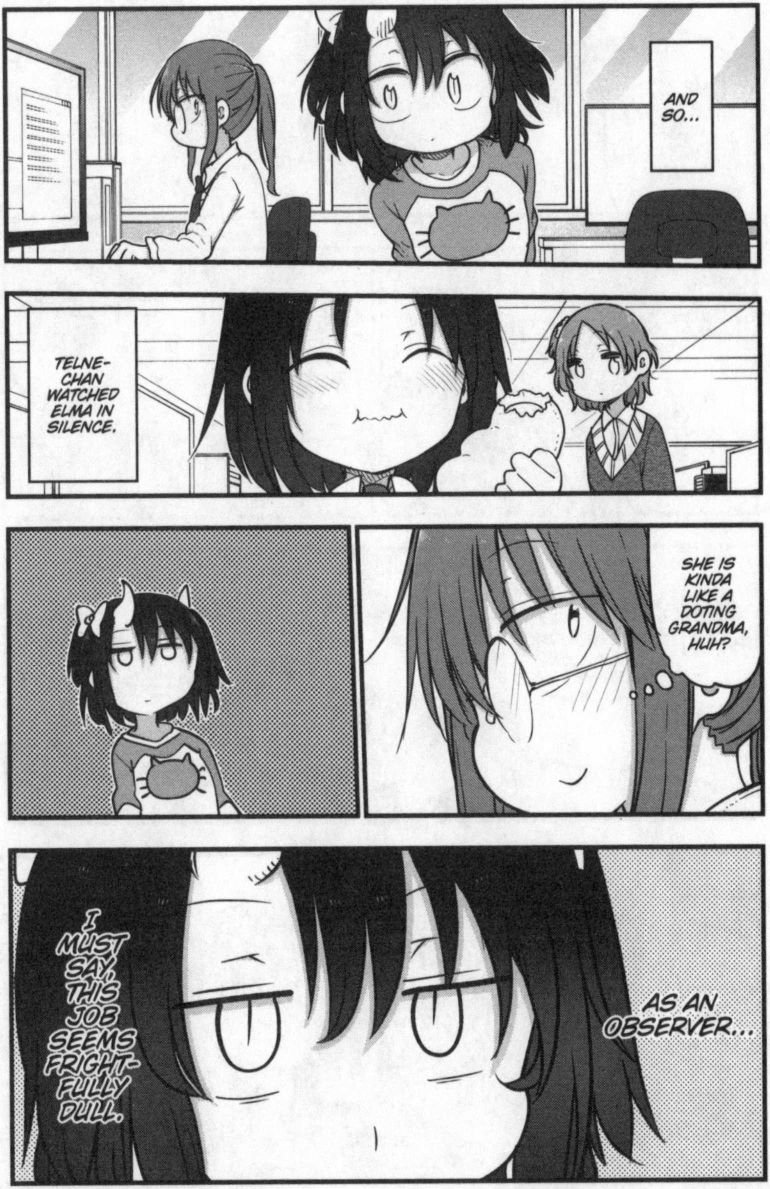
AND SO...
TELNE-CHAN WATCHED ELMA IN SILENCE.
SHE IS KINDA LIKE A DOTING GRANDMA, HUH?
AS AN OBSERVER...
I MUST SAY, THIS JOB SEEMS FRIGHT-FULLY DULL.

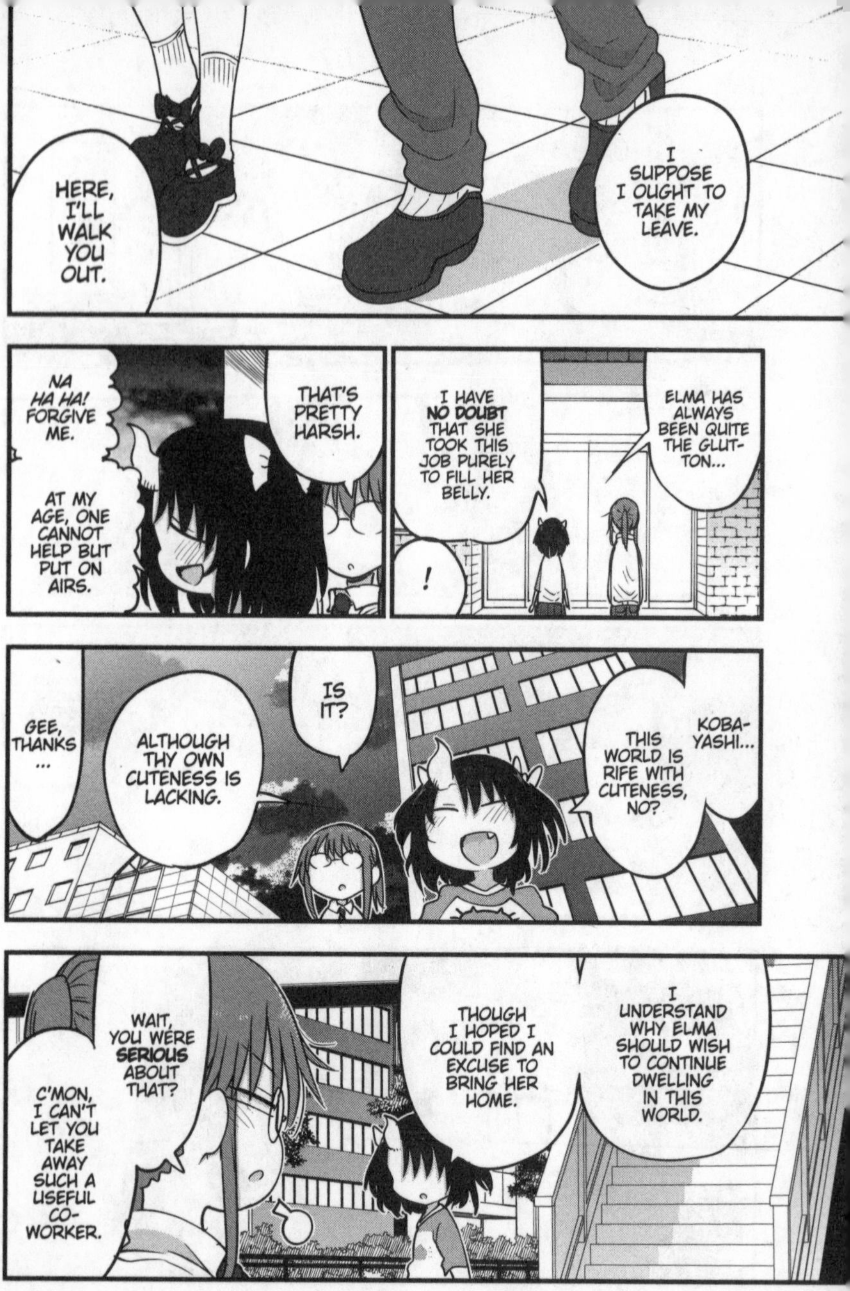
I SUPPOSE I OUGHT TO TAKE MY LEAVE.
HERE, I'LL WALK YOU OUT.
ELMA HAS ALWAYS BEEN QUITE THE GLUT-TON...
I HAVE NO DOUBT THAT SHE TOOK THIS JOB PURELY TO FILL HER BELLY.
!
THAT'S PRETTY HARSH.
NA HA HA! FORGIVE ME.
AT MY AGE, ONE CANNOT HELP BUT PUT ON AIRS.
KOBA-YASHI...
THIS WORLD IS RIFE WITH CUTENESS, NO?
IS IT?
ALTHOUGH THY OWN CUTENESS IS LACKING.
GEE, THANKS ...
I UNDERSTAND WHY ELMA SHOULD WISH TO CONTINUE DWELLING IN THIS WORLD.
THOUGH I HOPED I COULD FIND AN EXCUSE TO BRING HER HOME.
WAIT, YOU WERE SERIOUS ABOUT THAT?
C'MON, I CAN'T LET YOU TAKE AWAY SUCH A USEFUL CO-WORKER.

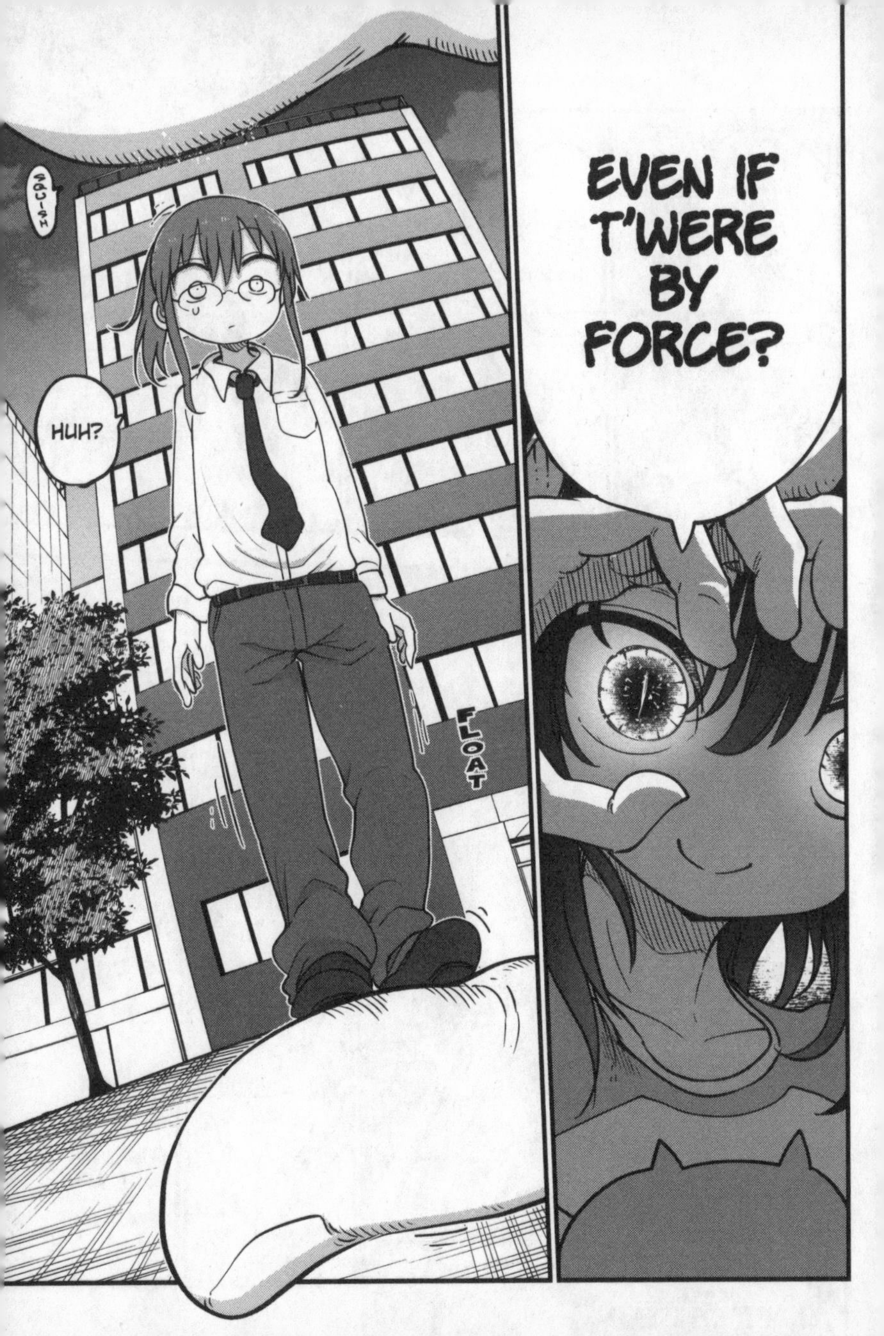
EVEN IF T'WERE BY FORCE?
SQUISH
HUH?
FLOAT

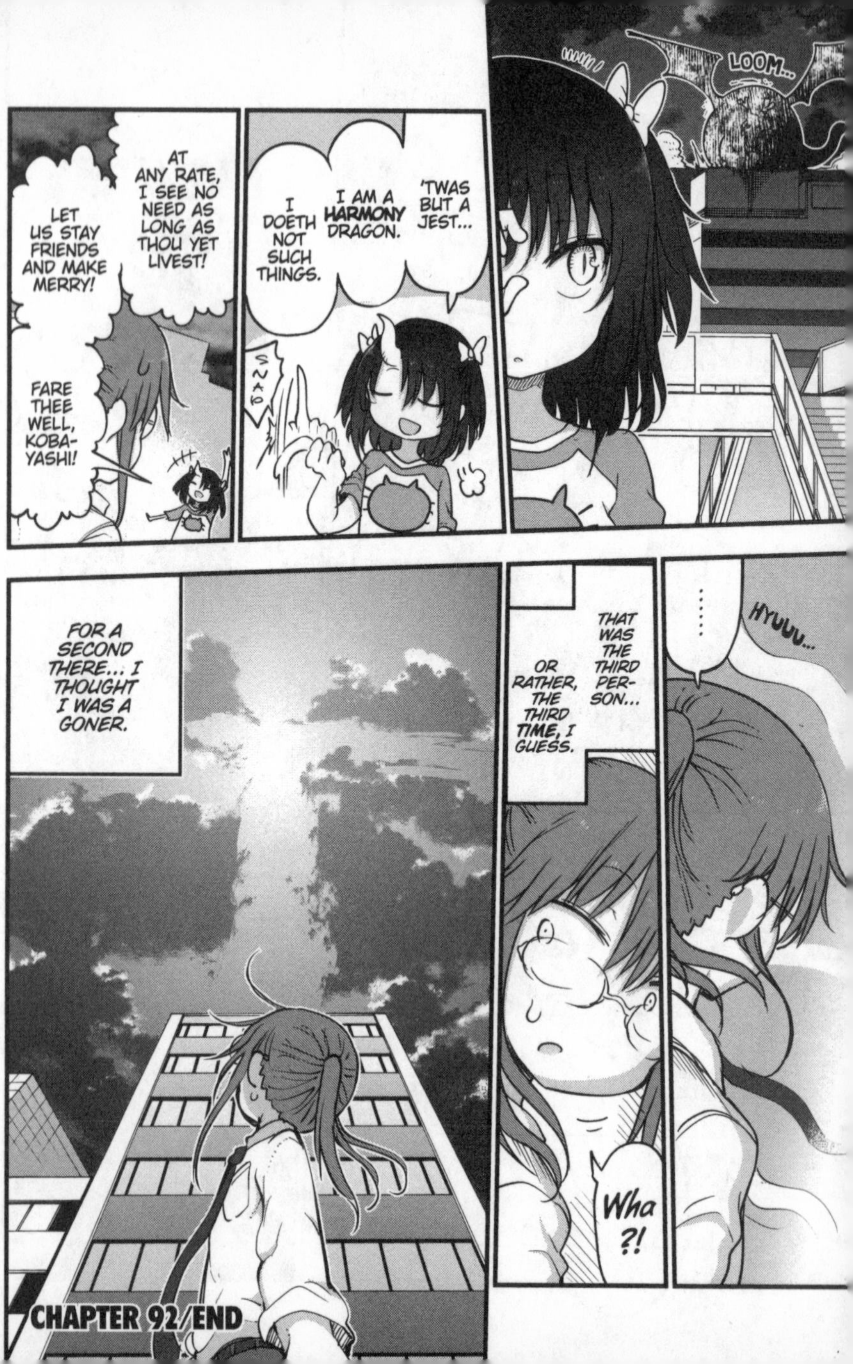
LOOM...
'TWAS BUT A JEST...
I AM A HARMONY DRAGON.
I DOETH NOT SUCH THINGS.
SNAP
AT ANY RATE, I SEE NO NEED AS LONG AS THOU YET LIVEST!
LET US STAY FRIENDS AND MAKE MERRY!
FARE THEE WELL, KOBA-YASHI!
HYUUU...
......
Wha?!
THAT WAS THE THIRD PERSON...
OR RATHER, THE THIRD TIME, I GUESS.
FOR A SECOND THERE... I THOUGHT I WAS A GONER.
CHAPTER 92/END

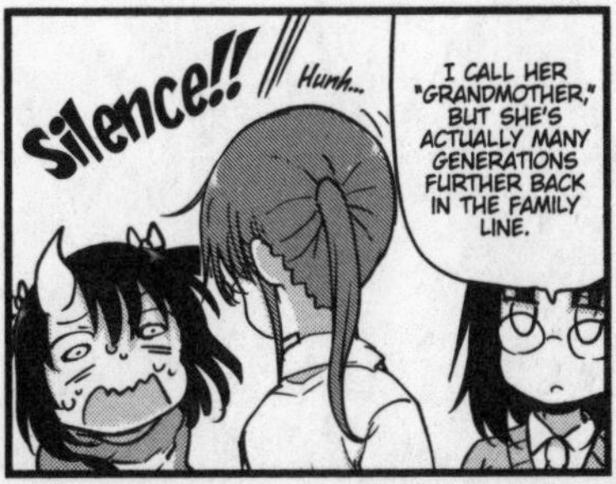
I CALL HER "GRANDMOTHER," BUT SHE'S ACTUALLY MANY GENERATIONS FURTHER BACK IN THE FAMILY LINE.
Hunh...
Silence!!

Miss Kobayashi's Dragon Maid

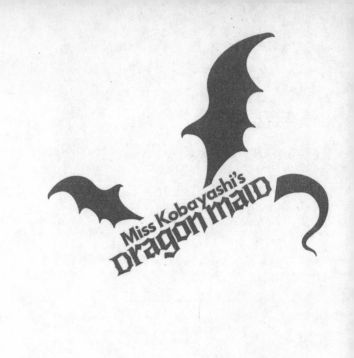

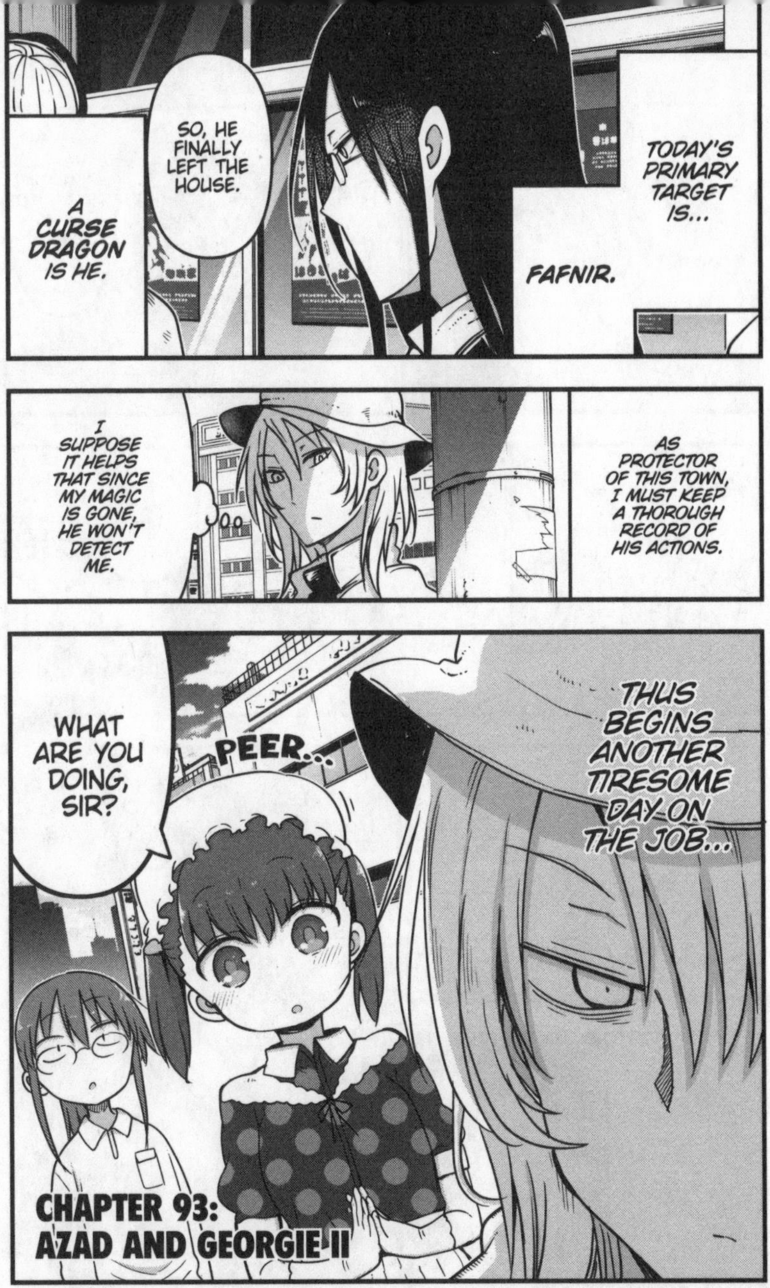
TODAY'S PRIMARY TARGET IS...
FAFNIR.
SO, HE FINALLY LEFT THE HOUSE.
A CURSE DRAGON IS HE.
AS PROTECTOR OF THIS TOWN, I MUST KEEP A THOROUGH RECORD OF HIS ACTIONS.
I SUPPOSE IT HELPS THAT SINCE MY MAGIC IS GONE, HE WON'T DETECT ME.
THUS BEGINS ANOTHER TIRESOME DAY ON THE JOB...
WHAT ARE YOU DOING, SIR?
PEER...
CHAPTER 93: AZAD AND GEORGIE II

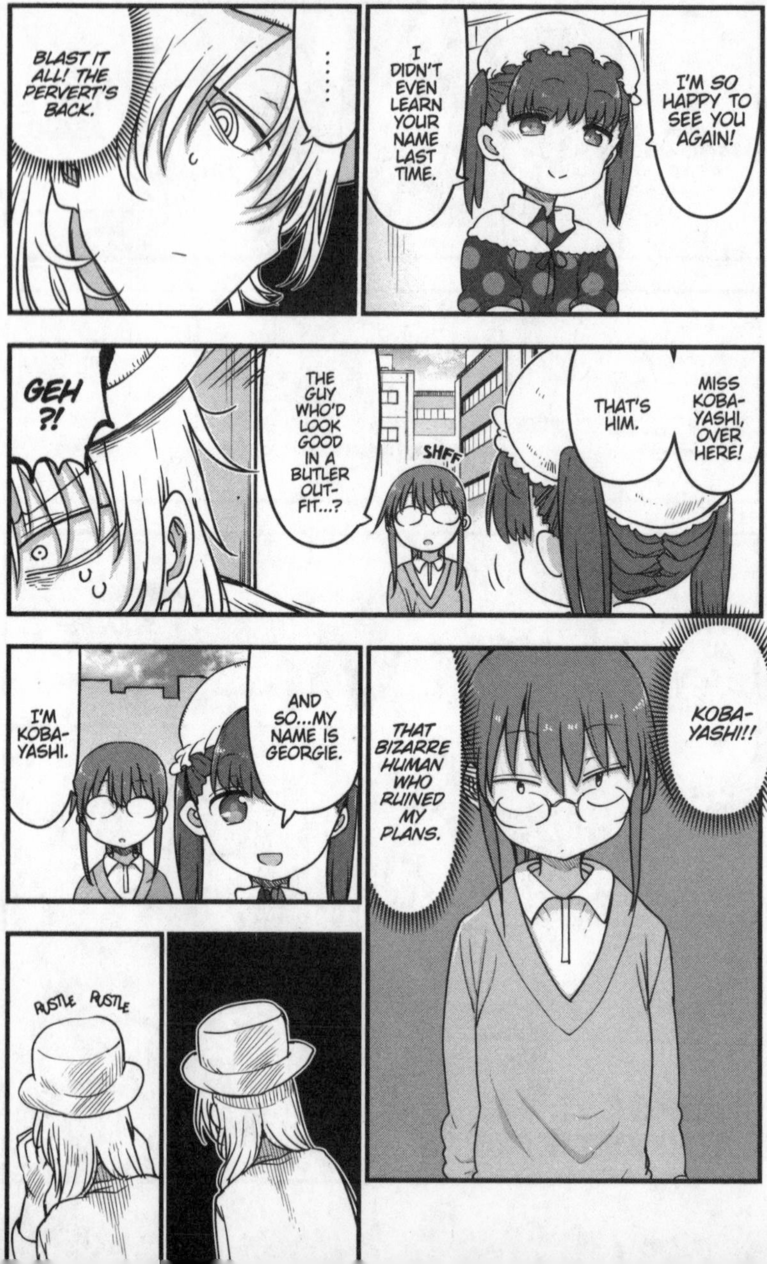
I'M SO HAPPY TO SEE YOU AGAIN!
I DIDN'T EVEN LEARN YOUR NAME LAST TIME.
......
BLAST IT ALL! THE PERVERT'S BACK.
MISS KOBA-YASHI, OVER HERE!
THAT'S HIM.
SHFF
THE GUY WHO'D LOOK GOOD IN A BUTLER OUT-FIT...?
GEH ?!
KOBA-YASHI!!
THAT BIZARRE HUMAN WHO RUINED MY PLANS.
AND SO...MY NAME IS GEORGIE.
I'M KOBA-YASHI.
RUSTLE RUSTLE

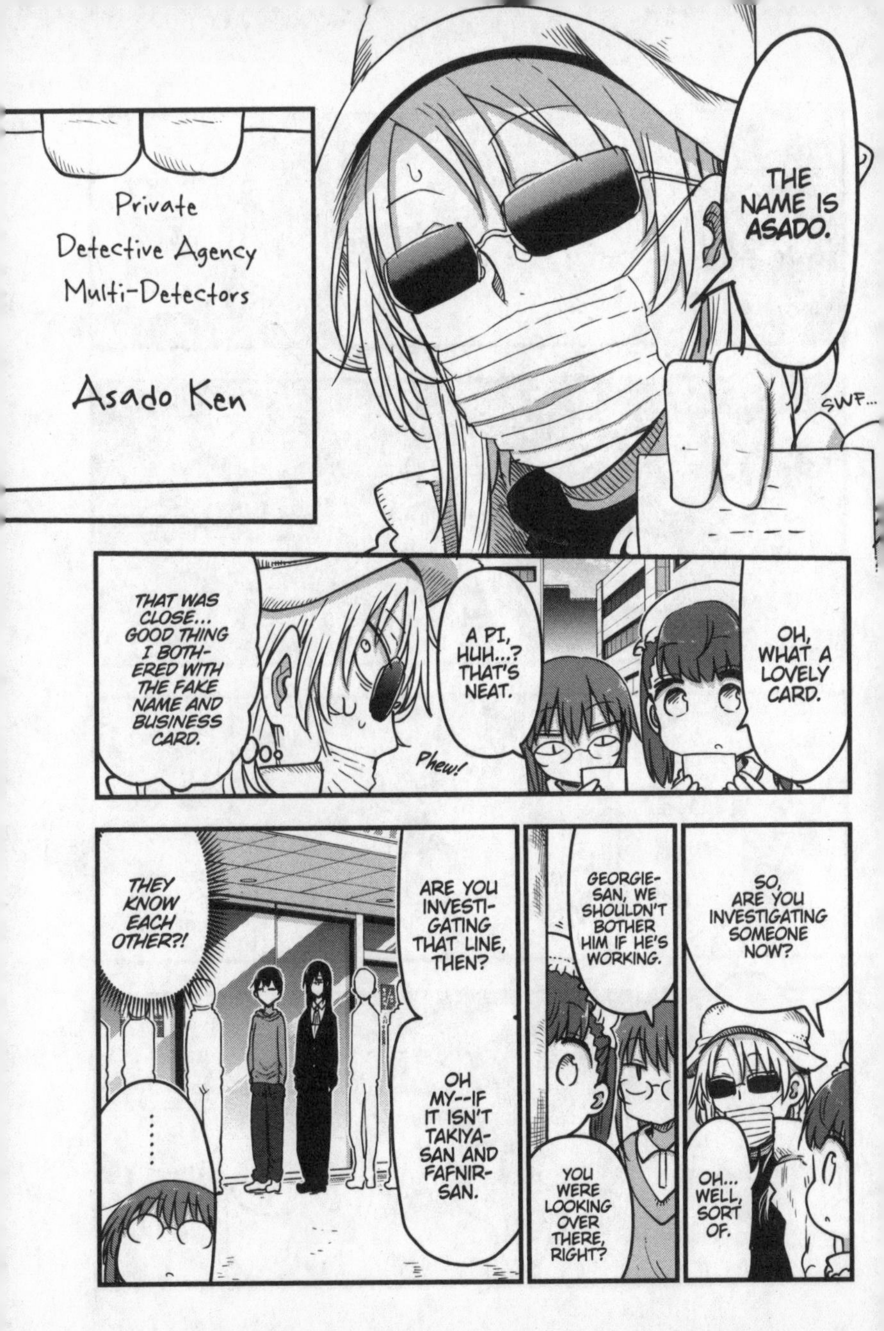
THE NAME IS ASADO.
SWF...
Private Detective Agency Multi-Detectors
Asado Ken
OH, WHAT A LOVELY CARD.
A PI, HUH...? THAT'S NEAT.
Phew!
THAT WAS CLOSE... GOOD THING I BOTHERED WITH THE FAKE NAME AND BUSINESS CARD.
SO, ARE YOU INVESTIGATING SOMEONE NOW?
OH... WELL, SORT OF.
GEORGIE-SAN, WE SHOULDN'T BOTHER HIM IF HE'S WORKING.
YOU WERE LOOKING OVER THERE, RIGHT?
ARE YOU INVESTIGATING THAT LINE, THEN?
OH MY--IF IT ISN'T TAKIYA-SAN AND FAFNIR-SAN.
THEY KNOW EACH OTHER?!
......

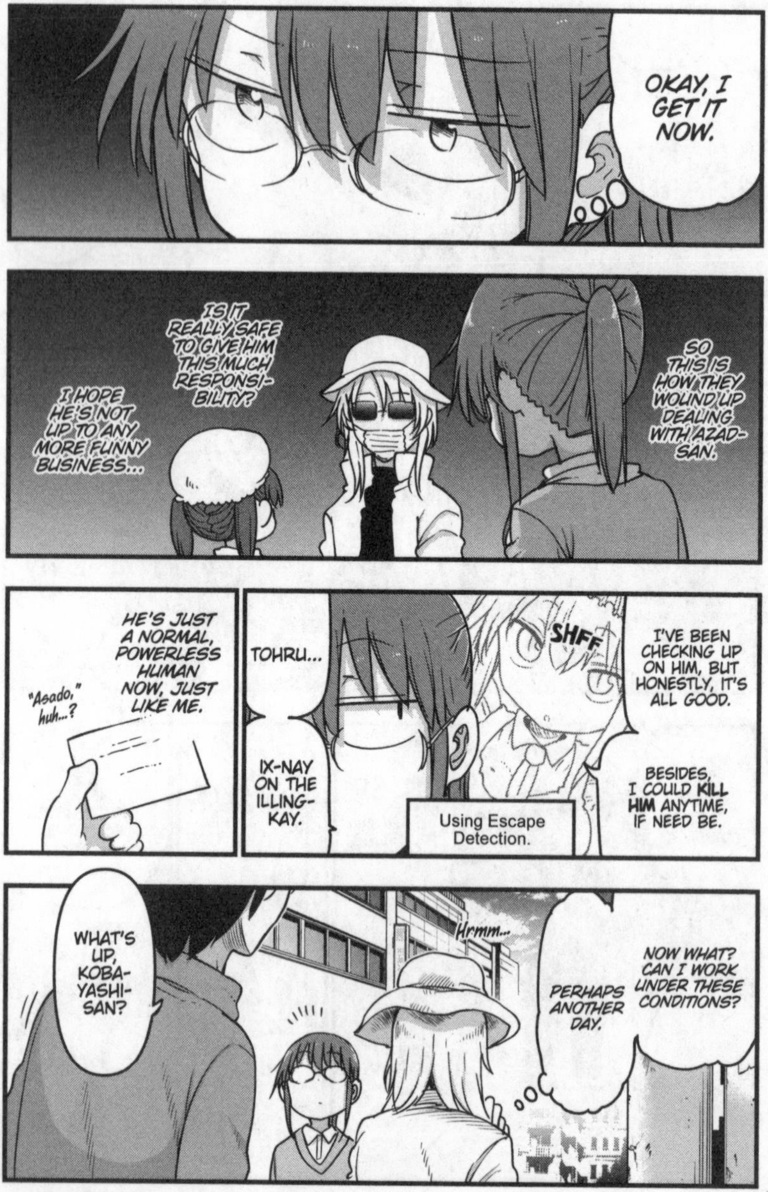
OKAY, I GET IT NOW.
SO THIS IS HOW THEY WOUND UP DEALING WITH AZAD-SAN.
IS IT REALLY SAFE TO GIVE HIM THIS MUCH RESPONSI-BILITY?
I HOPE HE'S NOT UP TO ANY MORE FUNNY BUSINESS...
I'VE BEEN CHECKING UP ON HIM, BUT HONESTLY, IT'S ALL GOOD.
SHFF
TOHRU...
BESIDES, I COULD KILL HIM ANYTIME, IF NEED BE.
IX-NAY ON THE ILLING-KAY.
Using Escape Detection.
HE'S JUST A NORMAL, POWERLESS HUMAN NOW, JUST LIKE ME.
"Asado," huh...?
NOW WHAT? CAN I WORK UNDER THESE CONDITIONS?
Hrmmm...
PERHAPS ANOTHER DAY.
WHAT'S UP, KOBA-YASHI-SAN?

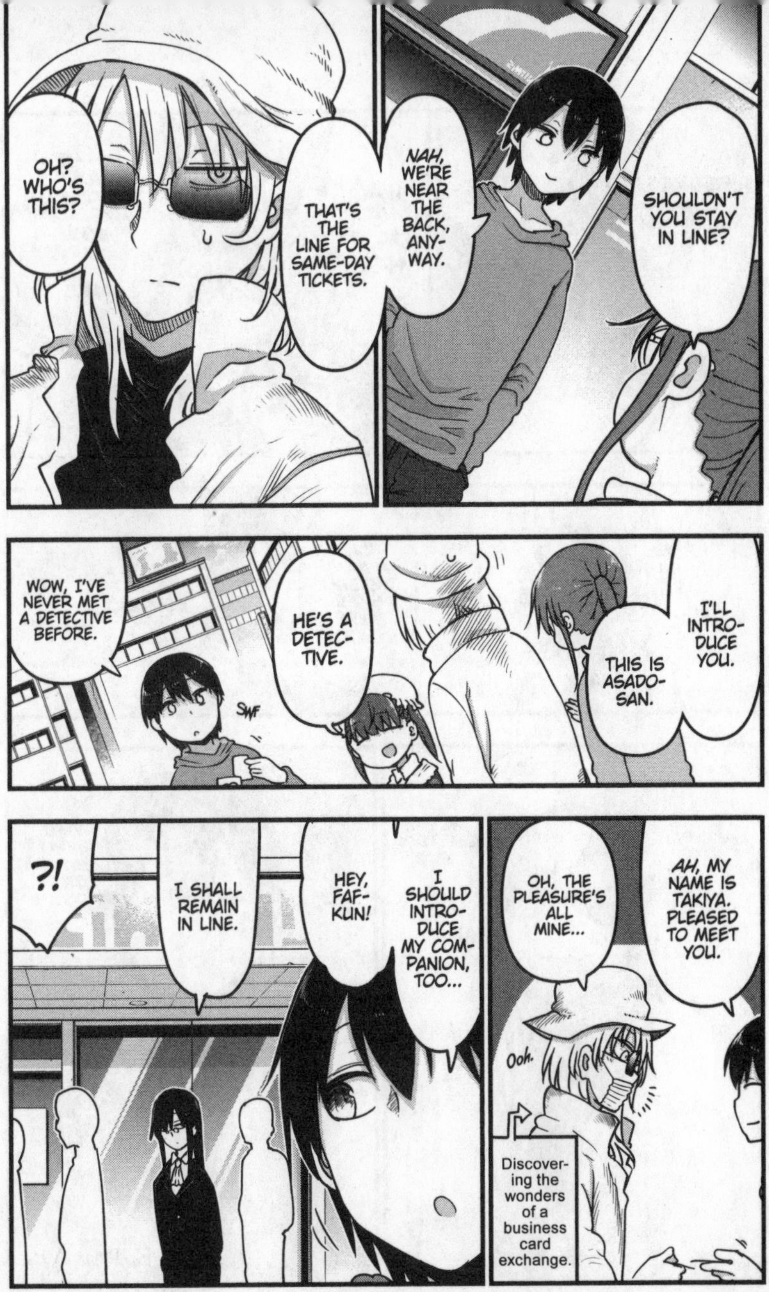
SHOULDN'T YOU STAY IN LINE?
NAH, WE'RE NEAR THE BACK, ANY-WAY.
THAT'S THE LINE FOR SAME-DAY TICKETS.
OH? WHO'S THIS?
I'LL INTRO-DUCE YOU.
THIS IS ASADO-SAN.
HE'S A DETEC-TIVE.
SWF
WOW, I'VE NEVER MET A DETECTIVE BEFORE.
AH, MY NAME IS TAKIYA. PLEASED TO MEET YOU.
OH, THE PLEASURE'S ALL MINE...
Ooh.
Discover-ing the wonders of a business card exchange.
I SHOULD INTRO-DUCE MY COM-PANION, TOO...
HEY, FAF-KUN!
I SHALL REMAIN IN LINE.
?!

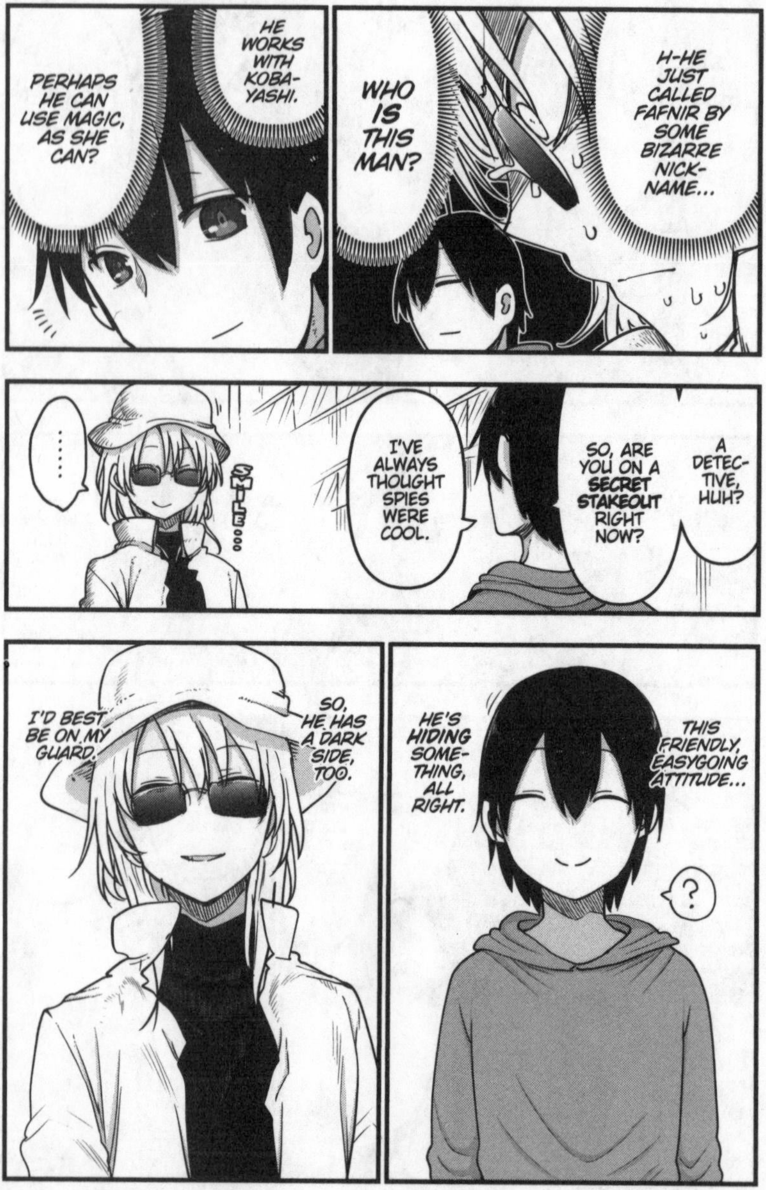
H-HE JUST CALLED FAFNIR BY SOME BIZARRE NICKNAME...
WHO IS THIS MAN?
HE WORKS WITH KOBAYASHI.
PERHAPS HE CAN USE MAGIC, AS SHE CAN?
A DETECTIVE, HUH?
SO, ARE YOU ON A SECRET STAKEOUT RIGHT NOW?
I'VE ALWAYS THOUGHT SPIES WERE COOL.
......
SMILE...
THIS FRIENDLY, EASYGOING ATTITUDE...
?
HE'S HIDING SOMETHING, ALL RIGHT.
SO, HE HAS A DARK SIDE, TOO.
I'D BEST BE ON MY GUARD.

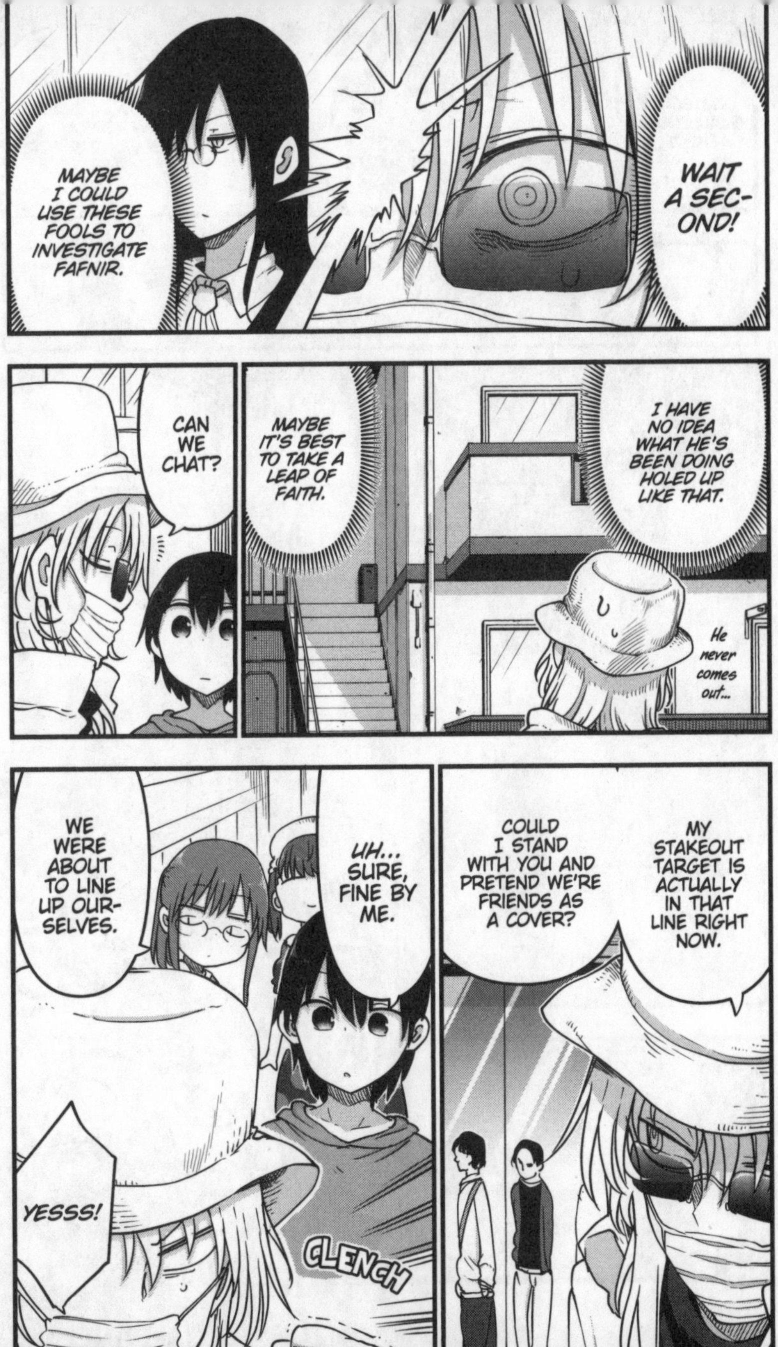
WAIT A SEC-OND!
MAYBE I COULD USE THESE FOOLS TO INVESTIGATE FAFNIR.
I HAVE NO IDEA WHAT HE'S BEEN DOING HOLED UP LIKE THAT.
He never comes out...
MAYBE IT'S BEST TO TAKE A LEAP OF FAITH.
CAN WE CHAT?
MY STAKEOUT TARGET IS ACTUALLY IN THAT LINE RIGHT NOW.
COULD I STAND WITH YOU AND PRETEND WE'RE FRIENDS AS A COVER?
UH... SURE, FINE BY ME.
WE WERE ABOUT TO LINE UP OUR-SELVES.
YESSS!
CLENCH

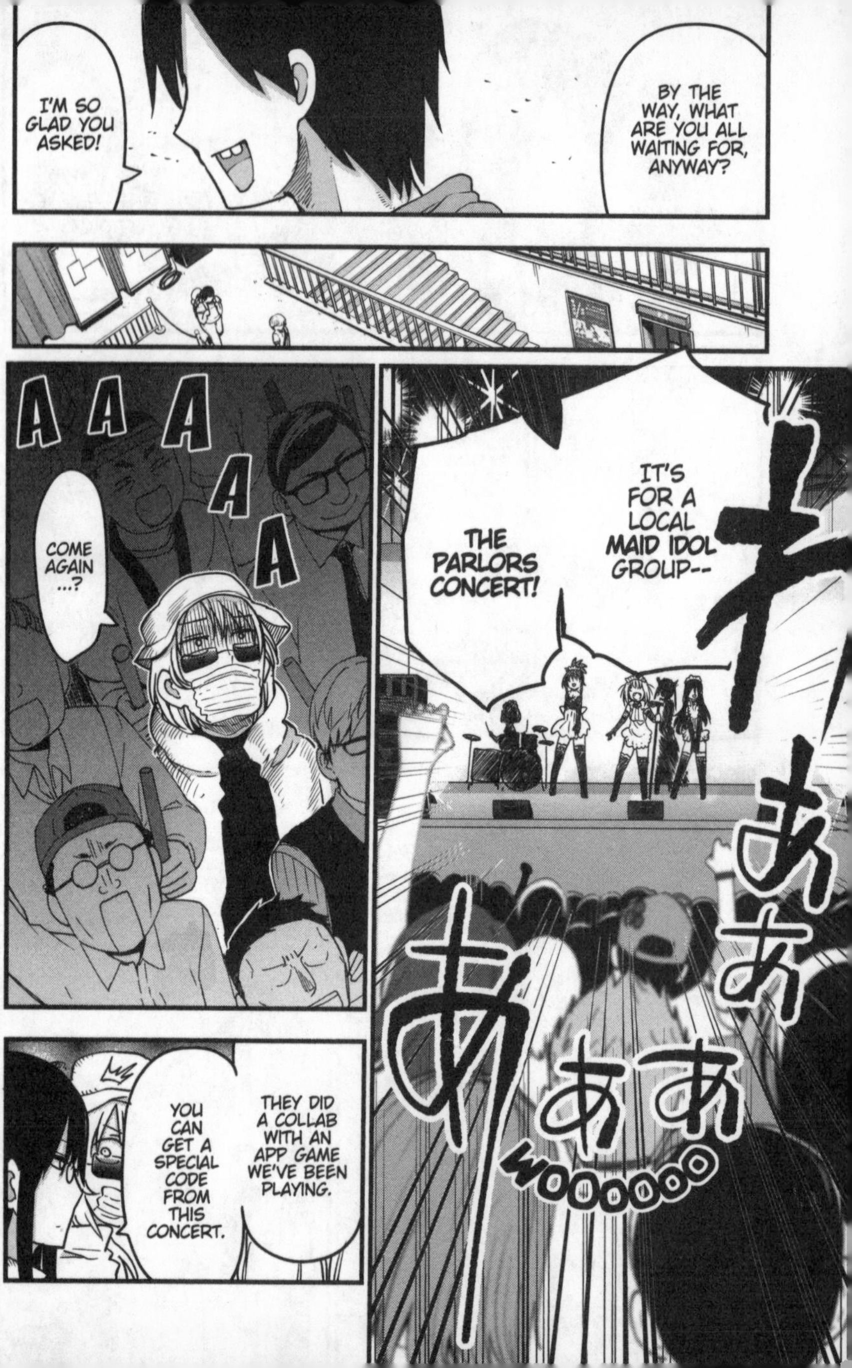
BY THE WAY, WHAT ARE YOU ALL WAITING FOR, ANYWAY?
I'M SO GLAD YOU ASKED!
IT'S FOR A LOCAL MAID IDOL GROUP--
THE PARLORS CONCERT!
WOOOOOOO
AAAAAA
COME AGAIN ...?
THEY DID A COLLAB WITH AN APP GAME WE'VE BEEN PLAYING.
YOU CAN GET A SPECIAL CODE FROM THIS CONCERT.

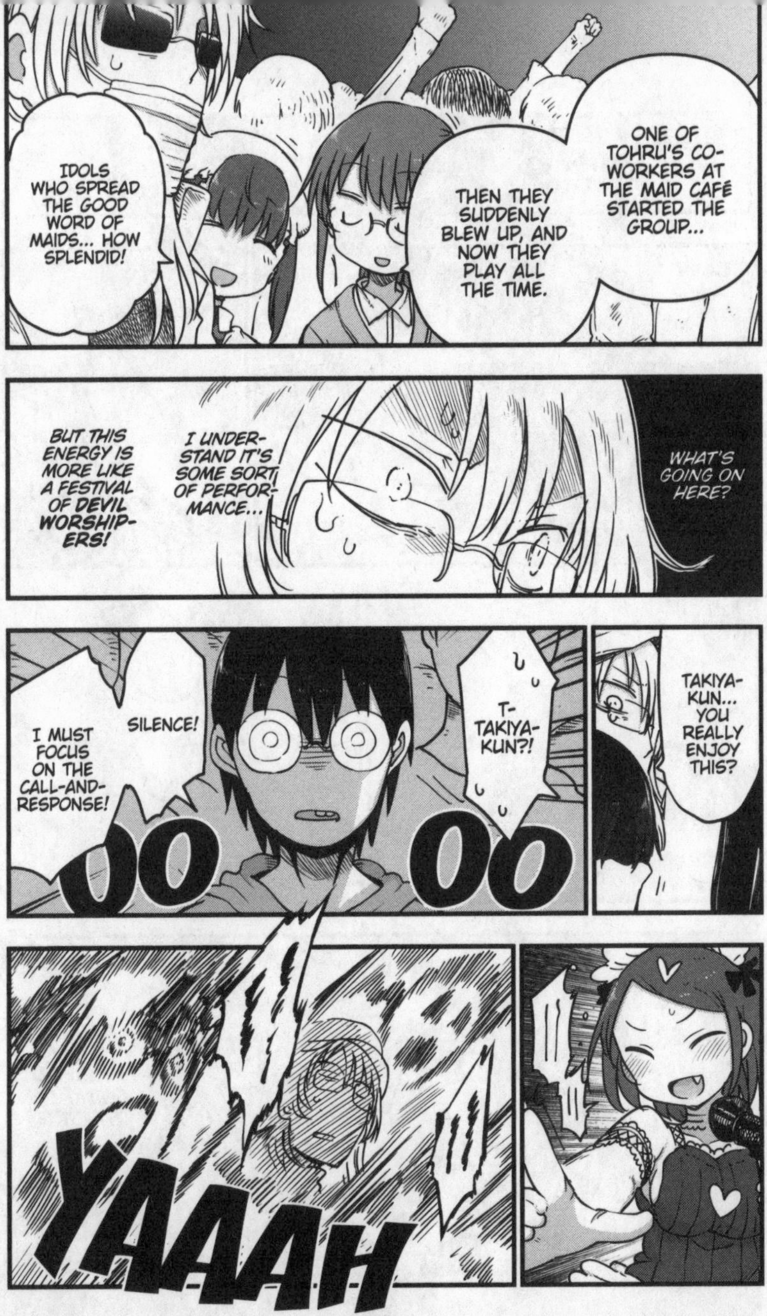
ONE OF TOHRU'S CO-WORKERS AT THE MAID CAFÉ STARTED THE GROUP...
THEN THEY SUDDENLY BLEW UP, AND NOW THEY PLAY ALL THE TIME.
IDOLS WHO SPREAD THE GOOD WORD OF MAIDS... HOW SPLENDID!
WHAT'S GOING ON HERE?
I UNDERSTAND IT'S SOME SORT OF PERFORMANCE...
BUT THIS ENERGY IS MORE LIKE A FESTIVAL OF DEVIL WORSHIPERS!
TAKIYA-KUN... YOU REALLY ENJOY THIS?
T-TAKIYA-KUN?!
SILENCE!
I MUST FOCUS ON THE CALL-AND-RESPONSE!
OO OO
YAAAH

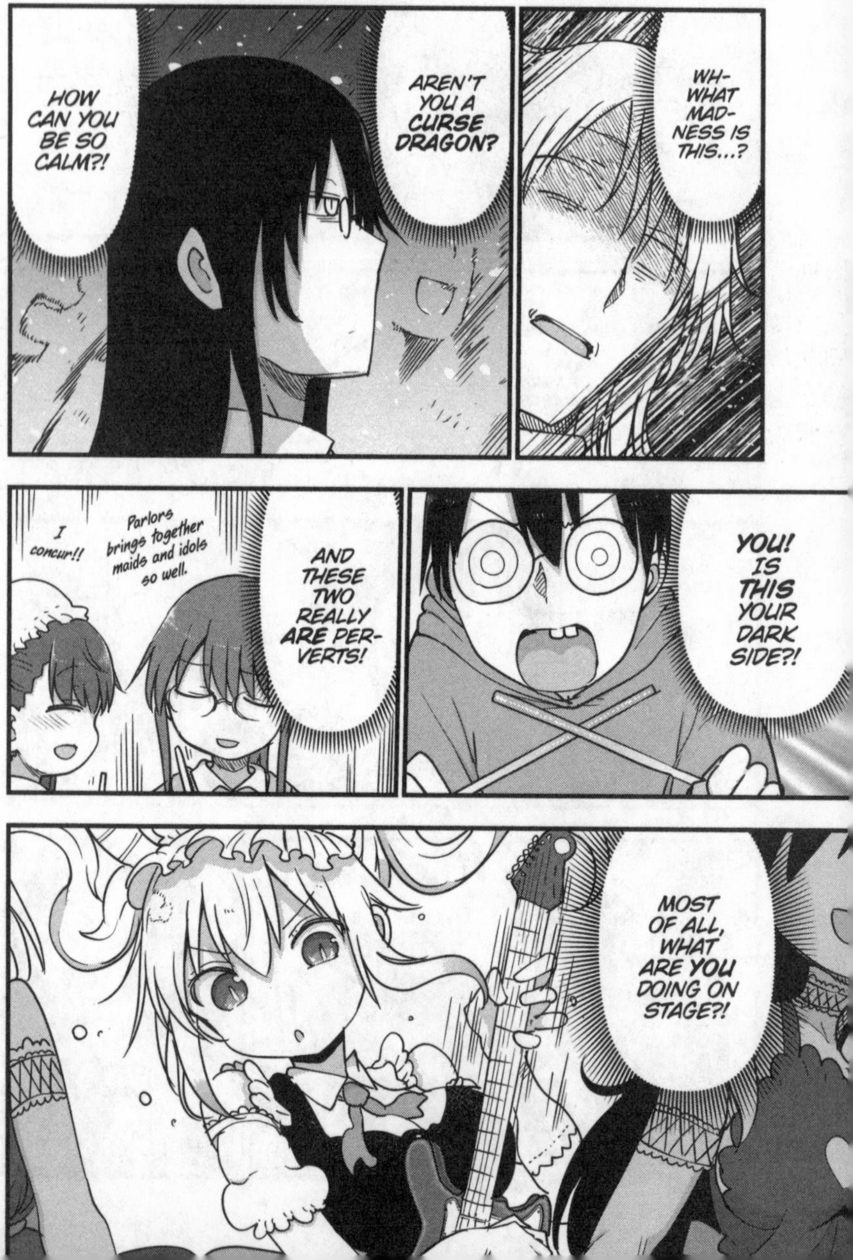
WH- WHAT MADNESS IS THIS...?
AREN'T YOU A CURSE DRAGON?
HOW CAN YOU BE SO CALM?!
YOU! IS THIS YOUR DARK SIDE?!
AND THESE TWO REALLY ARE PER-VERTS!
Parlors brings together maids and idols so well.
I concur!!
MOST OF ALL, WHAT ARE YOU DOING ON STAGE?!

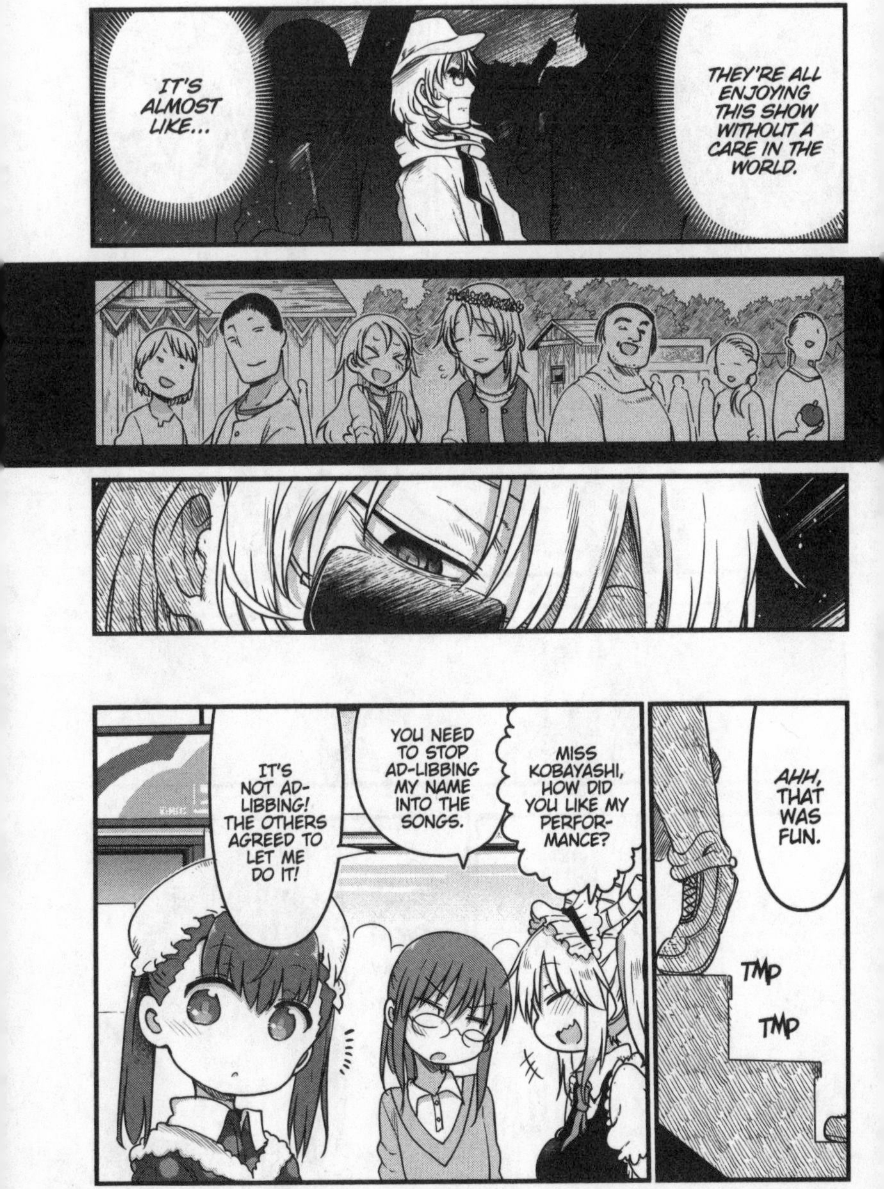
THEY'RE ALL ENJOYING THIS SHOW WITHOUT A CARE IN THE WORLD.
IT'S ALMOST LIKE...
AHH, THAT WAS FUN.
TMP
TMP
MISS KOBAYASHI, HOW DID YOU LIKE MY PERFORMANCE?
YOU NEED TO STOP AD-LIBBING MY NAME INTO THE SONGS.
IT'S NOT AD-LIBBING! THE OTHERS AGREED TO LET ME DO IT!

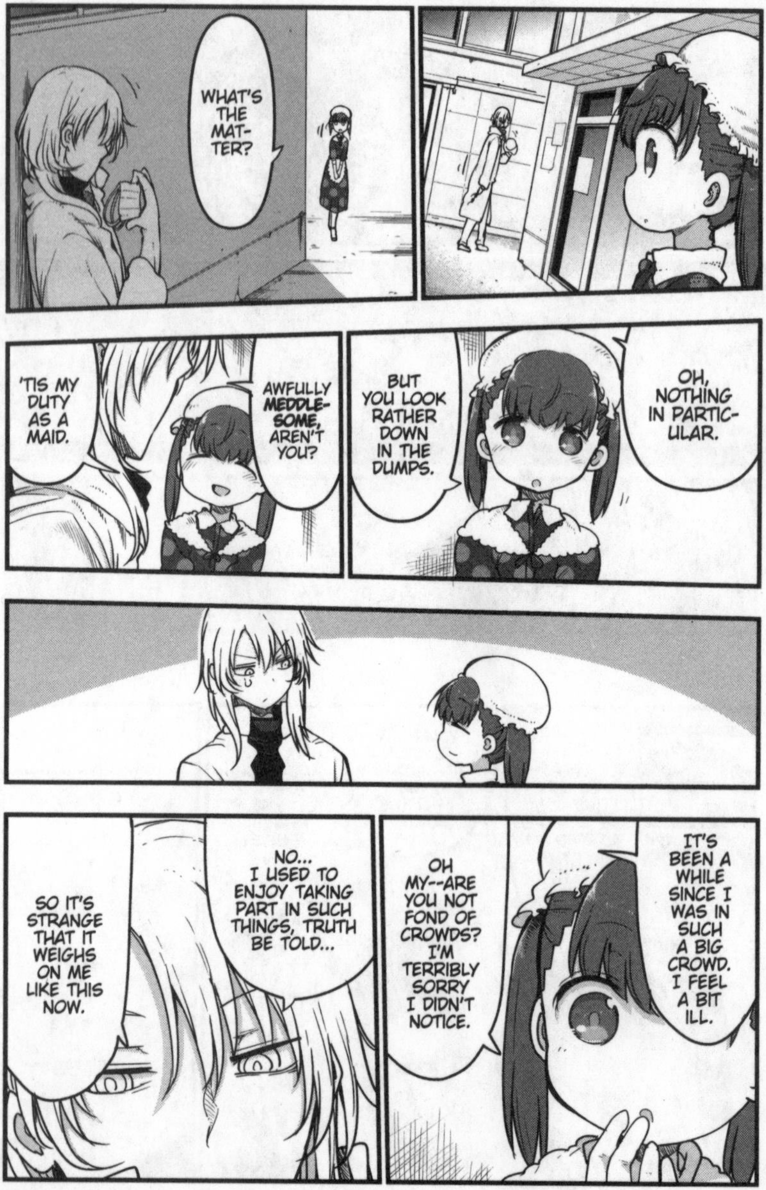
WHAT'S THE MAT-TER?
OH, NOTHING IN PARTIC-ULAR.
BUT YOU LOOK RATHER DOWN IN THE DUMPS.
AWFULLY MEDDLE-SOME, AREN'T YOU?
'TIS MY DUTY AS A MAID.
IT'S BEEN A WHILE SINCE I WAS IN SUCH A BIG CROWD. I FEEL A BIT ILL.
OH MY--ARE YOU NOT FOND OF CROWDS? I'M TERRIBLY SORRY I DIDN'T NOTICE.
NO... I USED TO ENJOY TAKING PART IN SUCH THINGS, TRUTH BE TOLD...
SO IT'S STRANGE THAT IT WEIGHS ON ME LIKE THIS NOW.

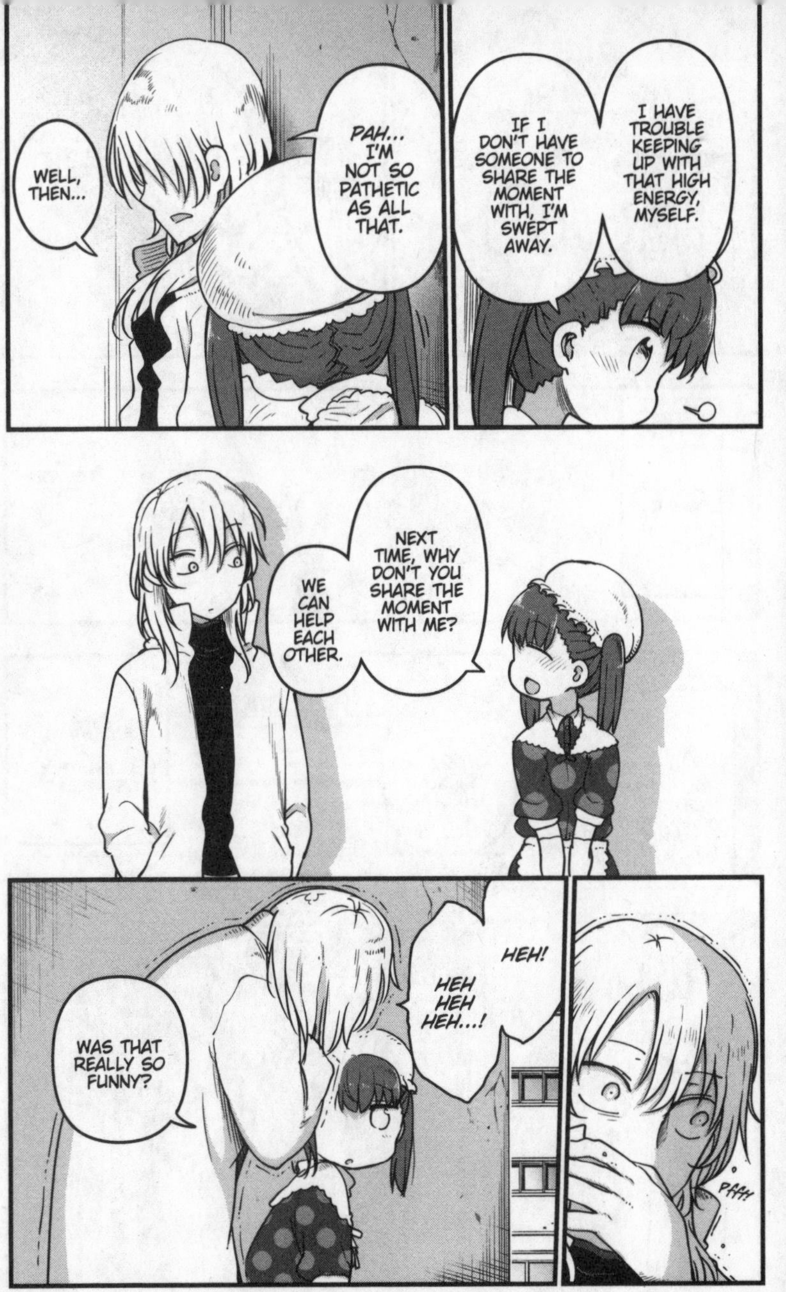
I HAVE TROUBLE KEEPING UP WITH THAT HIGH ENERGY, MYSELF.
IF I DON'T HAVE SOMEONE TO SHARE THE MOMENT WITH, I'M SWEPT AWAY.
PAH... I'M NOT SO PATHETIC AS ALL THAT.
WELL, THEN...
NEXT TIME, WHY DON'T YOU SHARE THE MOMENT WITH ME?
WE CAN HELP EACH OTHER.
PFFF
HEH!
HEH HEH HEH...!
WAS THAT REALLY SO FUNNY?

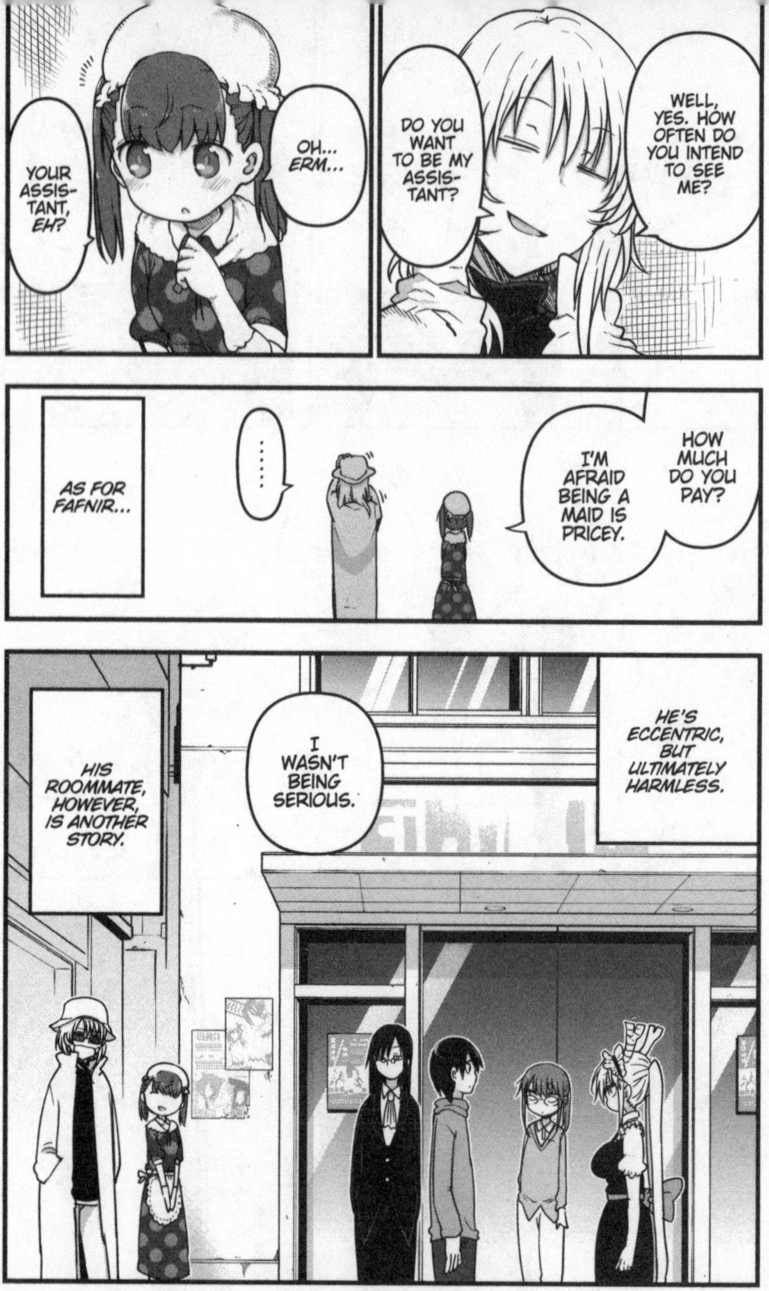
WELL, YES. HOW OFTEN DO YOU INTEND TO SEE ME?
DO YOU WANT TO BE MY ASSISTANT?
OH... ERM...
YOUR ASSISTANT, EH?
HOW MUCH DO YOU PAY?
I'M AFRAID BEING A MAID IS PRICEY.
......
AS FOR FAFNIR...
HE'S ECCENTRIC, BUT ULTIMATELY HARMLESS.
I WASN'T BEING SERIOUS.
HIS ROOMMATE, HOWEVER, IS ANOTHER STORY.

CHAPTER 93/END

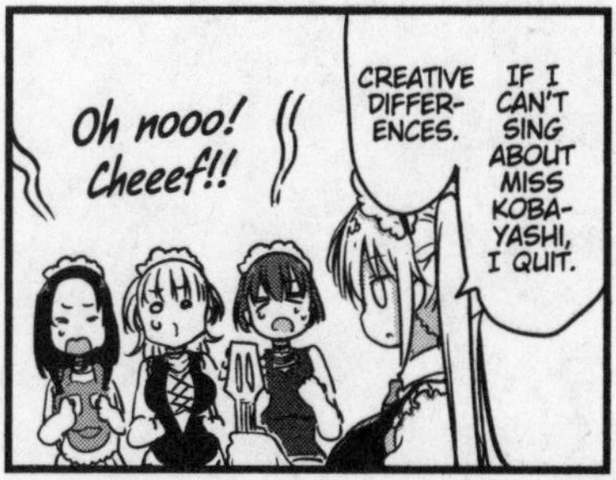
IF I CAN'T SING ABOUT MISS KOBA-YASHI, I QUIT.
CREATIVE DIFFER-ENCES.
Oh nooo! Cheeef!!

Miss Kobayashi's Dragon Maid

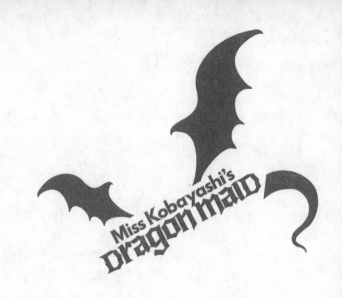

CHAPTER 94

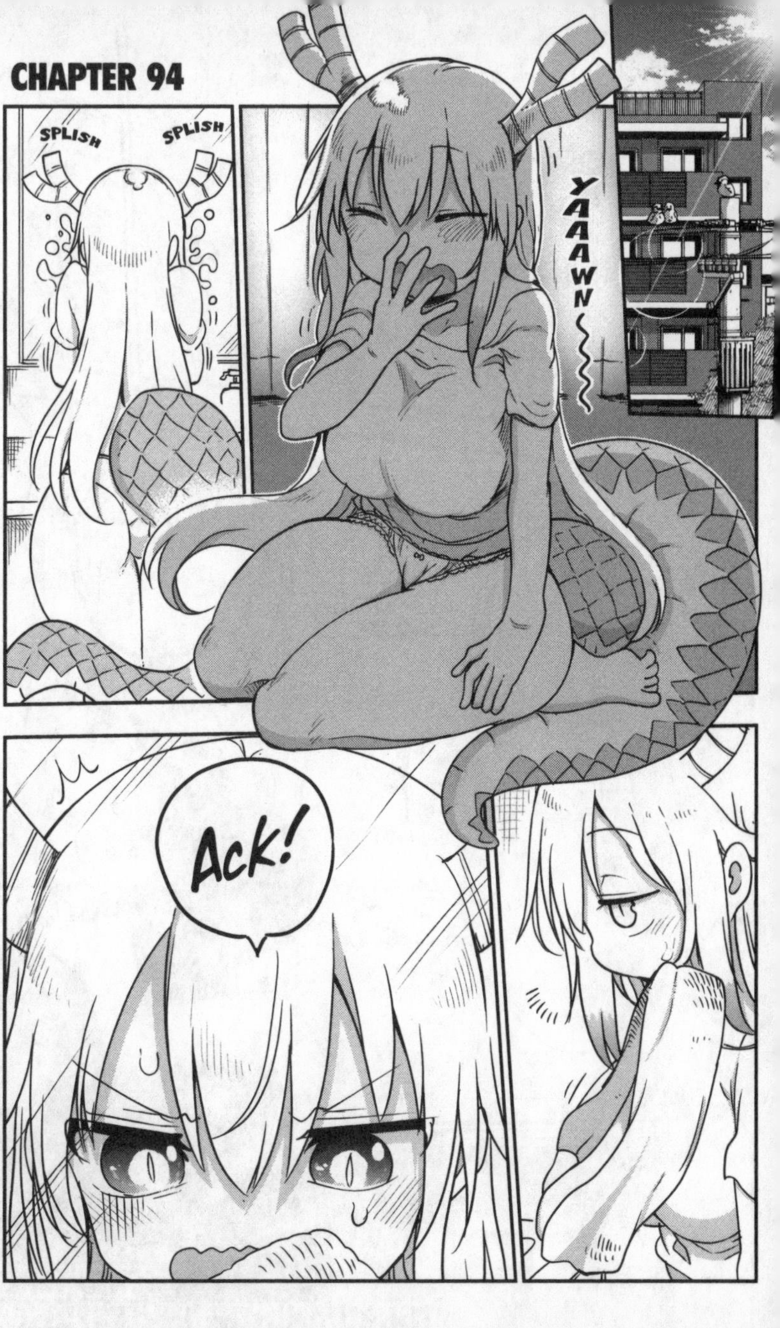
YAAAWN~
SPLISH
SPLISH
Ack!

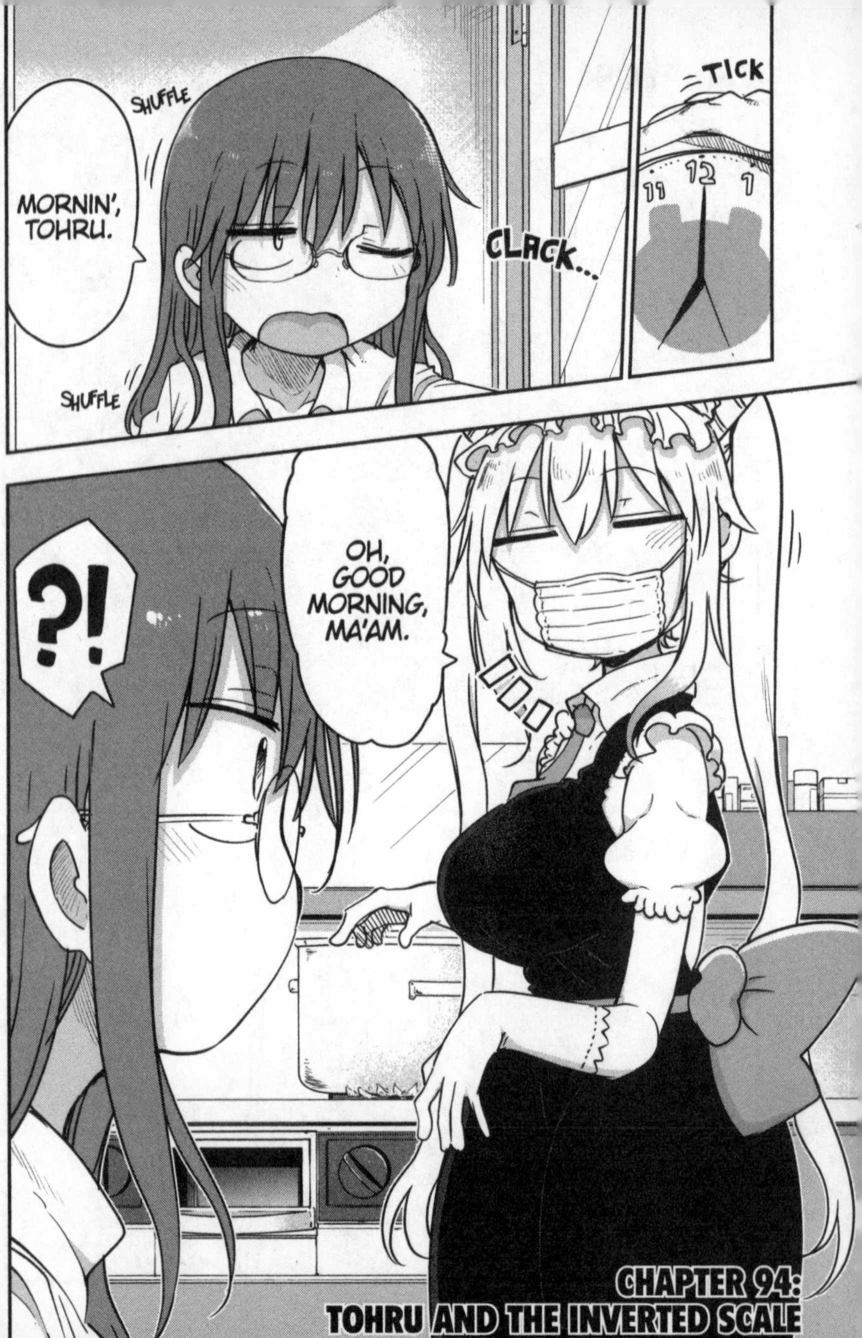
TICK
11 12 1
CLACK...
SHUFFLE
MORNIN', TOHRU.
SHUFFLE
OH, GOOD MORNING, MA'AM.
?!
CHAPTER 94:
TOHRU AND THE INVERTED SCALE

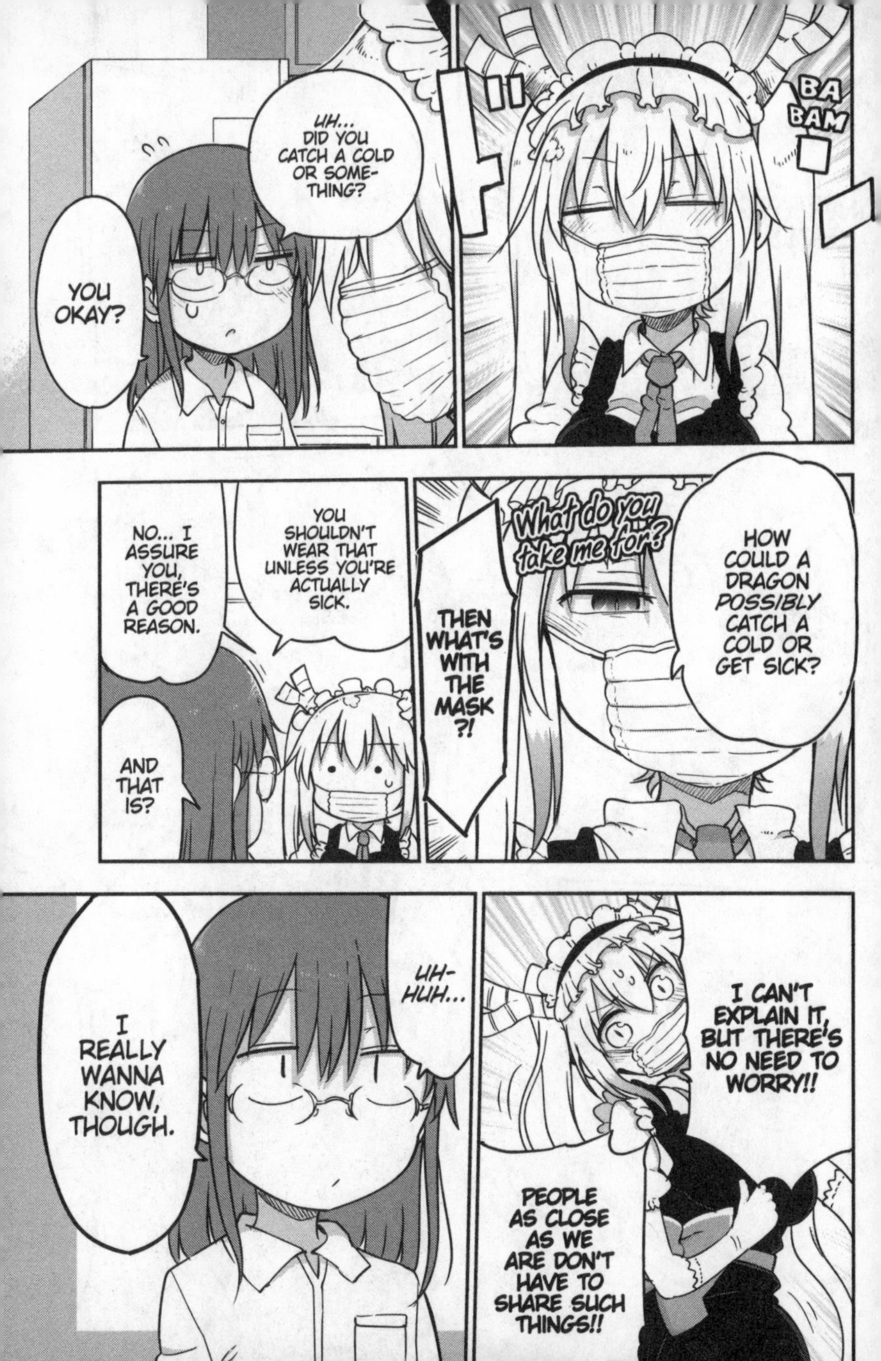
BA BAM
UH... DID YOU CATCH A COLD OR SOME-THING?
YOU OKAY?
HOW COULD A DRAGON *POSSIBLY* CATCH A COLD OR GET SICK?
What do you take me for?
THEN WHAT'S WITH THE MASK?!
YOU SHOULDN'T WEAR THAT UNLESS YOU'RE ACTUALLY SICK.
NO... I ASSURE YOU, THERE'S A GOOD REASON.
AND THAT IS?
I CAN'T EXPLAIN IT, BUT THERE'S NO NEED TO WORRY!!
PEOPLE AS CLOSE AS WE ARE DON'T HAVE TO SHARE SUCH THINGS!!
UH-HUH...
I REALLY WANNA KNOW, THOUGH.

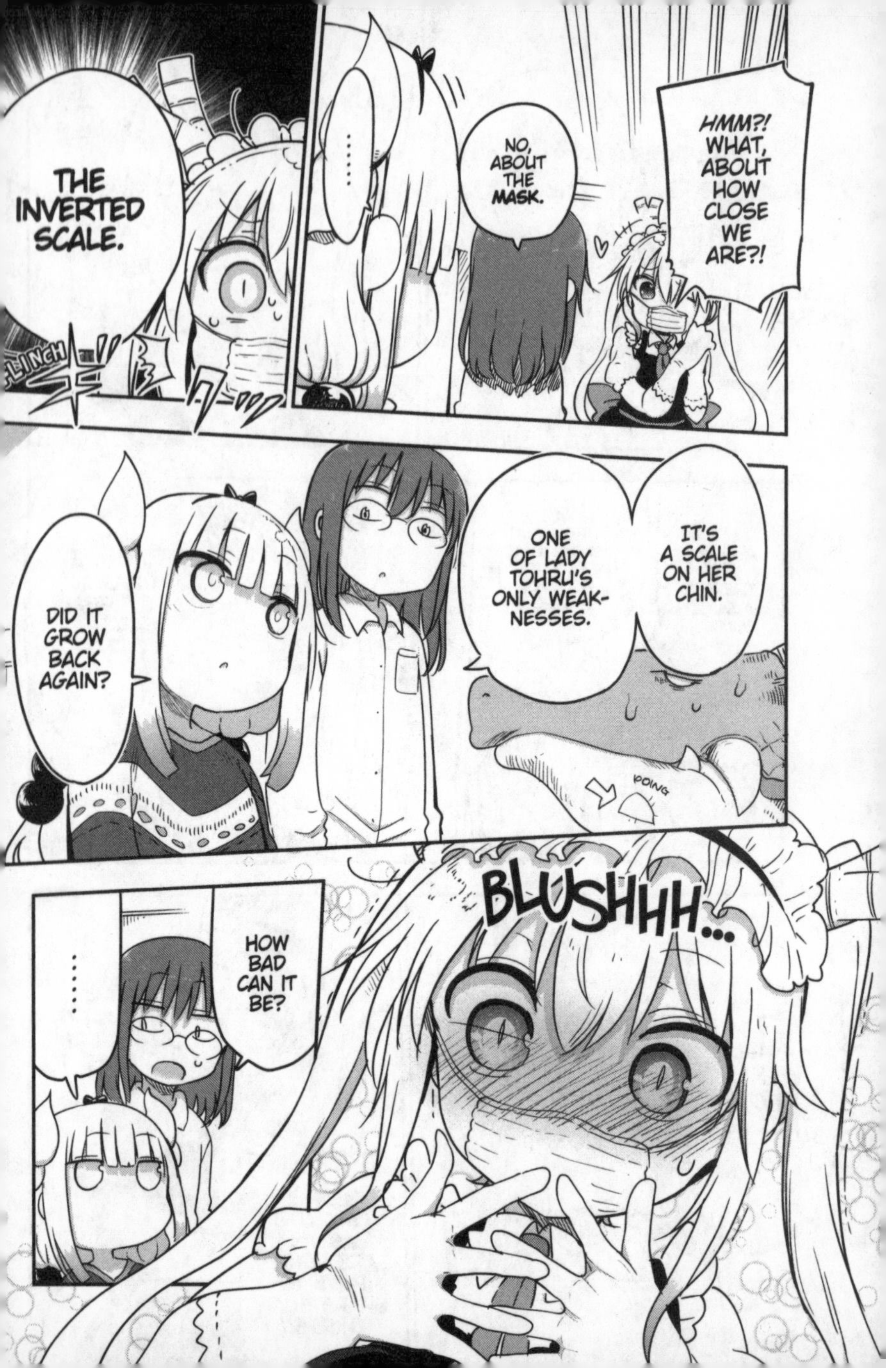
HMM?! WHAT, ABOUT HOW CLOSE WE ARE?!
NO, ABOUT THE MASK.
......
THE INVERTED SCALE.
FLINCH
IT'S A SCALE ON HER CHIN.
ONE OF LADY TOHRU'S ONLY WEAK-NESSES.
POING
DID IT GROW BACK AGAIN?
BLUSHHH...
HOW BAD CAN IT BE?
......

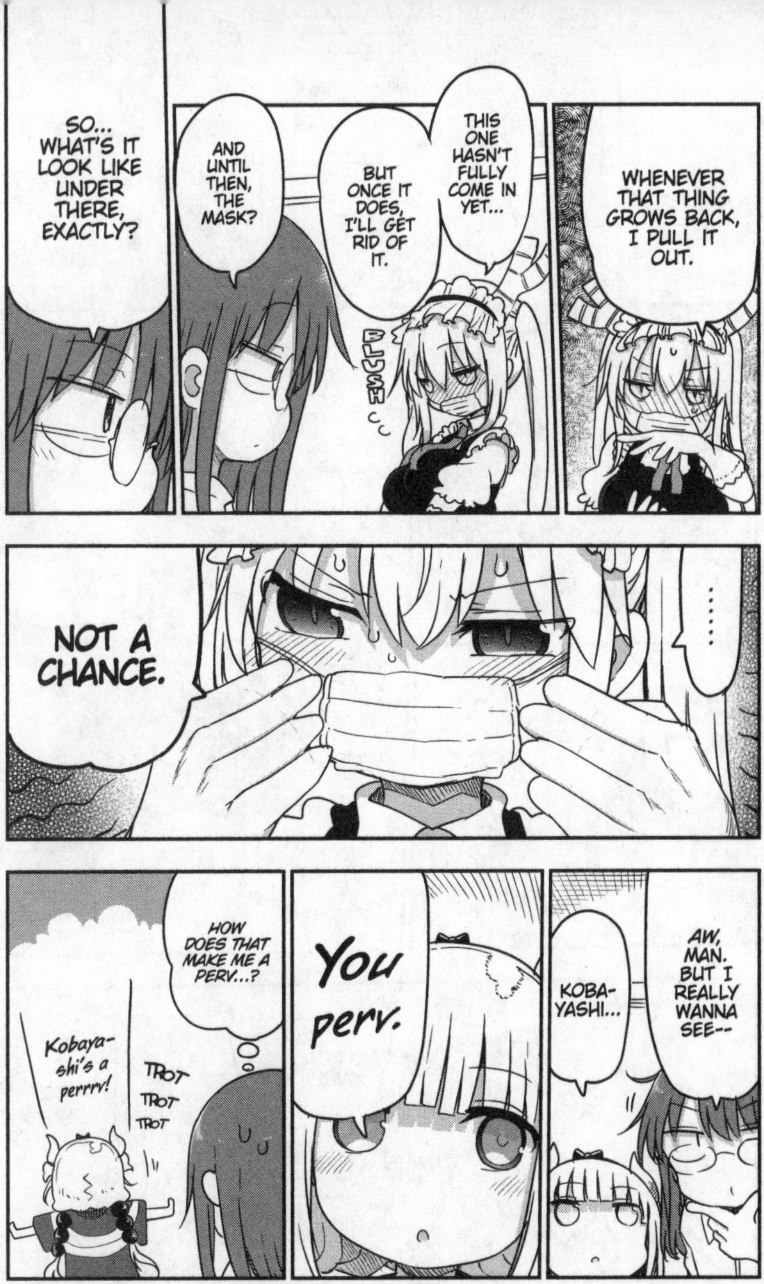
WHENEVER THAT THING GROWS BACK, I PULL IT OUT.
THIS ONE HASN'T FULLY COME IN YET...
BUT ONCE IT DOES, I'LL GET RID OF IT.
BLUSH
AND UNTIL THEN, THE MASK?
SO... WHAT'S IT LOOK LIKE UNDER THERE, EXACTLY?
......
NOT A CHANCE.
AW, MAN. BUT I REALLY WANNA SEE--
KOBA-YASHI...
You perv.
HOW DOES THAT MAKE ME A PERV...?
Kobaya-shi's a perrrv!
TROT TROT TROT

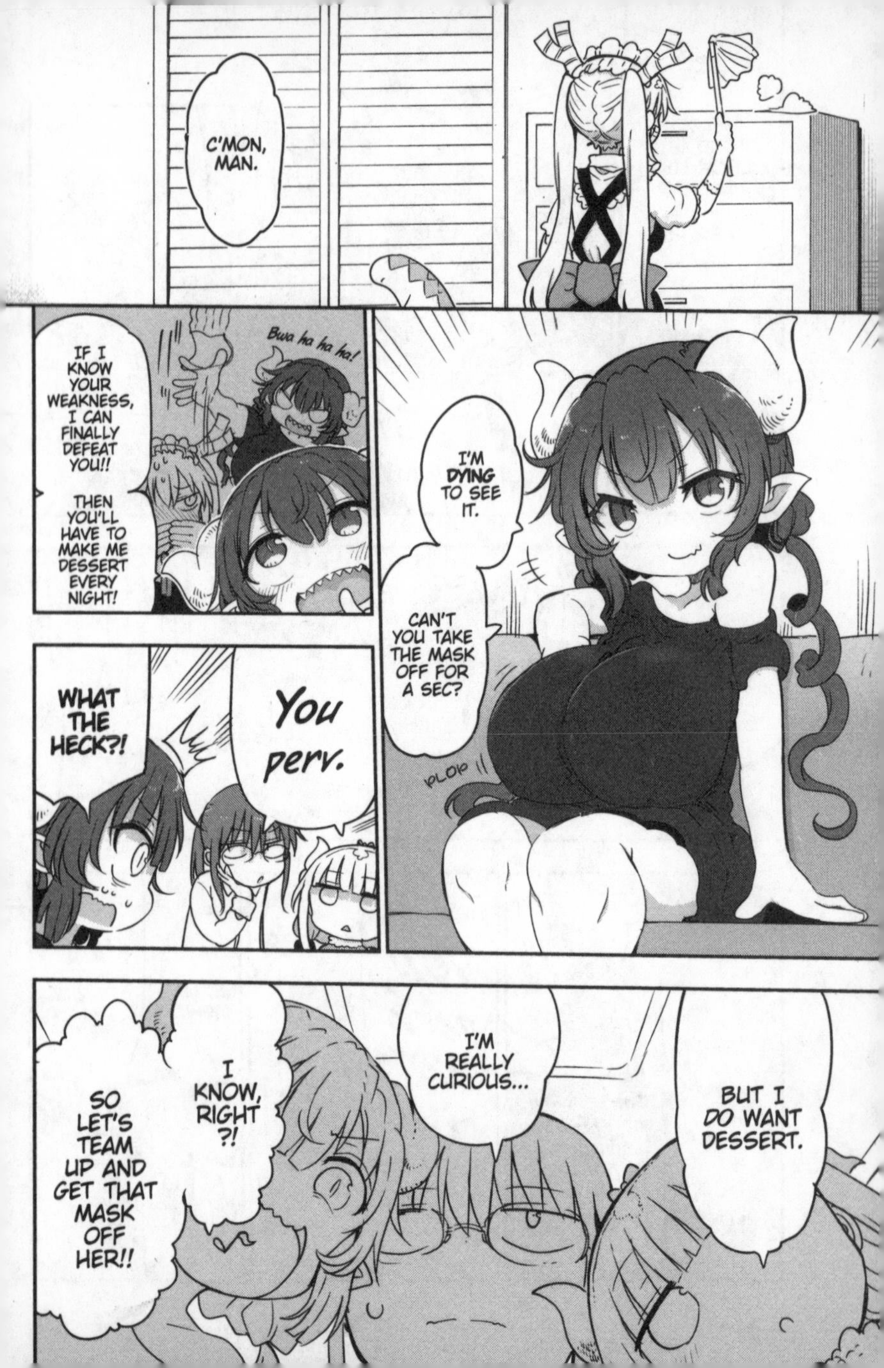
C'MON, MAN.
I'M DYING TO SEE IT.
CAN'T YOU TAKE THE MASK OFF FOR A SEC?
PLOP
Bwa ha ha ha!
IF I KNOW YOUR WEAKNESS, I CAN FINALLY DEFEAT YOU!!
THEN YOU'LL HAVE TO MAKE ME DESSERT EVERY NIGHT!
You perv.
WHAT THE HECK?!
BUT I DO WANT DESSERT.
I'M REALLY CURIOUS...
I KNOW, RIGHT?!
SO LET'S TEAM UP AND GET THAT MASK OFF HER!!

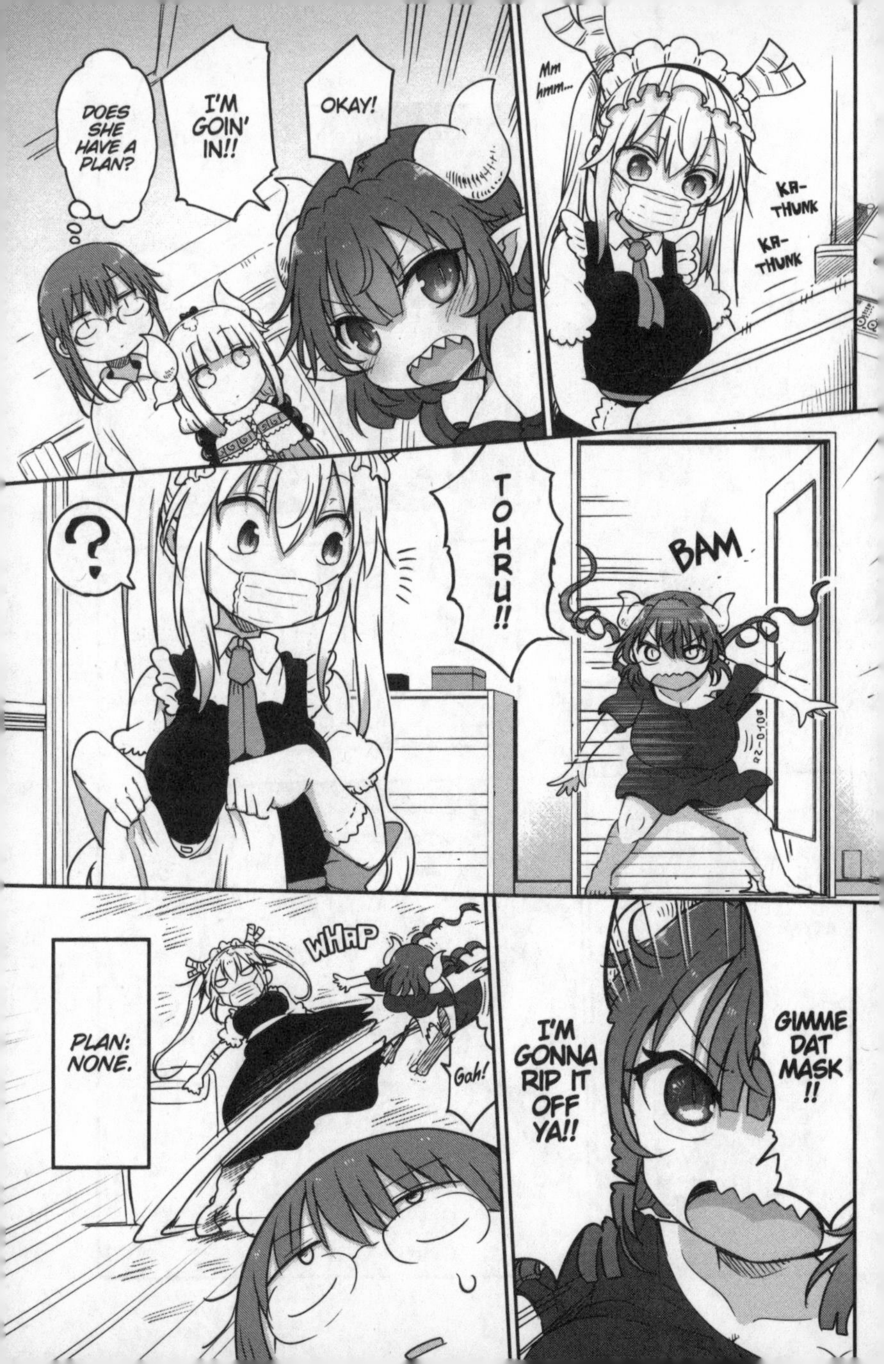
Mm hmm...
KA-THUNK
KA-THUNK
OKAY!
I'M GOIN' IN!!
DOES SHE HAVE A PLAN?
BAM
TOHRU!!
BOYOING
?
GIMME DAT MASK!!
I'M GONNA RIP IT OFF YA!!
WHAP
Gah!
PLAN: NONE.

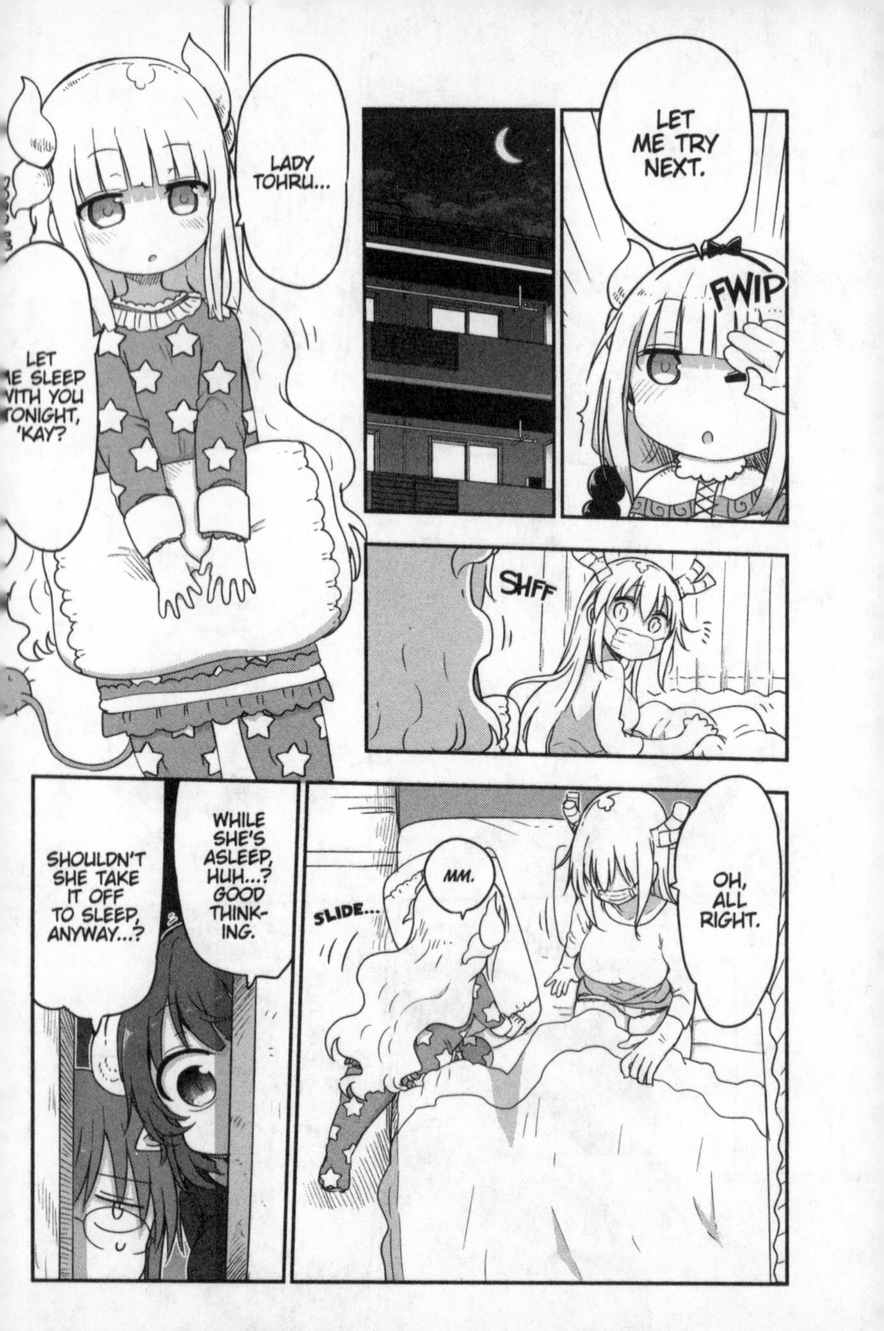
LET ME TRY NEXT.
FWIP
SHFF
LADY TOHRU...
LET ME SLEEP WITH YOU TONIGHT, 'KAY?
OH, ALL RIGHT.
MM.
SLIDE...
WHILE SHE'S ASLEEP, HUH...? GOOD THINKING.
SHOULDN'T SHE TAKE IT OFF TO SLEEP, ANYWAY...?

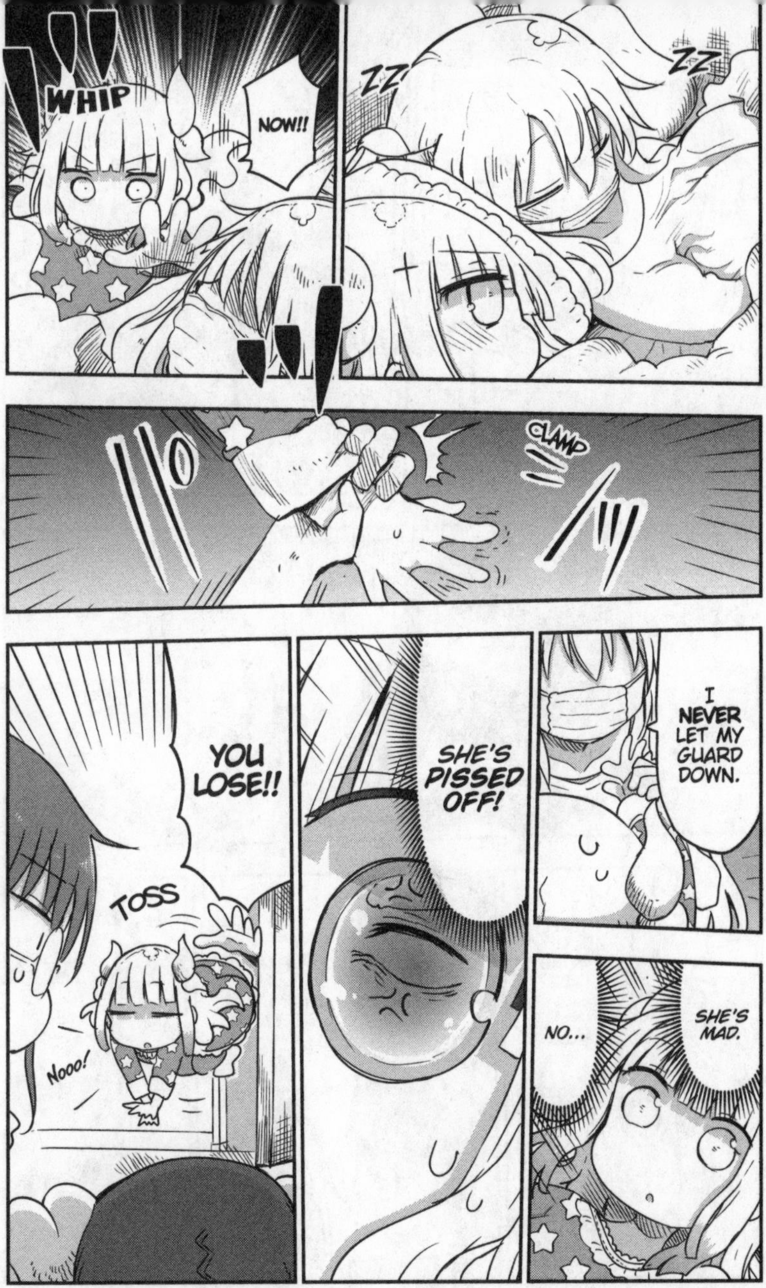
ZZZ
ZZZ
NOW!!
WHIP
CLAMP
I NEVER LET MY GUARD DOWN.
SHE'S MAD.
NO...
SHE'S PISSED OFF!
YOU LOSE!!
TOSS
Nooo!

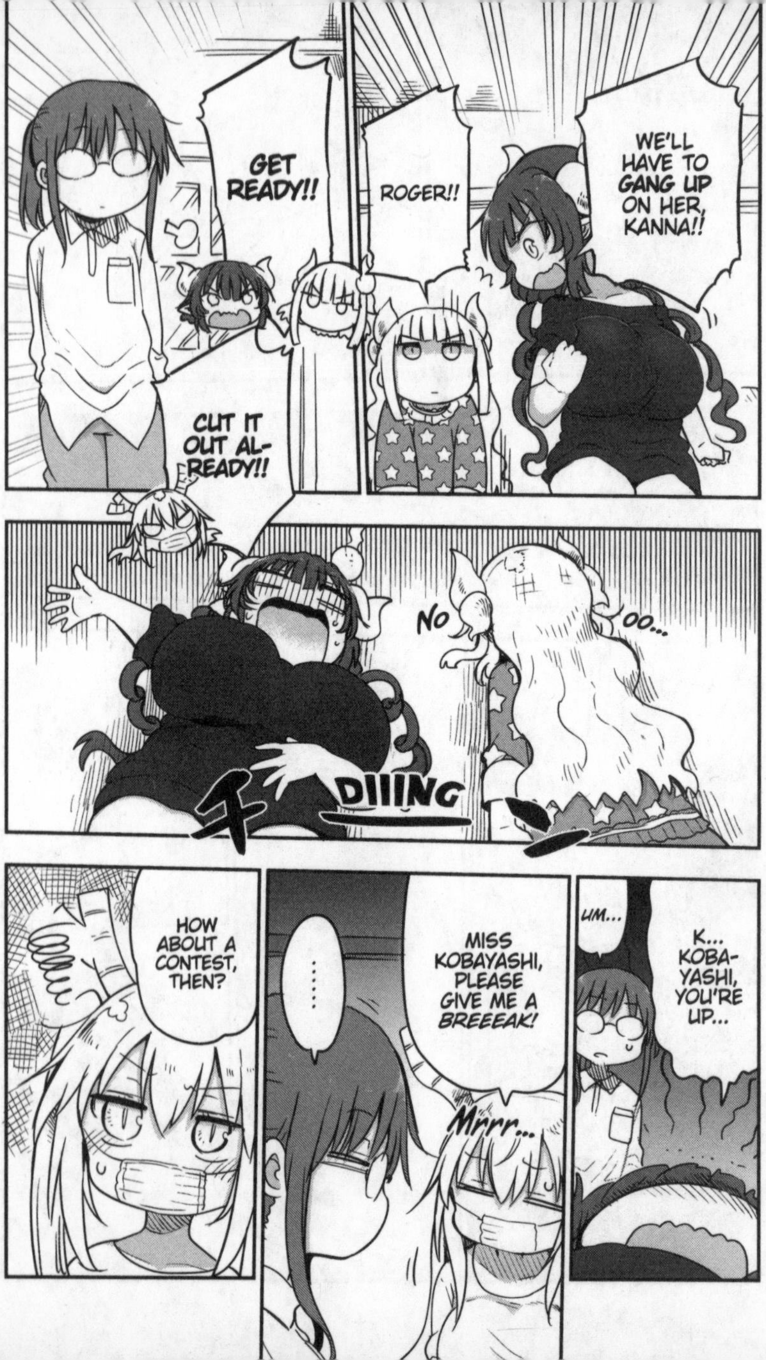
WE'LL HAVE TO GANG UP ON HER, KANNA!!
ROGER!!
GET READY!!
CUT IT OUT AL-READY!!
NO OO...
DIIING
UM...
K... KOBA-YASHI, YOU'RE UP...
MISS KOBAYASHI, PLEASE GIVE ME A BREEEAK!
Mrrr...
......
HOW ABOUT A CONTEST, THEN?

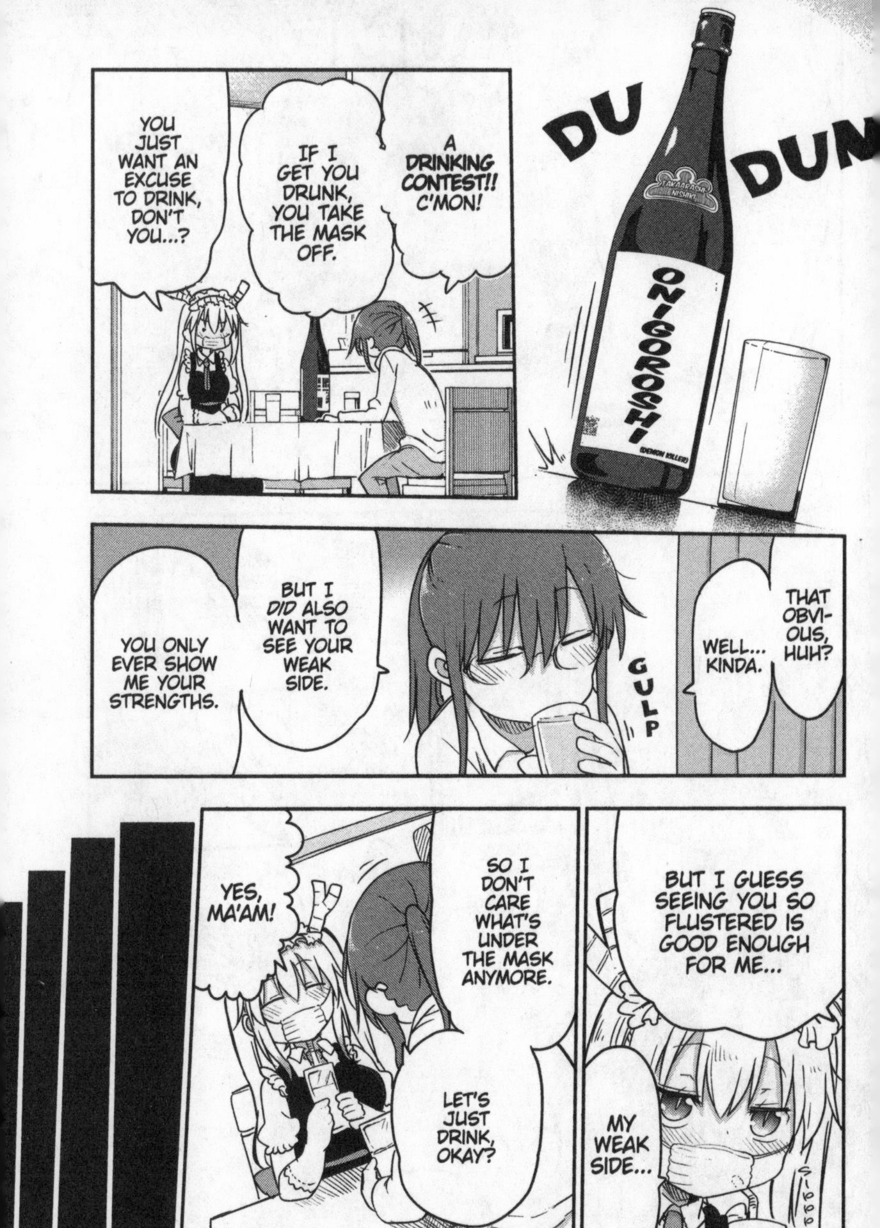
DU DUN
TAKAARASHI NISHIKI
ONIGOROSHI
(DEMON KILLER)
A DRINKING CONTEST!! C'MON!
IF I GET YOU DRUNK, YOU TAKE THE MASK OFF.
YOU JUST WANT AN EXCUSE TO DRINK, DON'T YOU...?
THAT OBVIOUS, HUH?
WELL... KINDA.
GULP
BUT I *DID* ALSO WANT TO SEE YOUR WEAK SIDE.
YOU ONLY EVER SHOW ME YOUR STRENGTHS.
BUT I GUESS SEEING YOU SO FLUSTERED IS GOOD ENOUGH FOR ME...
MY WEAK SIDE...
SO I DON'T CARE WHAT'S UNDER THE MASK ANYMORE.
LET'S JUST DRINK, OKAY?
YES, MA'AM!

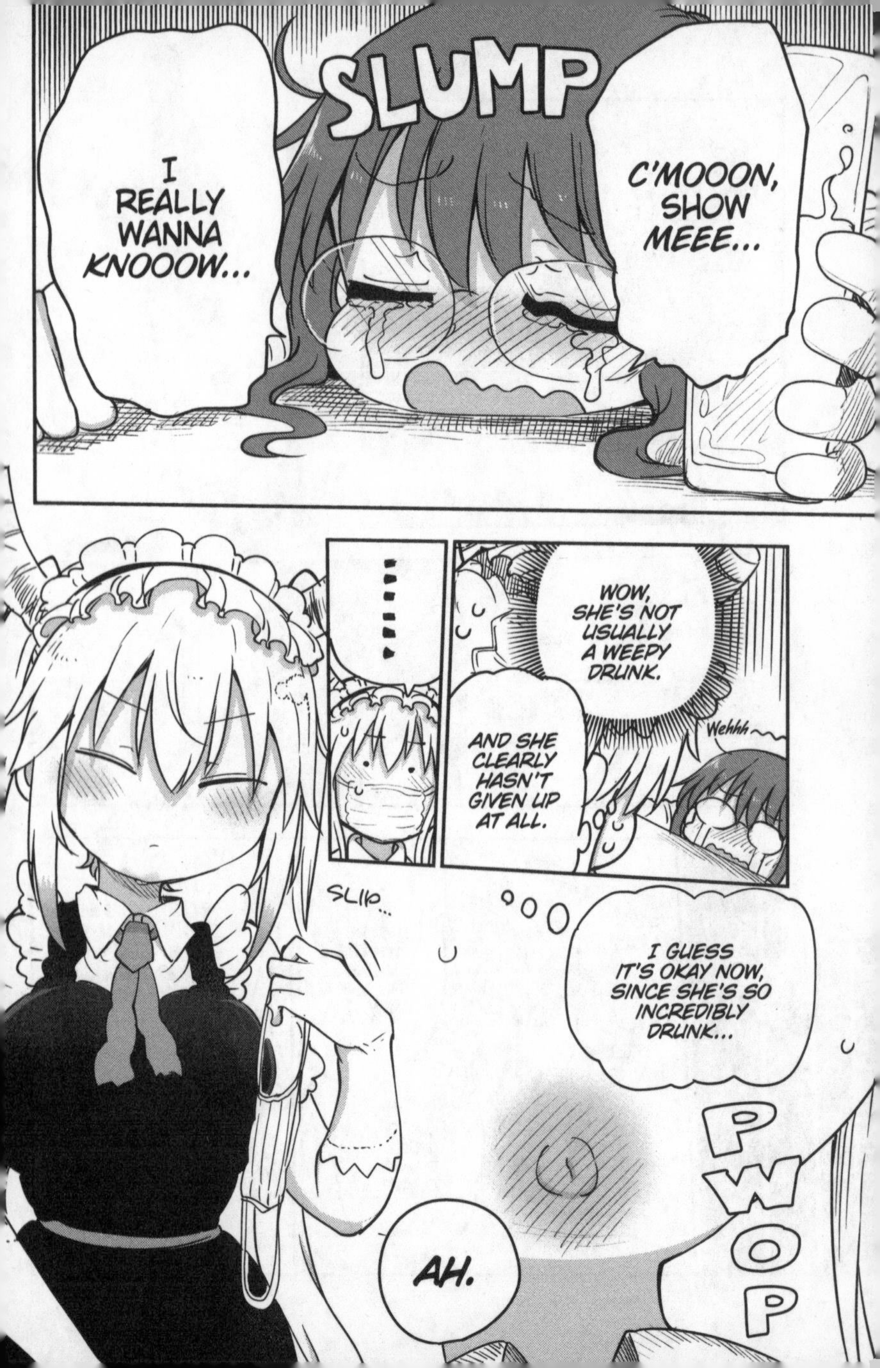
C'MOOON, SHOW MEEE...
SLUMP
I REALLY WANNA KNOOOW...
WOW, SHE'S NOT USUALLY A WEEPY DRUNK.
Wehhh~
AND SHE CLEARLY HASN'T GIVEN UP AT ALL.
......
I GUESS IT'S OKAY NOW, SINCE SHE'S SO INCREDIBLY DRUNK...
SLIP...
PWOP
AH.

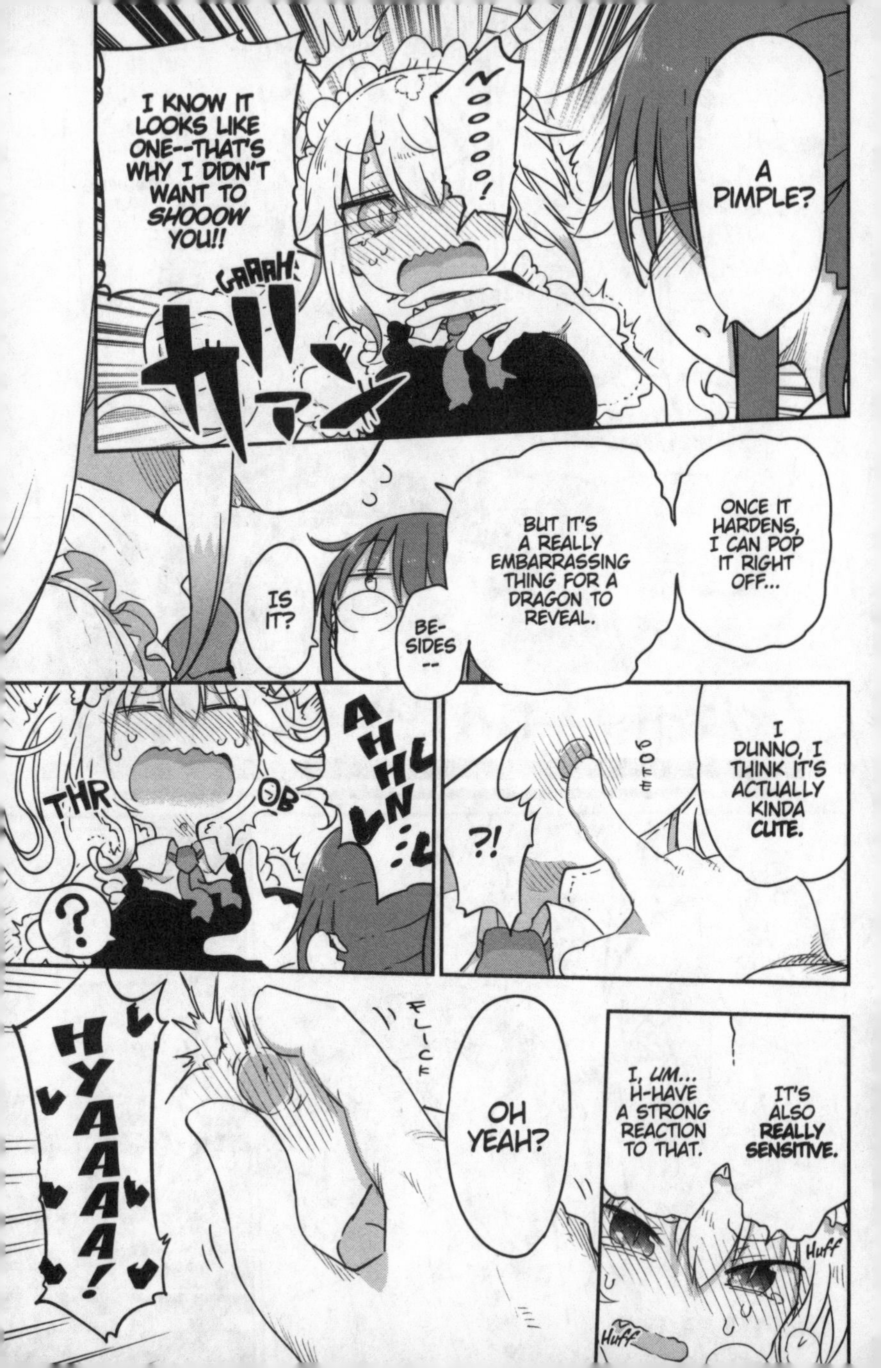
A PIMPLE?
NOOOOOO!
I KNOW IT LOOKS LIKE ONE--THAT'S WHY I DIDN'T WANT TO SHOOOW YOU!!
GRAAAH!
ONCE IT HARDENS, I CAN POP IT RIGHT OFF...
BUT IT'S A REALLY EMBARRASSING THING FOR A DRAGON TO REVEAL.
BE-SIDES --
IS IT?
I DUNNO, I THINK IT'S ACTUALLY KINDA CUTE.
POKE
?!
AHHN♥!
THROB
?
IT'S ALSO REALLY SENSITIVE.
I, UM... H-HAVE A STRONG REACTION TO THAT.
Huff
Huff
OH YEAH?
FLICK
HYAAAAA!

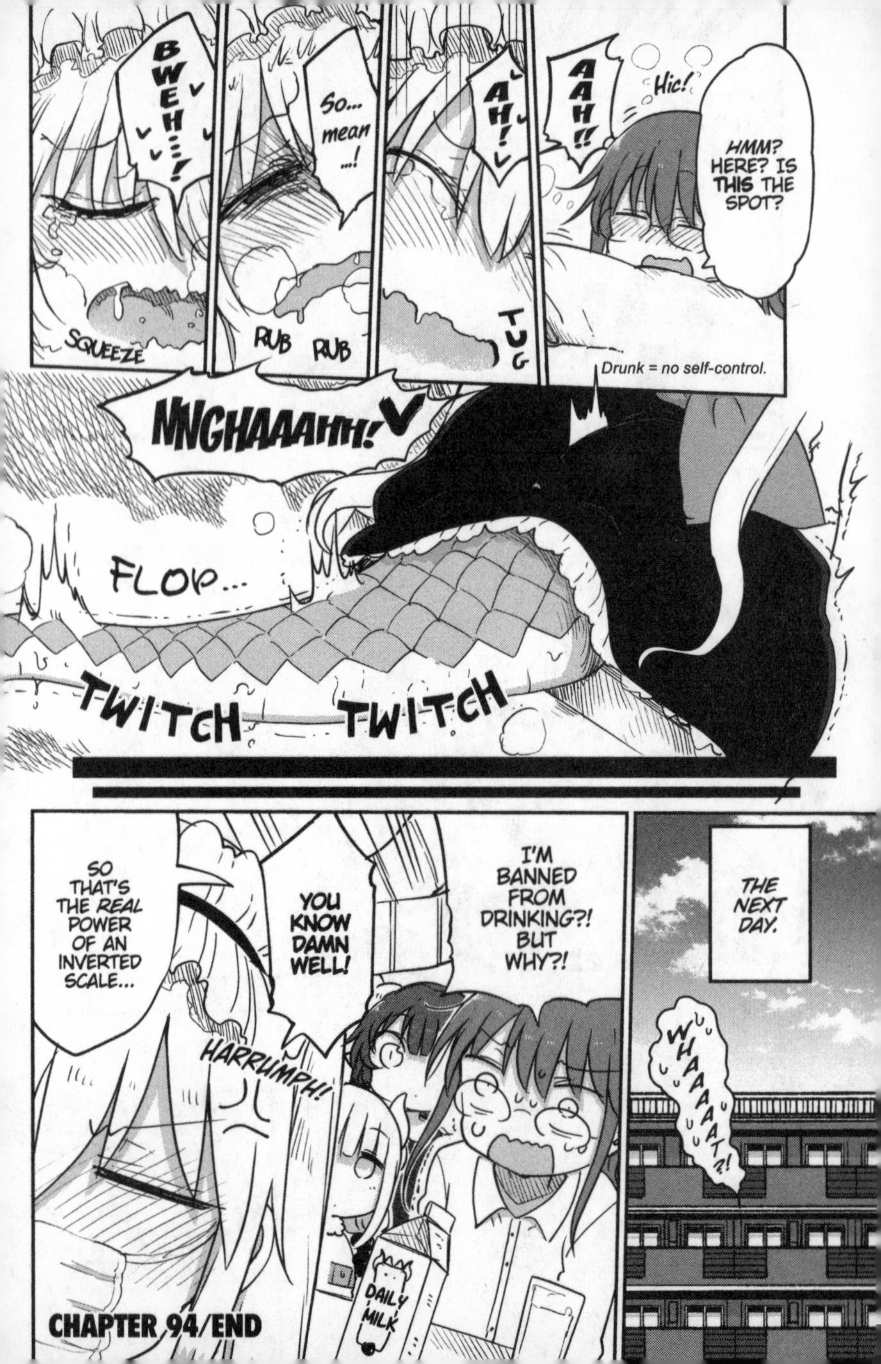
Hic!
HMM? HERE? IS THIS THE SPOT?
AAH!!
AH!
TUG
Drunk = no self-control.
So... mean ...!
RUB RUB
BWEH...!
SQUEEZE
NNGHAAAAHH!
FLOP...
TWITCH TWITCH
THE NEXT DAY.
WHAAAAAT?!
I'M BANNED FROM DRINKING?! BUT WHY?!
YOU KNOW DAMN WELL!
HARRUMPH!
SO THAT'S THE *REAL* POWER OF AN INVERTED SCALE...
DAILY MILK
CHAPTER 94/END

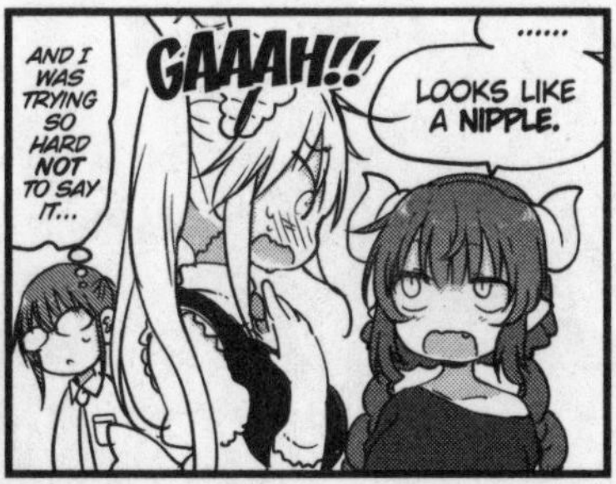
......
LOOKS LIKE A NIPPLE.
GAAAH!!
AND I WAS TRYING SO HARD NOT TO SAY IT...

Miss Kobayashi's
Dragon Maid

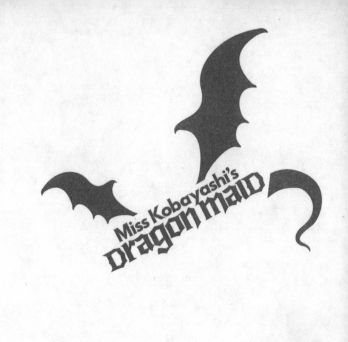

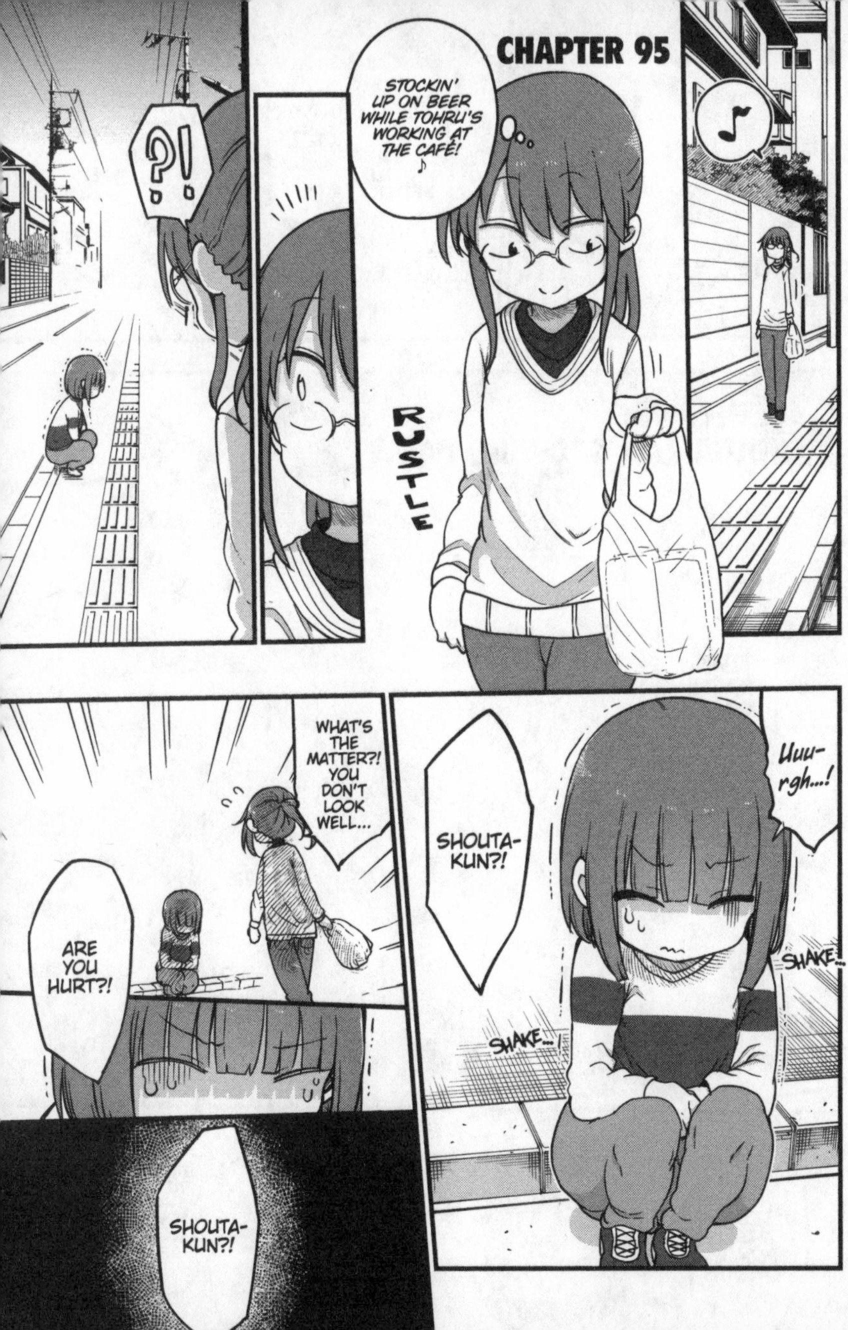
♪
CHAPTER 95
STOCKIN' UP ON BEER WHILE TOHRU'S WORKING AT THE CAFÉ! ♪
RUSTLE
?!
Uuu-rgh...!
SHOUTA-KUN?!
SHAKE...
SHAKE...
WHAT'S THE MATTER?! YOU DON'T LOOK WELL...
ARE YOU HURT?!
SHOUTA-KUN?!

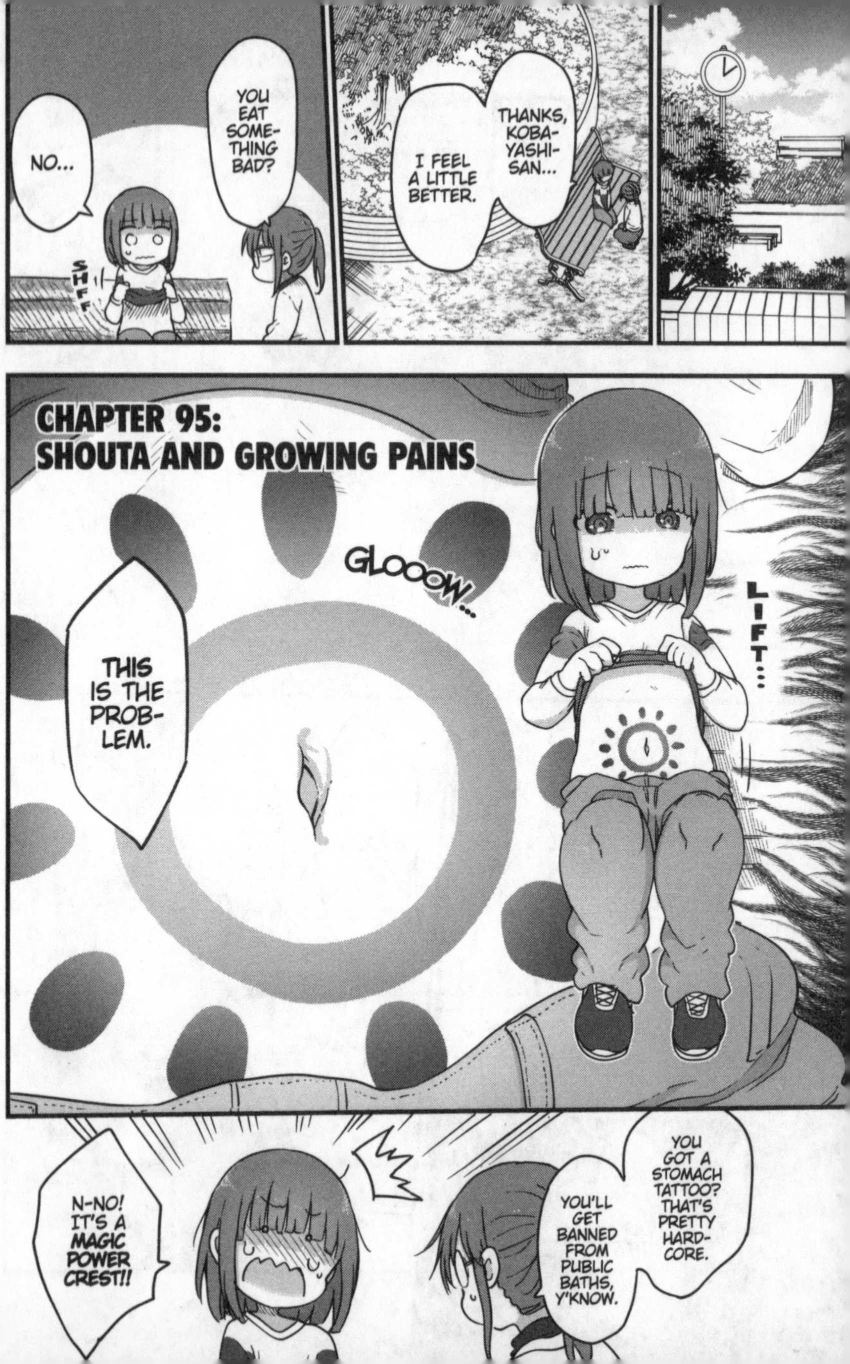
THANKS, KOBAYASHI-SAN...
I FEEL A LITTLE BETTER.
YOU EAT SOMETHING BAD?
NO...
SHFF
CHAPTER 95: SHOUTA AND GROWING PAINS
LIFT...
GLOOOW...
THIS IS THE PROBLEM.
YOU GOT A STOMACH TATTOO? THAT'S PRETTY HARDCORE.
YOU'LL GET BANNED FROM PUBLIC BATHS, Y'KNOW.
N-NO! IT'S A *MAGIC POWER* CREST!!

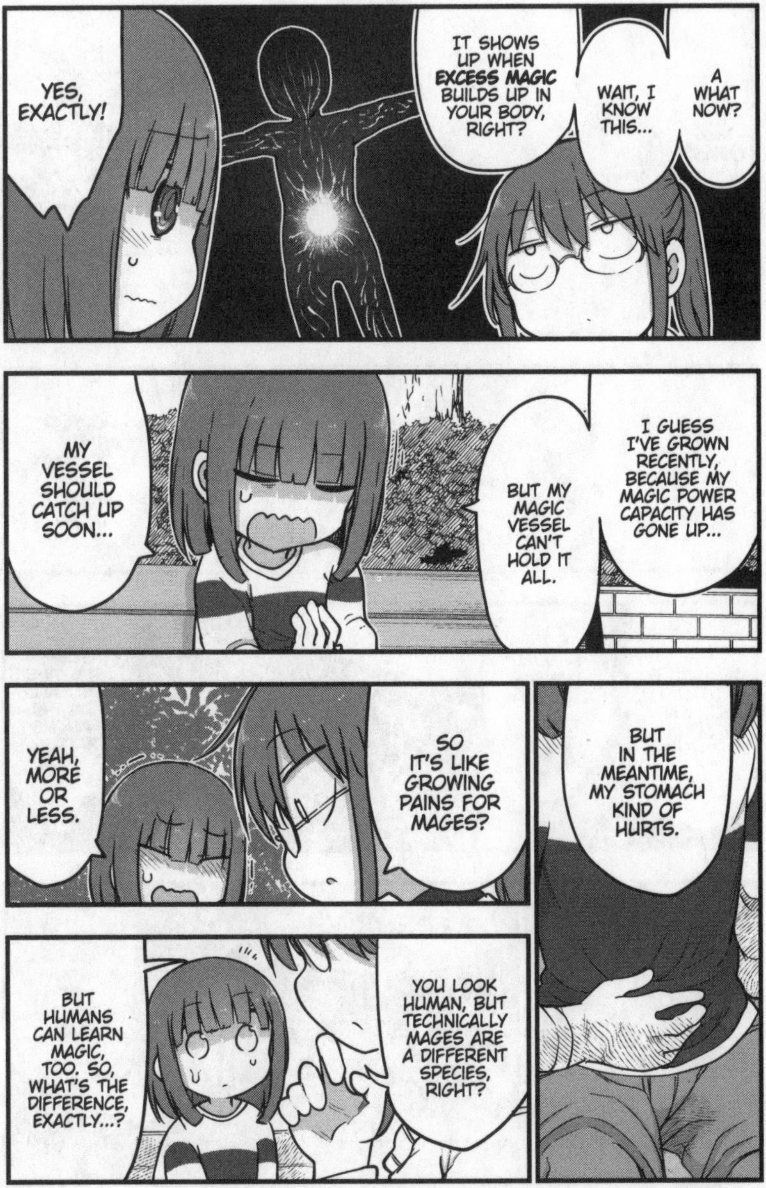
A WHAT NOW?
WAIT, I KNOW THIS...
IT SHOWS UP WHEN EXCESS MAGIC BUILDS UP IN YOUR BODY, RIGHT?
YES, EXACTLY!
I GUESS I'VE GROWN RECENTLY, BECAUSE MY MAGIC POWER CAPACITY HAS GONE UP...
BUT MY MAGIC VESSEL CAN'T HOLD IT ALL.
MY VESSEL SHOULD CATCH UP SOON...
BUT IN THE MEANTIME, MY STOMACH KIND OF HURTS.
SO IT'S LIKE GROWING PAINS FOR MAGES?
YEAH, MORE OR LESS.
YOU LOOK HUMAN, BUT TECHNICALLY MAGES ARE A DIFFERENT SPECIES, RIGHT?
BUT HUMANS CAN LEARN MAGIC, TOO. SO, WHAT'S THE DIFFERENCE, EXACTLY...?

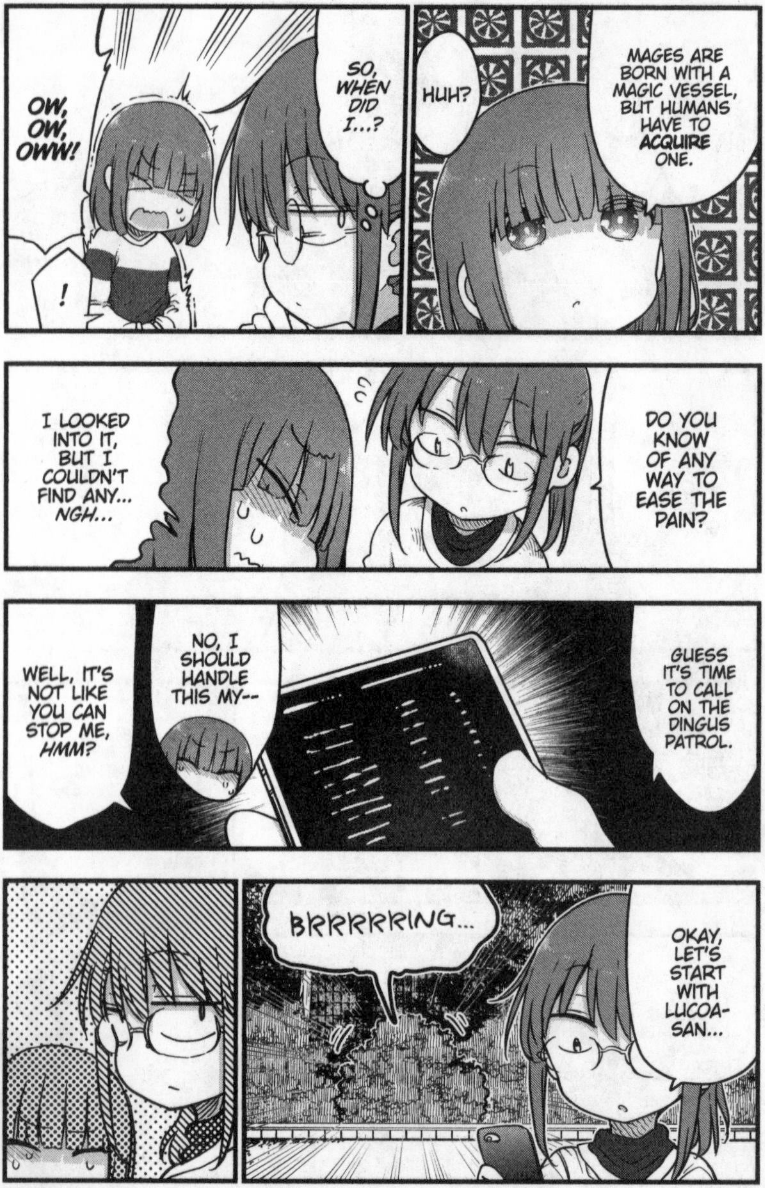

MAGES ARE BORN WITH A MAGIC VESSEL, BUT HUMANS HAVE TO ACQUIRE ONE.
HUH?
SO, WHEN DID I...?
OW, OW, OWW!
!
DO YOU KNOW OF ANY WAY TO EASE THE PAIN?
I LOOKED INTO IT, BUT I COULDN'T FIND ANY... NGH...
GUESS IT'S TIME TO CALL ON THE DINGUS PATROL.
NO, I SHOULD HANDLE THIS MY--
WELL, IT'S NOT LIKE YOU CAN STOP ME, HMM?
OKAY, LET'S START WITH LUCOA-SAN...
BRRRRRING...

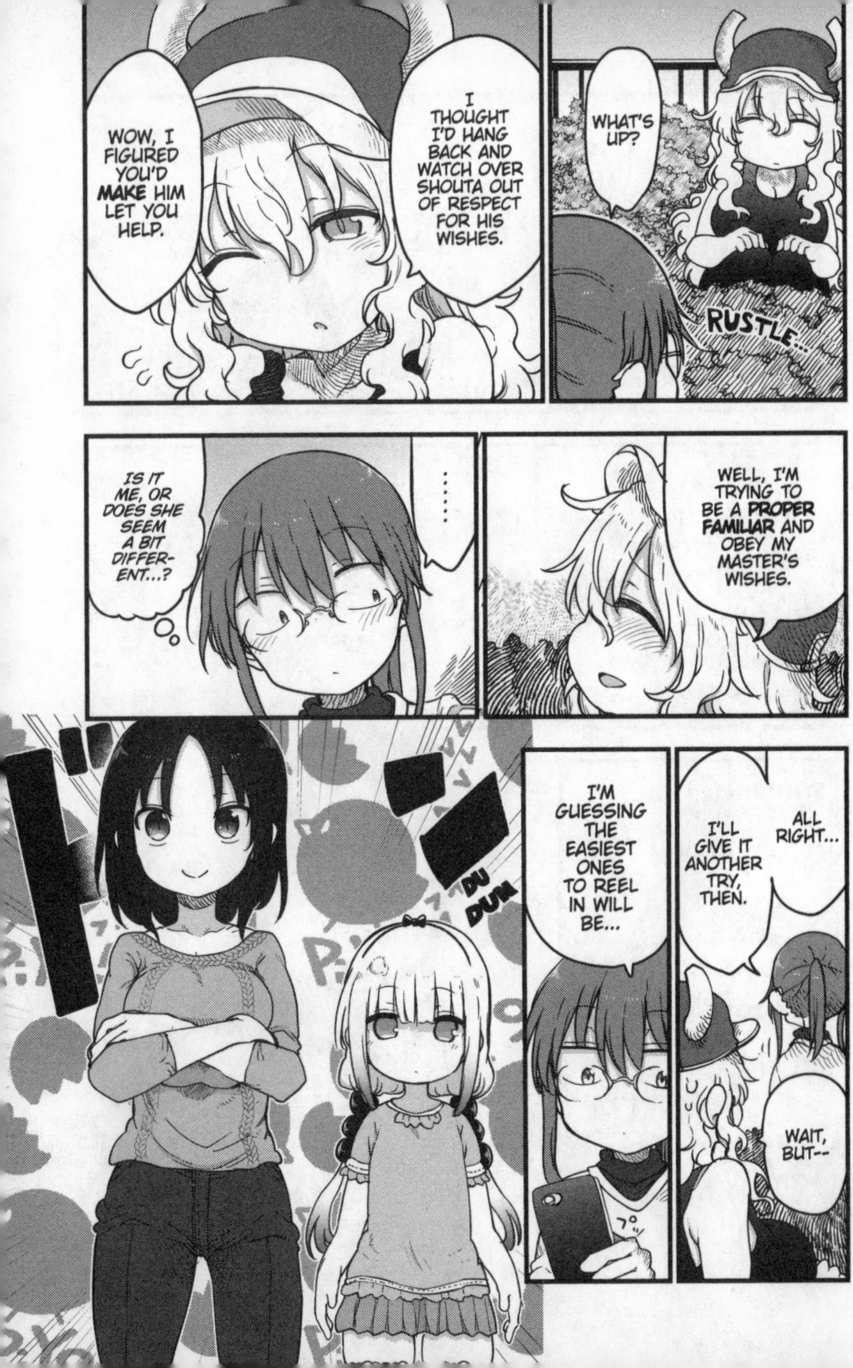
WHAT'S UP?
RUSTLE...
I THOUGHT I'D HANG BACK AND WATCH OVER SHOUTA OUT OF RESPECT FOR HIS WISHES.
WOW, I FIGURED YOU'D **MAKE** HIM LET YOU HELP.
WELL, I'M TRYING TO BE A **PROPER FAMILIAR** AND OBEY MY MASTER'S WISHES.
......
IS IT ME, OR DOES SHE SEEM A BIT DIFFERENT...?
ALL RIGHT...
I'LL GIVE IT ANOTHER TRY, THEN.
WAIT, BUT--
I'M GUESSING THE EASIEST ONES TO REEL IN WILL BE...
DU DUM

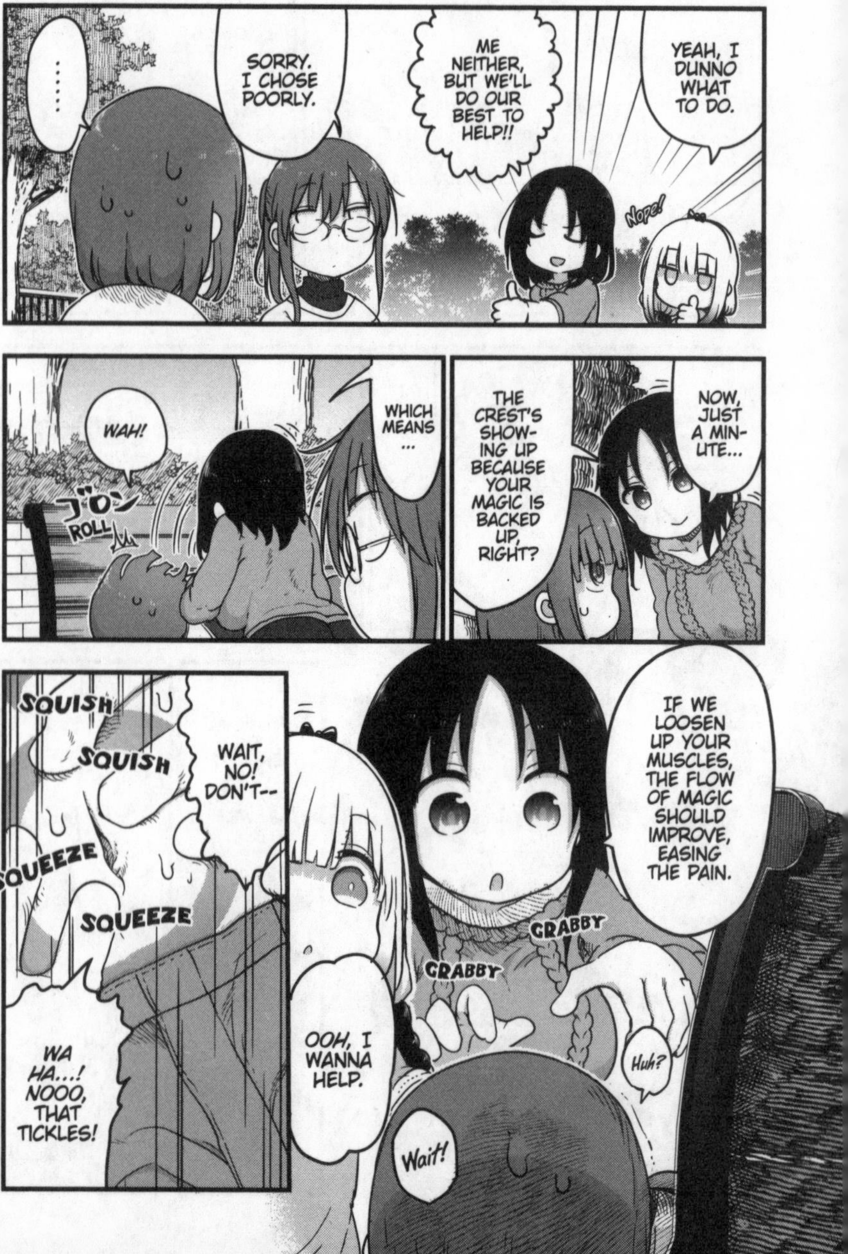
YEAH, I DUNNO WHAT TO DO.
Nope!
ME NEITHER, BUT WE'LL DO OUR BEST TO HELP!!
SORRY. I CHOSE POORLY.
......
NOW, JUST A MIN-UTE...
THE CREST'S SHOW-ING UP BECAUSE YOUR MAGIC IS BACKED UP, RIGHT?
WHICH MEANS ...
WAH!
ゴロン
ROLL
IF WE LOOSEN UP YOUR MUSCLES, THE FLOW OF MAGIC SHOULD IMPROVE, EASING THE PAIN.
GRABBY
GRABBY
Huh?
OOH, I WANNA HELP.
Wait!
WAIT, NO! DON'T--
SQUISH
SQUISH
SQUEEZE
SQUEEZE
WA HA...! NOOO, THAT TICKLES!

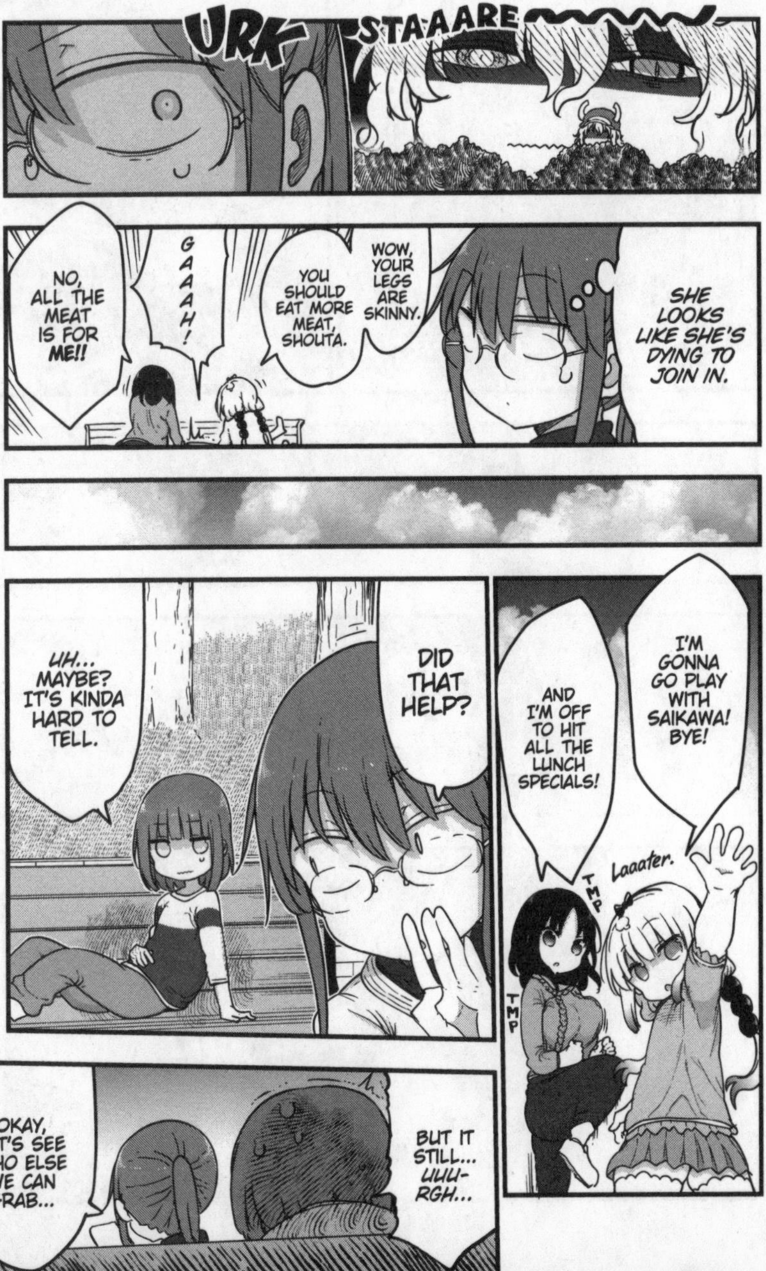
STAAARE
URK
SHE LOOKS LIKE SHE'S DYING TO JOIN IN.
WOW, YOUR LEGS ARE SKINNY.
YOU SHOULD EAT MORE MEAT, SHOUTA.
GAAAAH!
NO, ALL THE MEAT IS FOR ME!!
I'M GONNA GO PLAY WITH SAIKAWA! BYE!
AND I'M OFF TO HIT ALL THE LUNCH SPECIALS!
Laaater.
TMP
TMP
DID THAT HELP?
UH... MAYBE? IT'S KINDA HARD TO TELL.
BUT IT STILL... UUU-RGH...
OKAY, LET'S SEE WHO ELSE WE CAN GRAB...

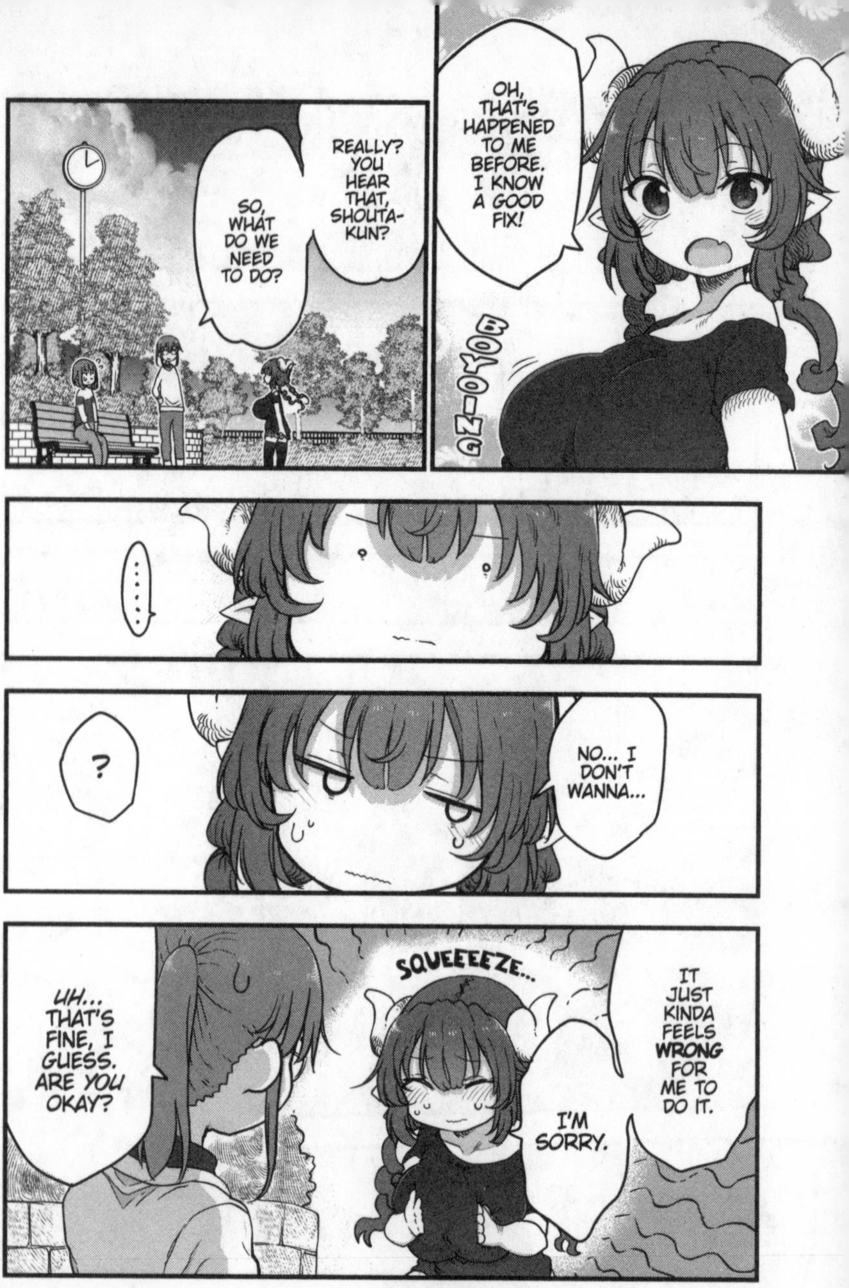
OH, THAT'S HAPPENED TO ME BEFORE. I KNOW A GOOD FIX!
BOYOING
REALLY? YOU HEAR THAT, SHOUTA-KUN?
SO, WHAT DO WE NEED TO DO?
......
NO... I DON'T WANNA...
?
IT JUST KINDA FEELS WRONG FOR ME TO DO IT.
I'M SORRY.
SQUEEEEZE...
UH... THAT'S FINE, I GUESS. ARE YOU OKAY?

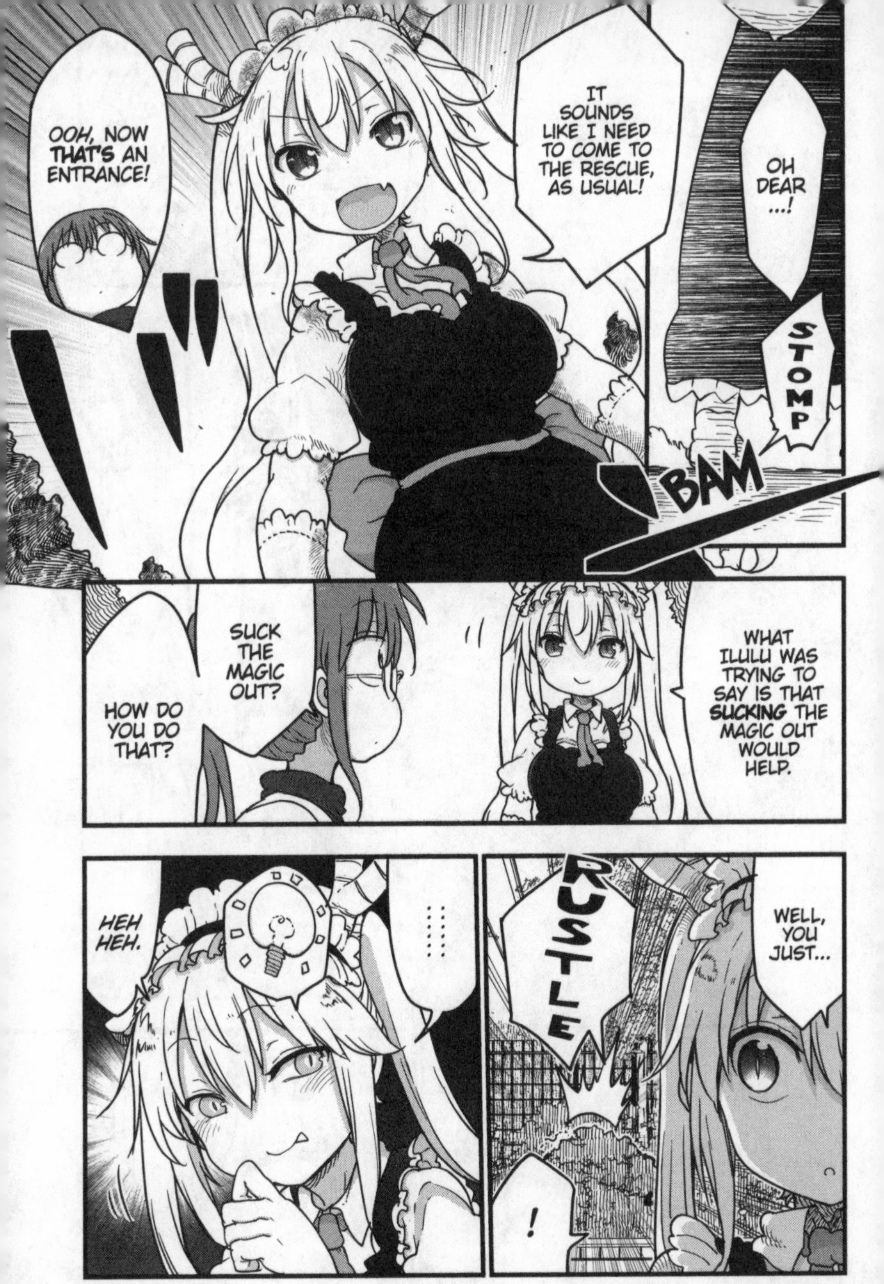
OH DEAR ...!
STOMP
BAM
IT SOUNDS LIKE I NEED TO COME TO THE RESCUE, AS USUAL!
OOH, NOW THAT'S AN ENTRANCE!
WHAT ILULU WAS TRYING TO SAY IS THAT **SUCKING** THE MAGIC OUT WOULD HELP.
SUCK THE MAGIC OUT?
HOW DO YOU DO THAT?
WELL, YOU JUST...
RUSTLE
!
......
HEH HEH.

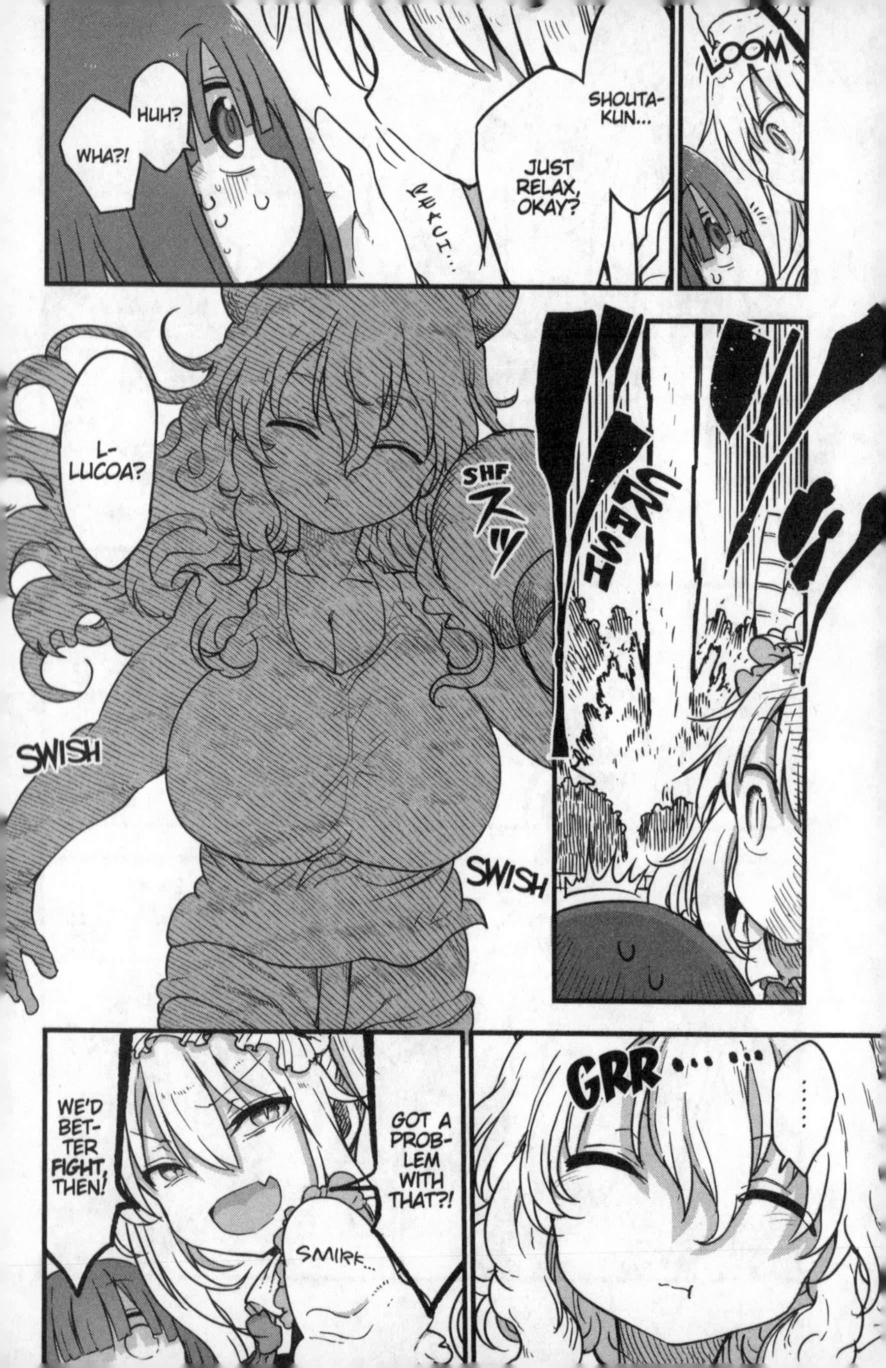

LOOM
SHOUTA-KUN...
JUST RELAX, OKAY?
REACH...
HUH?
WHA?!
CRASH
SWISH
SHF
スッ
L-LUCOA?
SWISH
GRR... ...
......
GOT A PROBLEM WITH THAT?!
WE'D BETTER FIGHT, THEN!
SMIRK...

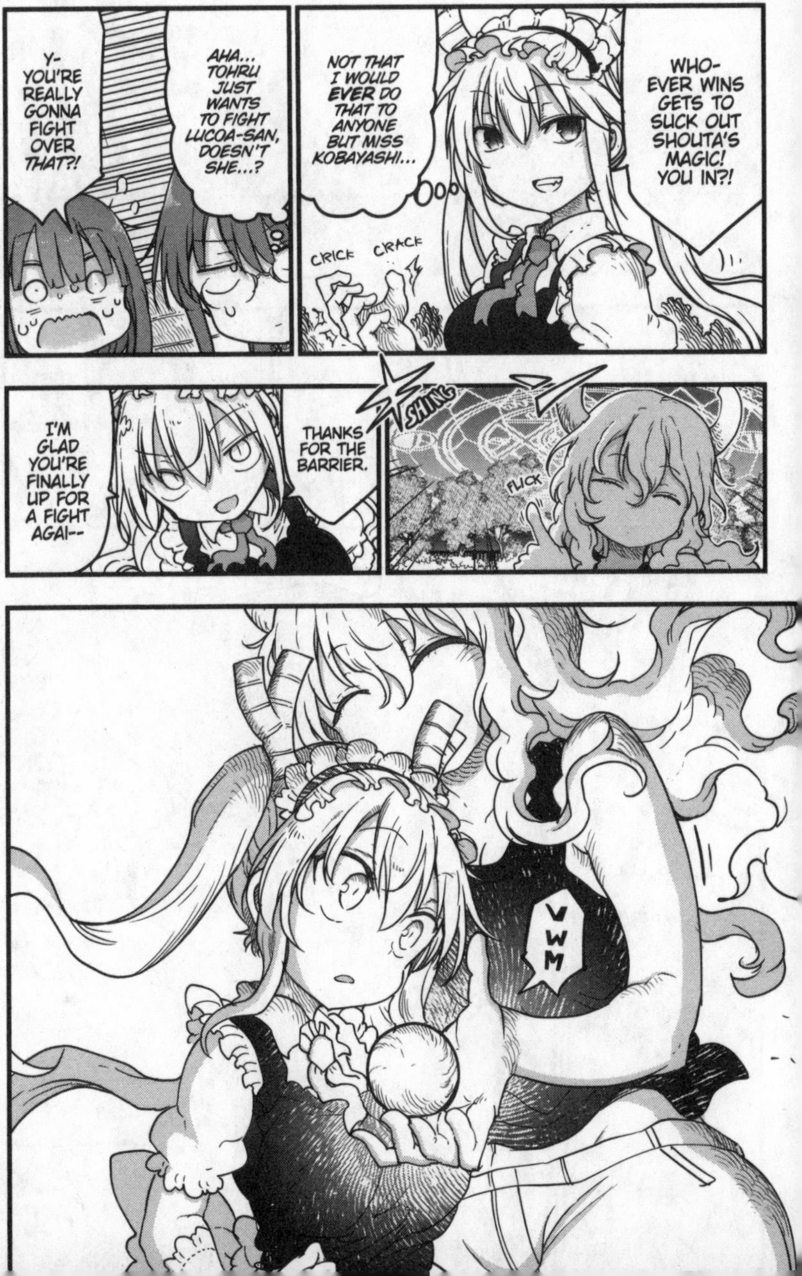
WHO-EVER WINS GETS TO SUCK OUT SHOUTA'S MAGIC! YOU IN?!
NOT THAT I WOULD EVER DO THAT TO ANYONE BUT MISS KOBAYASHI...
CRICK CRACK
AHA... TOHRU JUST WANTS TO FIGHT LUCOA-SAN, DOESN'T SHE...?
Y- YOU'RE REALLY GONNA FIGHT OVER THAT?!
SHING
FLICK
THANKS FOR THE BARRIER.
I'M GLAD YOU'RE FINALLY UP FOR A FIGHT AGAI--
VWM

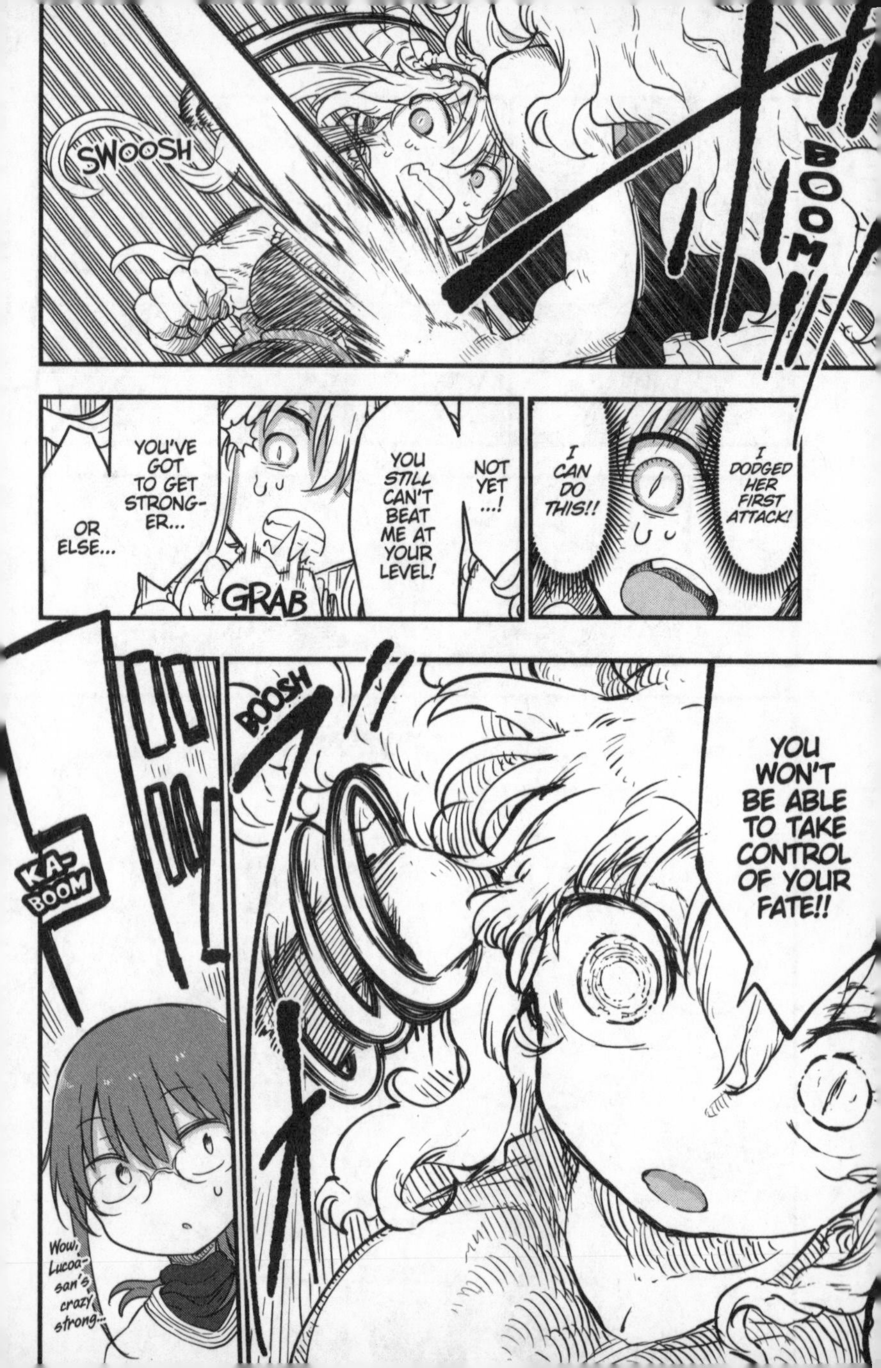
BOOM
SWOOSH
I DODGED HER FIRST ATTACK!
I CAN DO THIS!!
NOT YET ...!
YOU STILL CAN'T BEAT ME AT YOUR LEVEL!
GRAB
YOU'VE GOT TO GET STRONGER...
OR ELSE...
YOU WON'T BE ABLE TO TAKE CONTROL OF YOUR FATE!!
BOOSH
KA-BOOM
Wow, Lucoa-san's crazy strong...

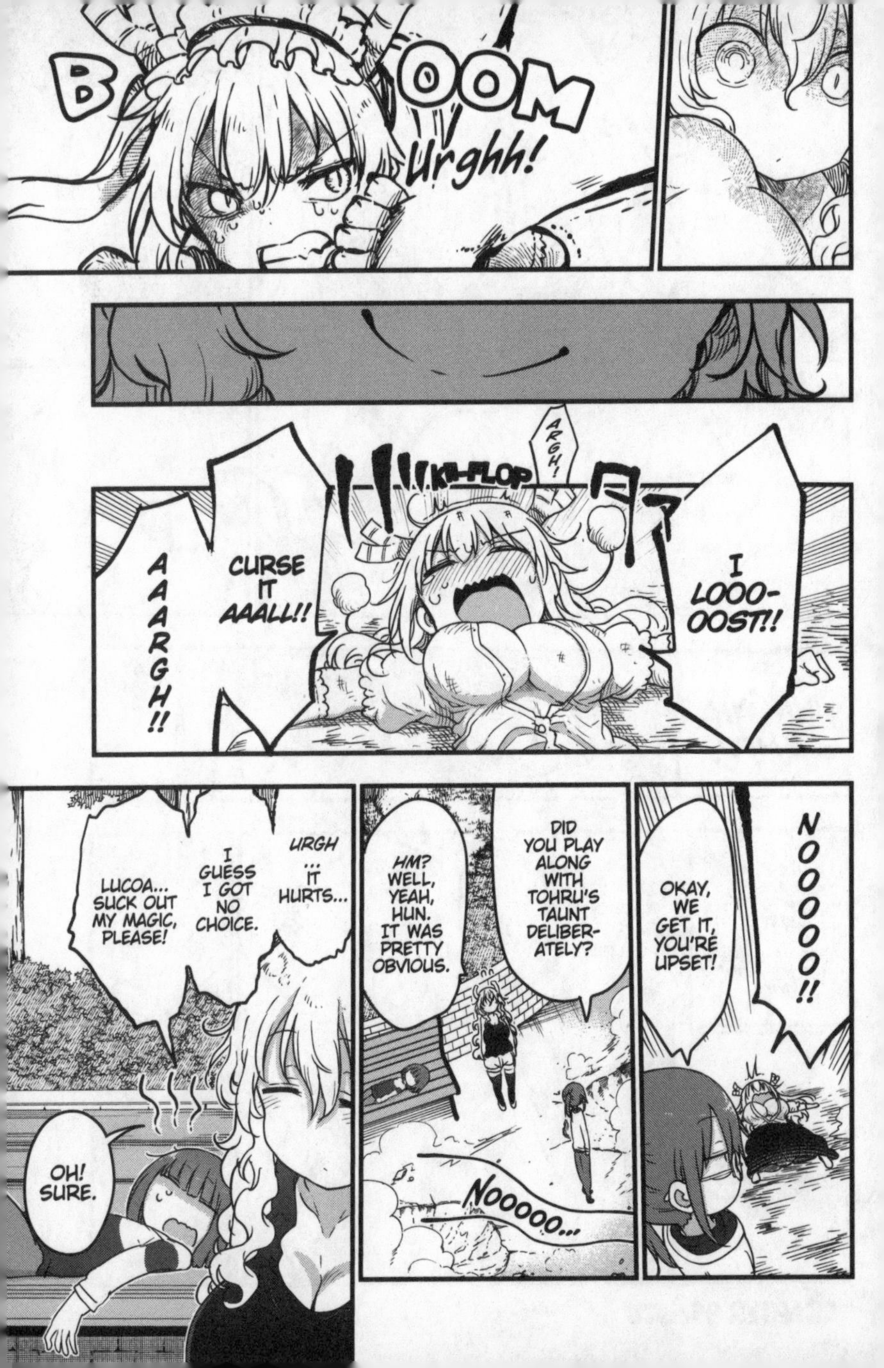

BOOOM
Urghh!
I LOOOO-OOST!!
ARGH!
KH-FLOP
CURSE IT AAALL!!
AAAARGH!!
NOOOOOO!!
OKAY, WE GET IT, YOU'RE UPSET!
DID YOU PLAY ALONG WITH TOHRU'S TAUNT DELIBER-ATELY?
HM? WELL, YEAH, HUN. IT WAS PRETTY OBVIOUS.
NOOOOO...
URGH... IT HURTS...
I GUESS I GOT NO CHOICE.
LUCOA... SUCK OUT MY MAGIC, PLEASE!
OH! SURE.

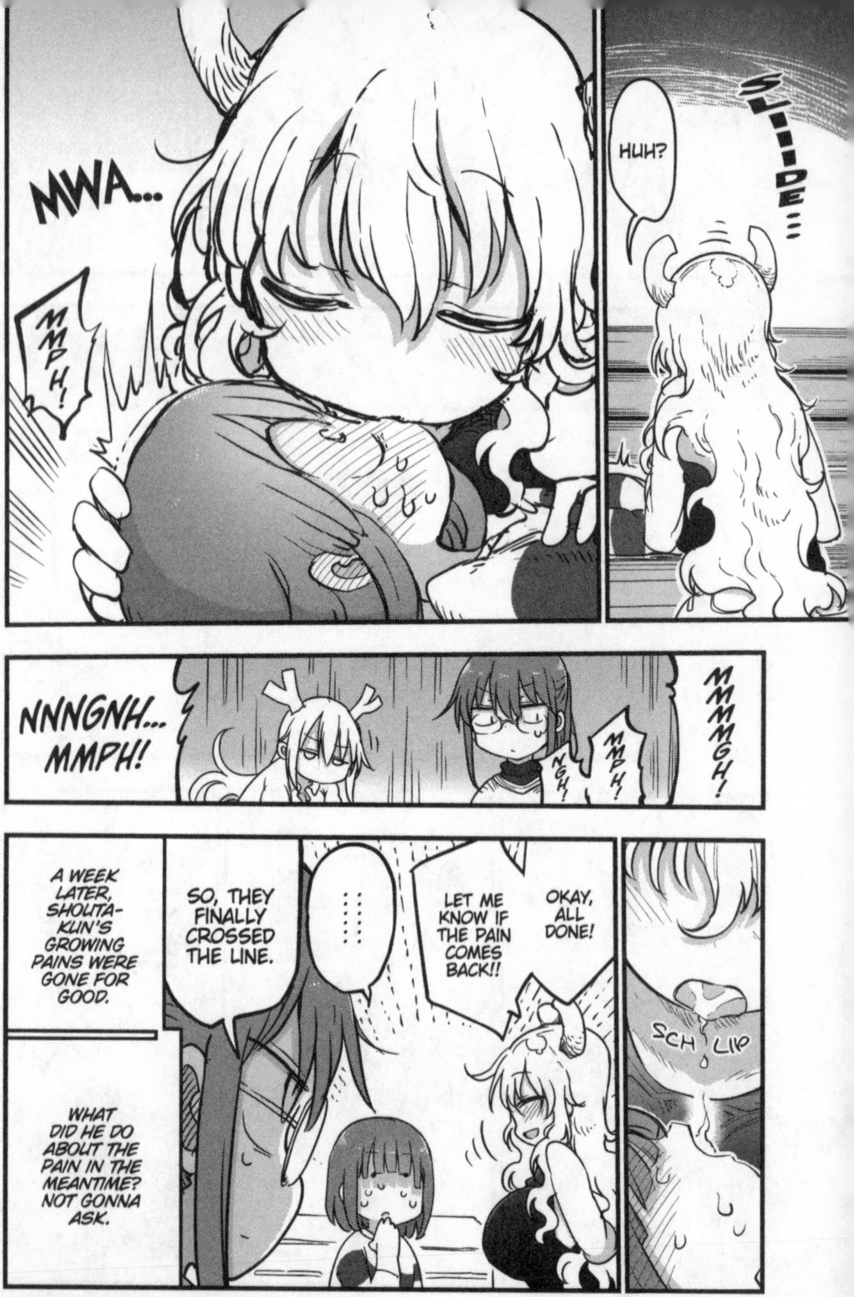
SLIIIDE
HUH?
MWA...
MMPH!
MMMMGH!
MMPH!
NGH!
NNNGNH... MMPH!
SCH LIP
OKAY, ALL DONE!
LET ME KNOW IF THE PAIN COMES BACK!!
......
SO, THEY FINALLY CROSSED THE LINE.
A WEEK LATER, SHOUTA-KUN'S GROWING PAINS WERE GONE FOR GOOD.
WHAT DID HE DO ABOUT THE PAIN IN THE MEANTIME? NOT GONNA ASK.

CHAPTER 95/END

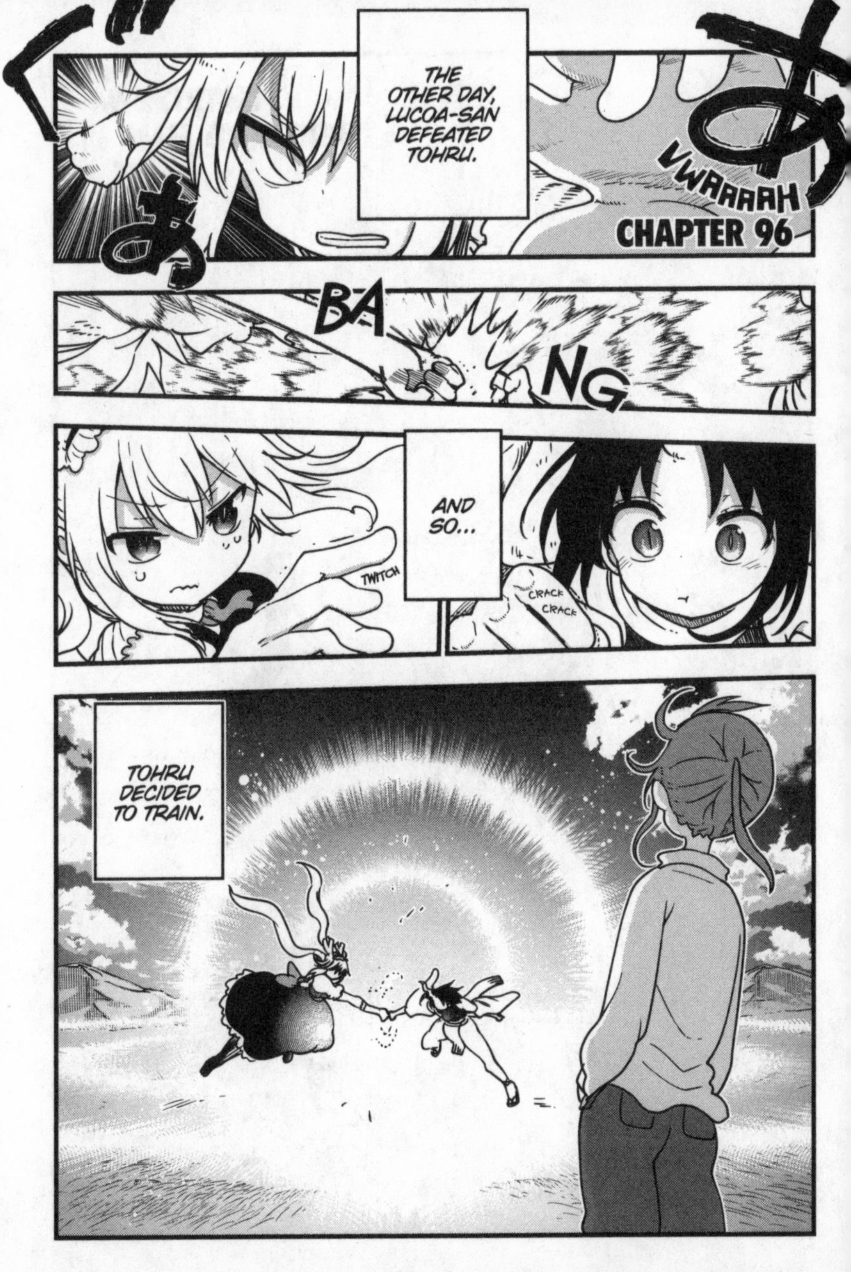
VWAAAAH
CHAPTER 96
THE OTHER DAY, LUCOA-SAN DEFEATED TOHRU.
BA
NG
CRACK CRACK
AND SO...
TWITCH
TOHRU DECIDED TO TRAIN.

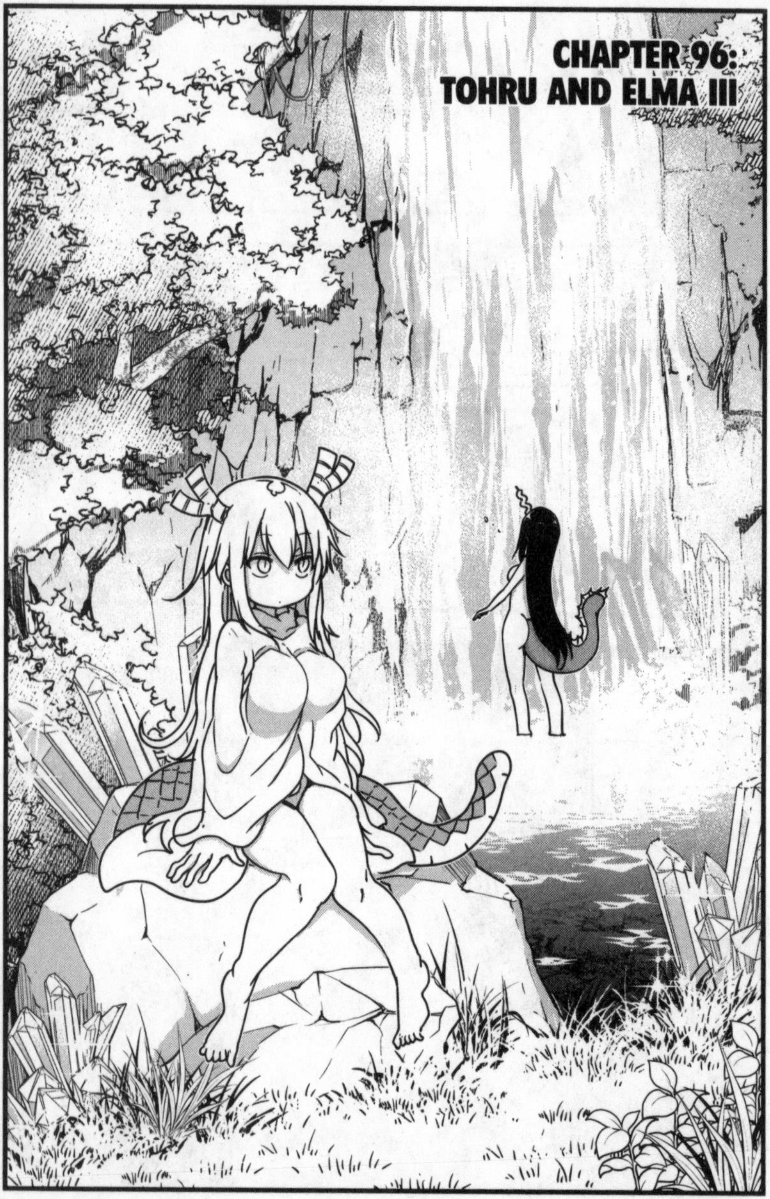
CHAPTER 96:
TOHRU AND ELMA III

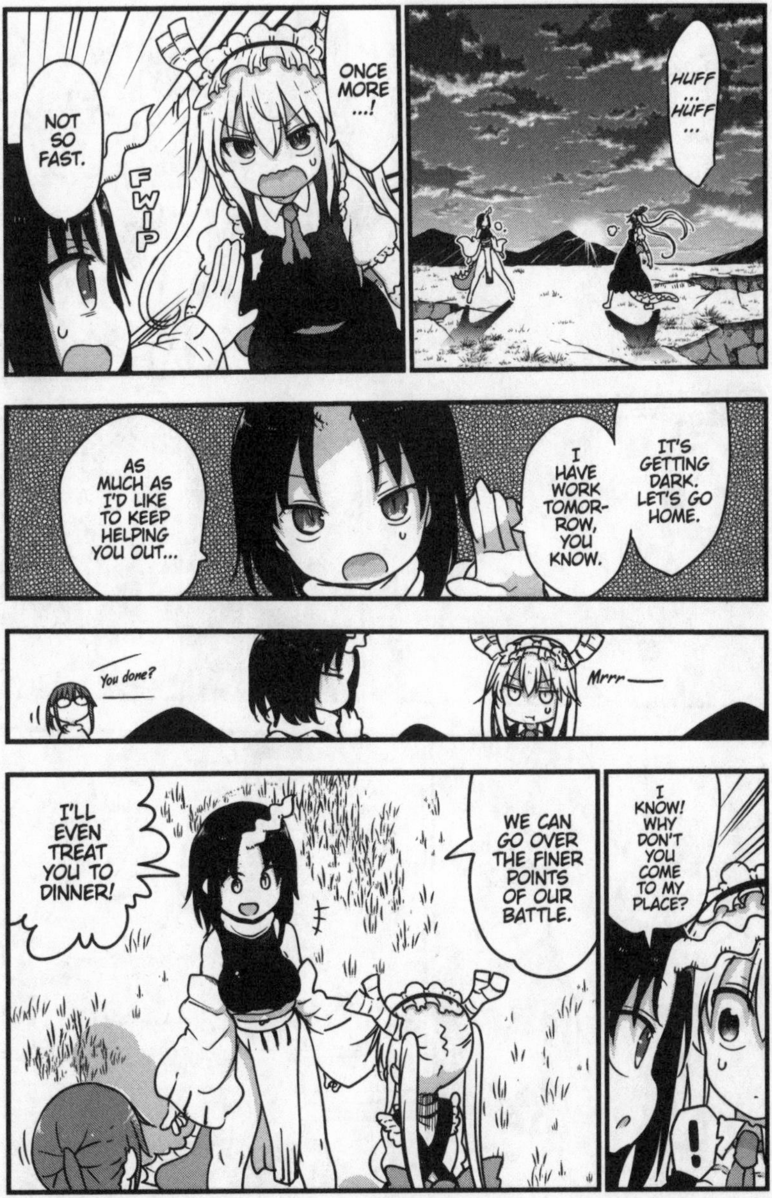
HUFF ... HUFF ...
ONCE MORE ...!
NOT SO FAST.
FWIP
IT'S GETTING DARK. LET'S GO HOME.
I HAVE WORK TOMOR-ROW, YOU KNOW.
AS MUCH AS I'D LIKE TO KEEP HELPING YOU OUT...
Mrrr—
You done?
I KNOW! WHY DON'T YOU COME TO MY PLACE?
WE CAN GO OVER THE FINER POINTS OF OUR BATTLE.
I'LL EVEN TREAT YOU TO DINNER!

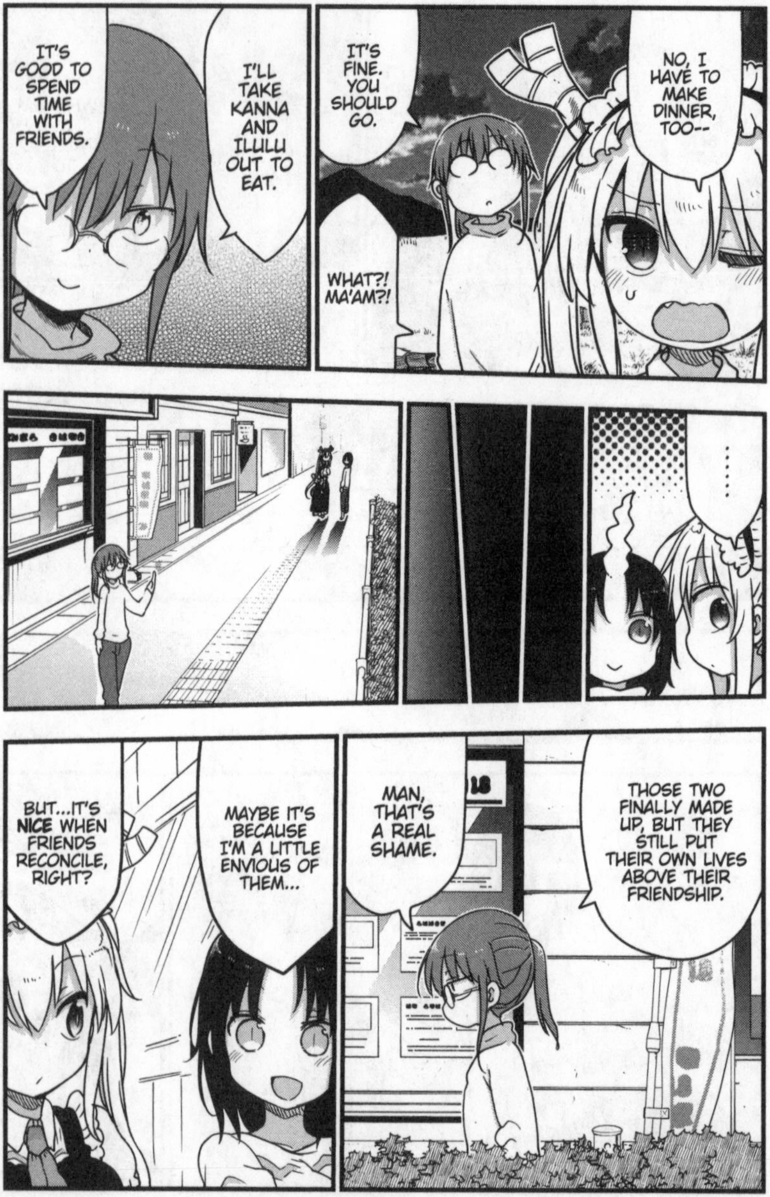
NO, I HAVE TO MAKE DINNER, TOO--
IT'S FINE. YOU SHOULD GO.
WHAT?! MA'AM?!
I'LL TAKE KANNA AND ILULU OUT TO EAT.
IT'S GOOD TO SPEND TIME WITH FRIENDS.
......
THOSE TWO FINALLY MADE UP, BUT THEY STILL PUT THEIR OWN LIVES ABOVE THEIR FRIENDSHIP.
MAN, THAT'S A REAL SHAME.
MAYBE IT'S BECAUSE I'M A LITTLE ENVIOUS OF THEM...
BUT...IT'S **NICE** WHEN FRIENDS RECONCILE, RIGHT?

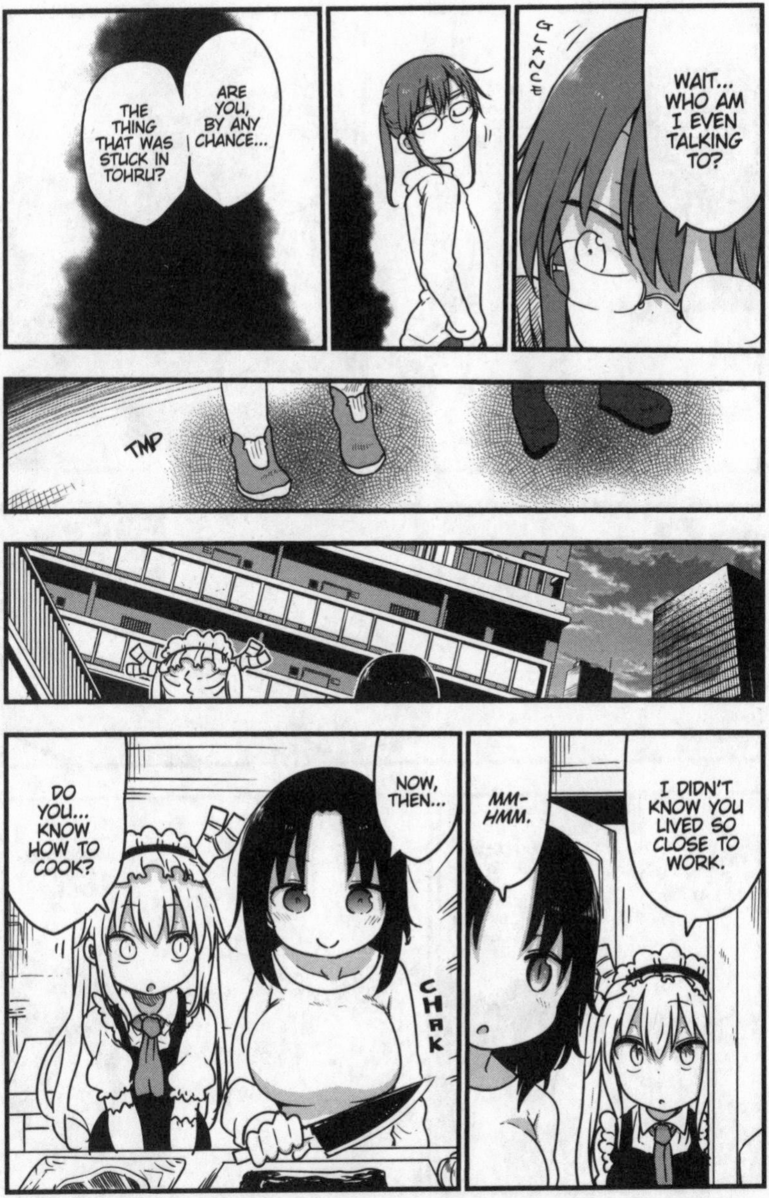
WAIT... WHO AM I EVEN TALKING TO?
GLANCE
ARE YOU, BY ANY CHANCE...
THE THING THAT WAS STUCK IN TOHRU?
TMP
I DIDN'T KNOW YOU LIVED SO CLOSE TO WORK.
MM-HMM.
NOW, THEN...
DO YOU... KNOW HOW TO COOK?
CHAK

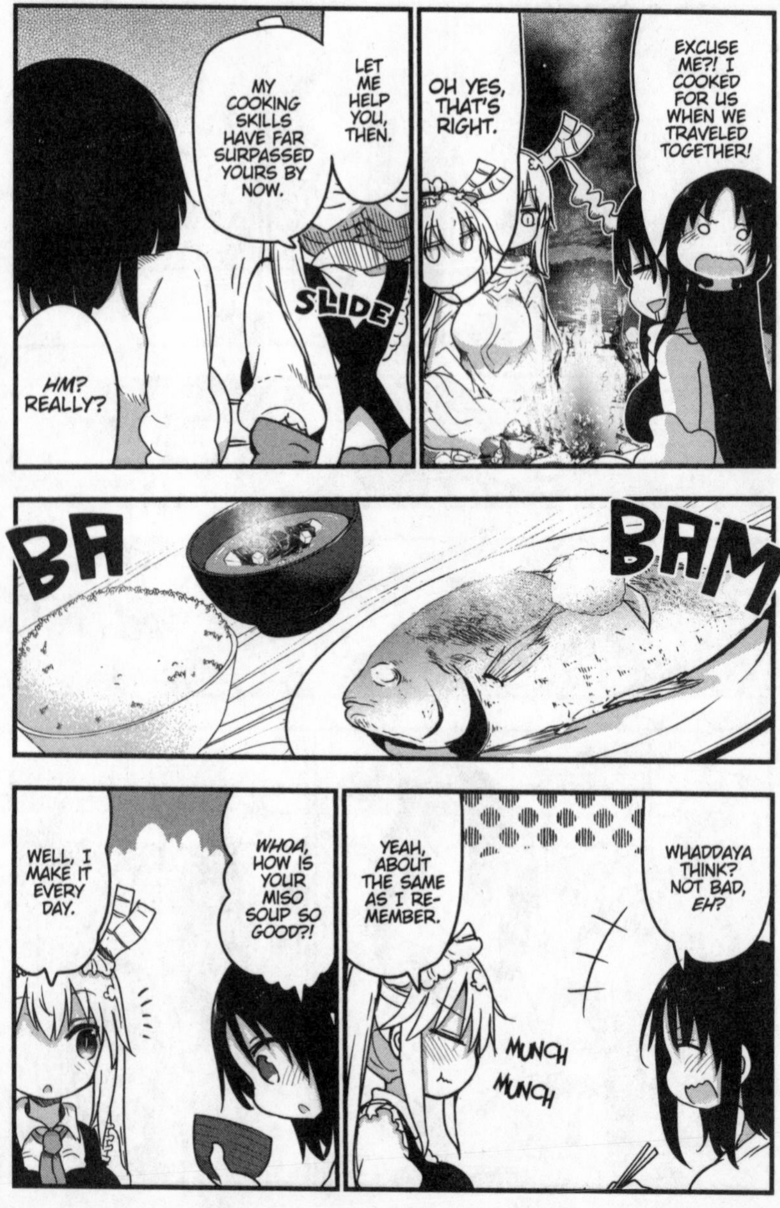
EXCUSE ME?! I COOKED FOR US WHEN WE TRAVELED TOGETHER!
OH YES, THAT'S RIGHT.
LET ME HELP YOU, THEN.
MY COOKING SKILLS HAVE FAR SURPASSED YOURS BY NOW.
SLIDE
HM? REALLY?
BA
BAM
WHADDAYA THINK? NOT BAD, EH?
YEAH, ABOUT THE SAME AS I RE-MEMBER.
MUNCH
MUNCH
WHOA, HOW IS YOUR MISO SOUP SO GOOD?!
WELL, I MAKE IT EVERY DAY.

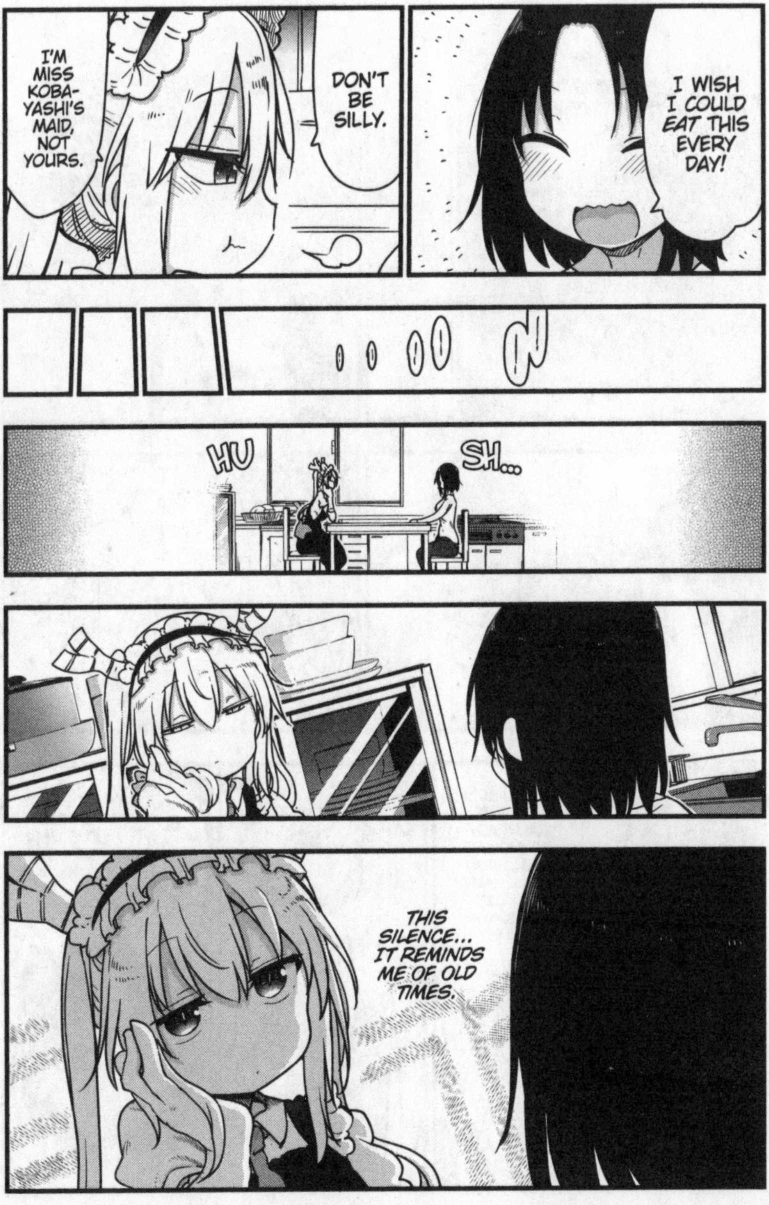
I WISH I COULD EAT THIS EVERY DAY!
DON'T BE SILLY.
I'M MISS KOBA-YASHI'S MAID, NOT YOURS.
HU SH...
THIS SILENCE... IT REMINDS ME OF OLD TIMES.

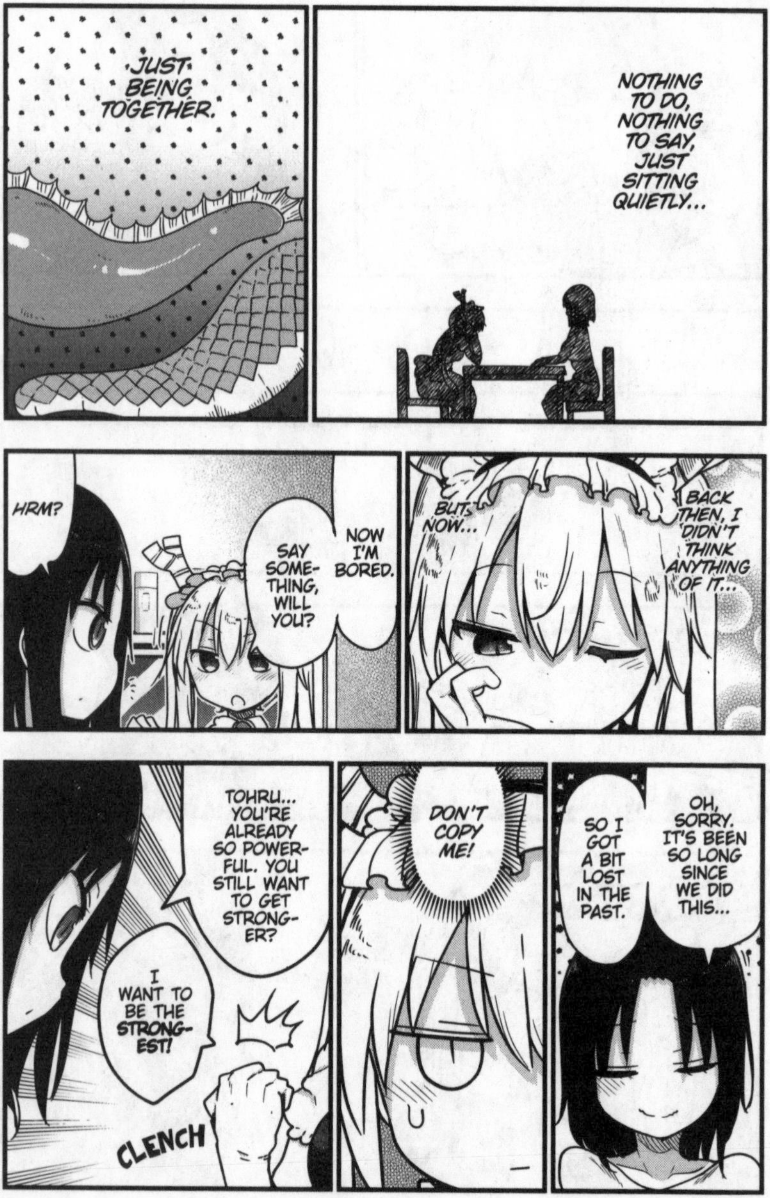
NOTHING TO DO, NOTHING TO SAY, JUST SITTING QUIETLY...
JUST BEING TOGETHER.
BACK THEN, I DIDN'T THINK ANYTHING OF IT...
BUT NOW...
NOW I'M BORED.
SAY SOME-THING, WILL YOU?
HRM?
OH, SORRY. IT'S BEEN SO LONG SINCE WE DID THIS...
SO I GOT A BIT LOST IN THE PAST.
DON'T COPY ME!
TOHRU... YOU'RE ALREADY SO POWER-FUL. YOU STILL WANT TO GET STRONG-ER?
I WANT TO BE THE STRONG-EST!
CLENCH

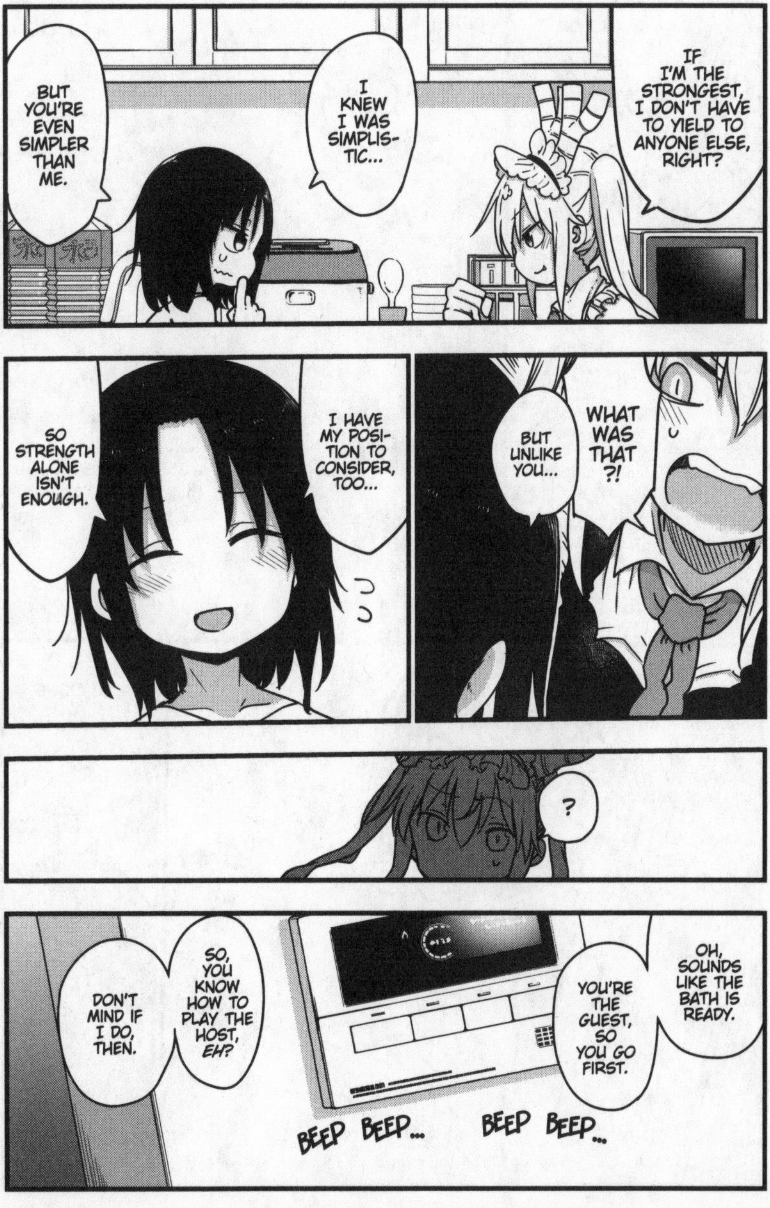
IF I'M THE STRONGEST, I DON'T HAVE TO YIELD TO ANYONE ELSE, RIGHT?
I KNEW I WAS SIMPLISTIC...
BUT YOU'RE EVEN SIMPLER THAN ME.
WHAT WAS THAT?!
BUT UNLIKE YOU...
I HAVE MY POSITION TO CONSIDER, TOO...
SO STRENGTH ALONE ISN'T ENOUGH.
?
OH, SOUNDS LIKE THE BATH IS READY.
YOU'RE THE GUEST, SO YOU GO FIRST.
BEEP BEEP...
BEEP BEEP...
SO, YOU KNOW HOW TO PLAY THE HOST, *EH*?
DON'T MIND IF I DO, THEN.

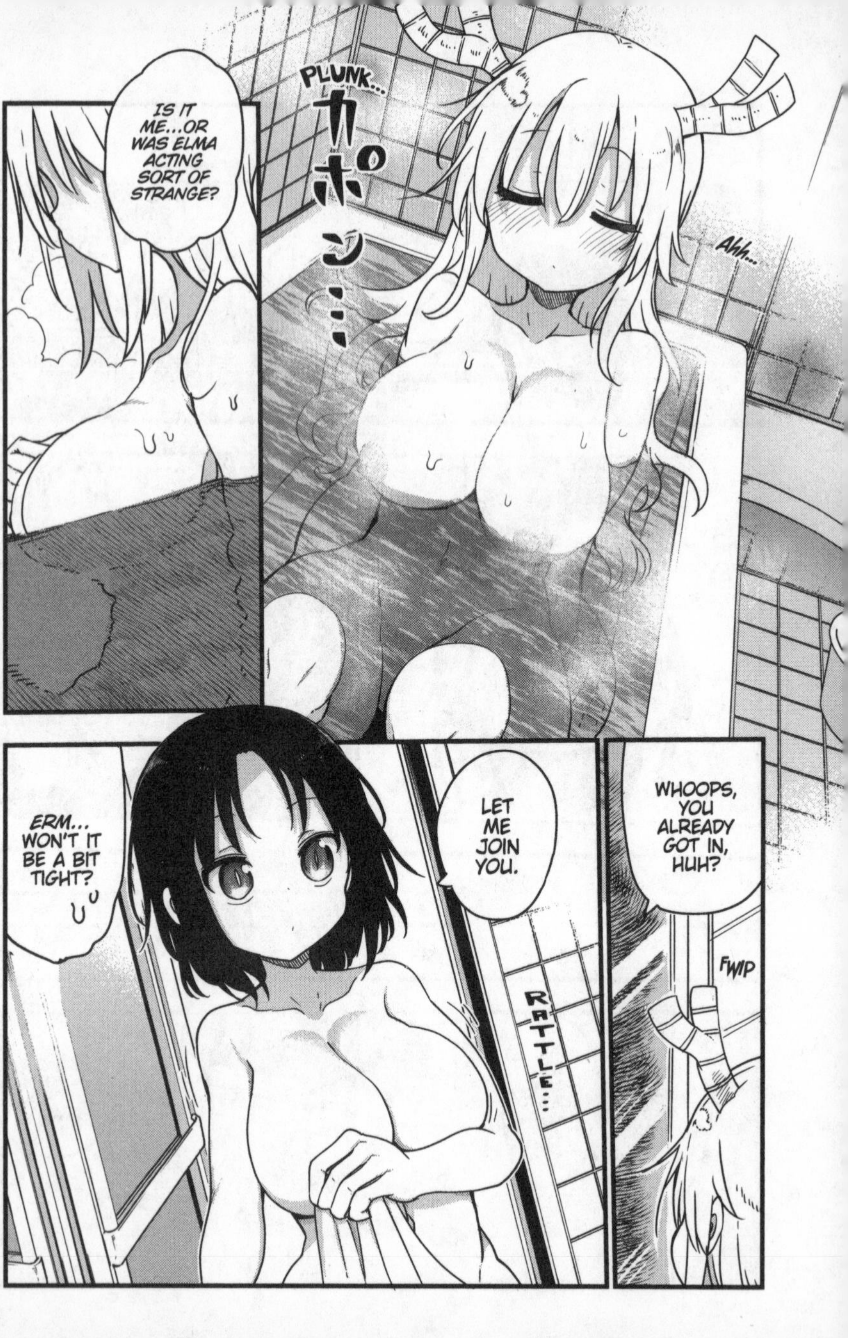
PLUNK...
カポン...
Ahh...
IS IT ME...OR WAS ELMA ACTING SORT OF STRANGE?
WHOOPS, YOU ALREADY GOT IN, HUH?
FWIP
LET ME JOIN YOU.
RATTLE...
ERM... WON'T IT BE A BIT TIGHT?

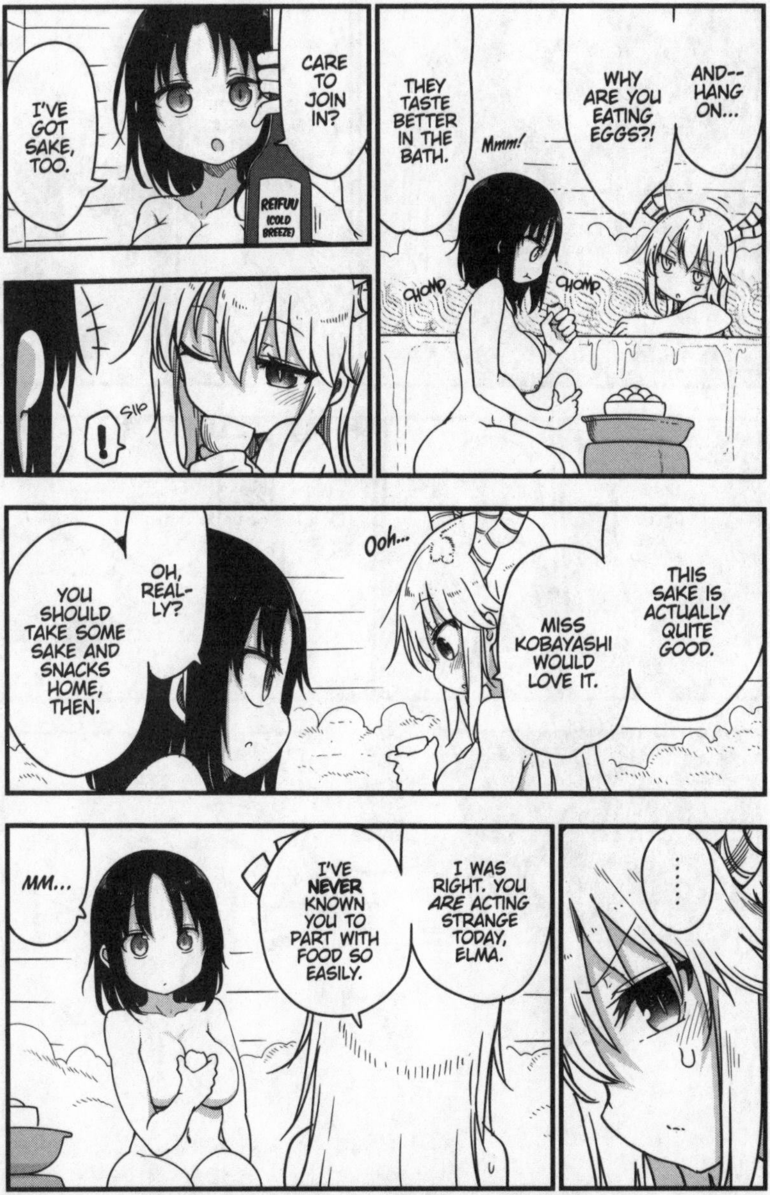
AND-- HANG ON...
WHY ARE YOU EATING EGGS?!
Mmm!
THEY TASTE BETTER IN THE BATH.
CHOMP
CHOMP
CARE TO JOIN IN?
I'VE GOT SAKE, TOO.
REIFUU (COLD BREEZE)
SIP
!
THIS SAKE IS ACTUALLY QUITE GOOD.
MISS KOBAYASHI WOULD LOVE IT.
Ooh...
OH, REALLY?
YOU SHOULD TAKE SOME SAKE AND SNACKS HOME, THEN.
......
I WAS RIGHT. YOU *ARE* ACTING STRANGE TODAY, ELMA.
I'VE **NEVER** KNOWN YOU TO PART WITH FOOD SO EASILY.
MM...

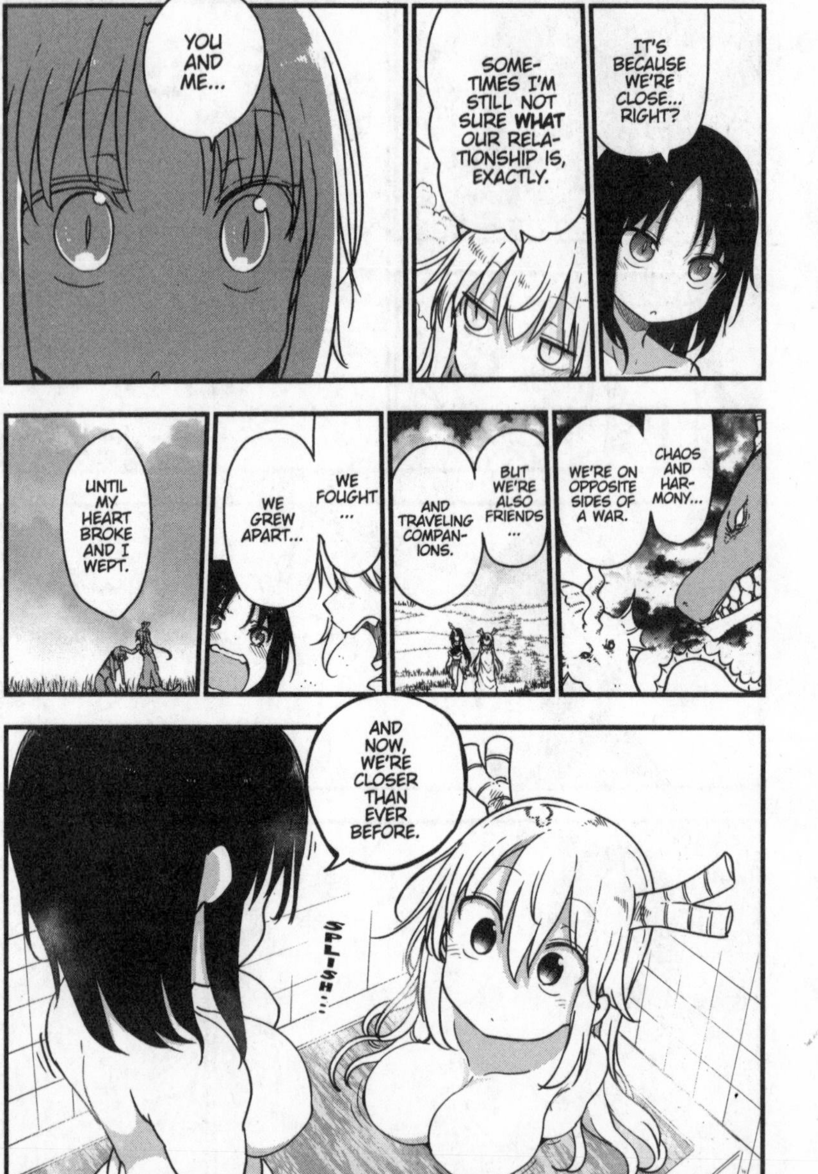
IT'S BECAUSE WE'RE CLOSE... RIGHT?
SOME-TIMES I'M STILL NOT SURE **WHAT** OUR RELA-TIONSHIP IS, EXACTLY.
YOU AND ME...
CHAOS AND HAR-MONY...
WE'RE ON OPPOSITE SIDES OF A WAR.
BUT WE'RE ALSO FRIENDS ...
AND TRAVELING COMPAN-IONS.
WE FOUGHT ...
WE GREW APART...
UNTIL MY HEART BROKE AND I WEPT.
AND NOW, WE'RE CLOSER THAN EVER BEFORE.
SPLISH...

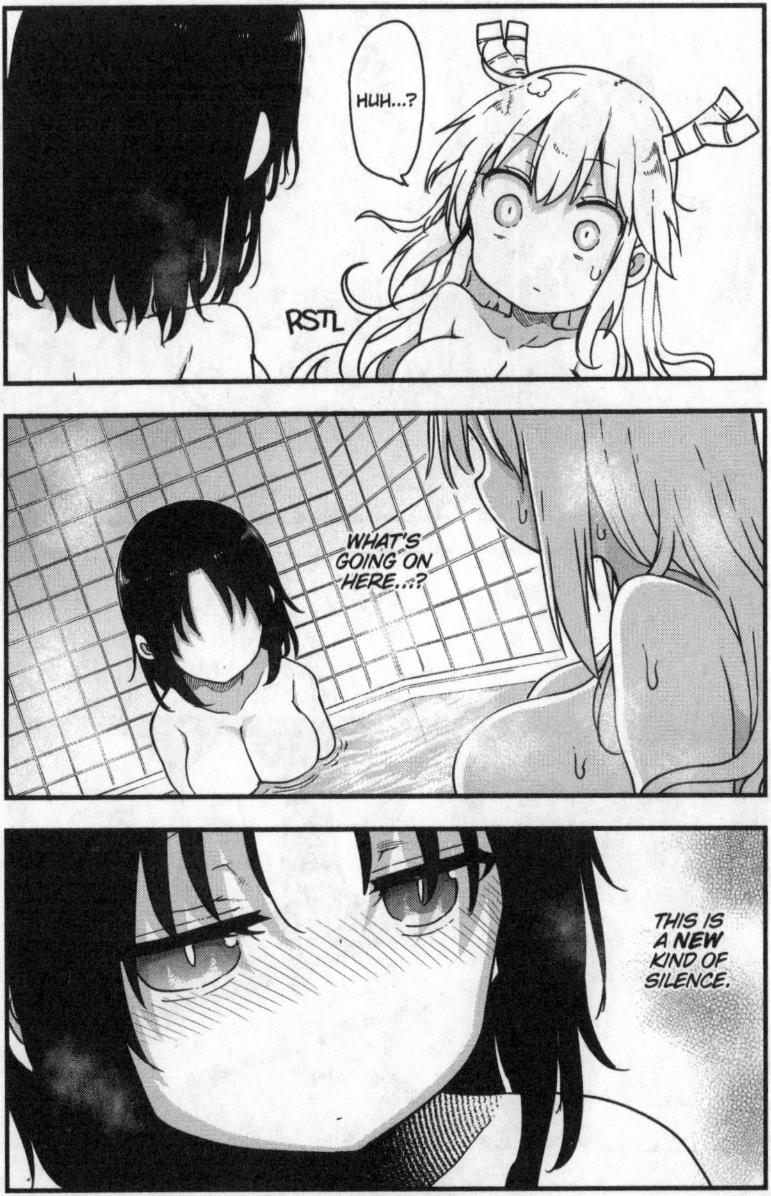
HUH...?
RSTL
WHAT'S GOING ON HERE...?
THIS IS A NEW KIND OF SILENCE.

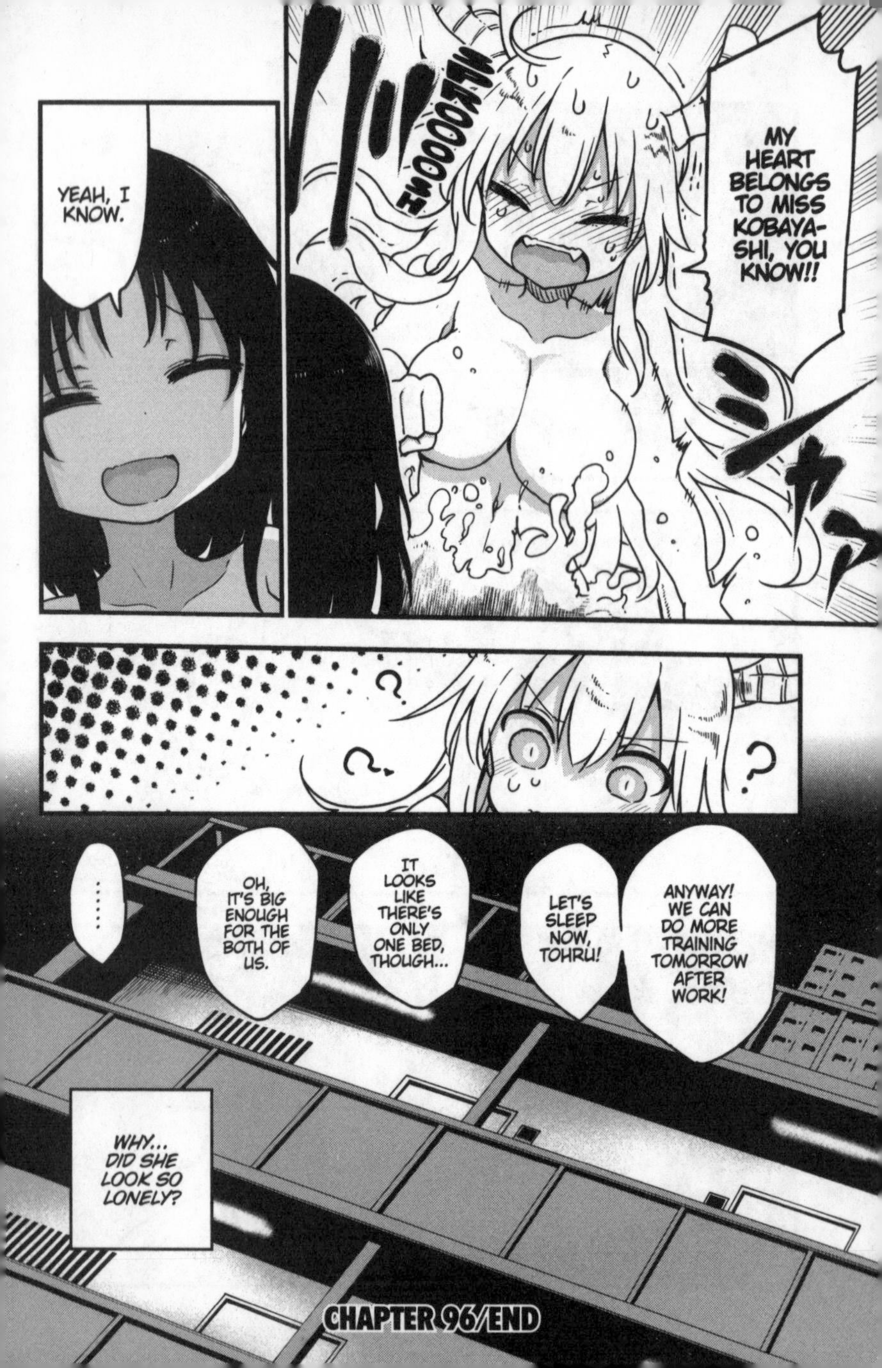
MY HEART BELONGS TO MISS KOBAYASHI, YOU KNOW!!
YEAH, I KNOW.
ANYWAY! WE CAN DO MORE TRAINING TOMORROW AFTER WORK!
LET'S SLEEP NOW, TOHRU!
IT LOOKS LIKE THERE'S ONLY ONE BED, THOUGH...
OH, IT'S BIG ENOUGH FOR THE BOTH OF US.
......
WHY... DID SHE LOOK SO LONELY?
CHAPTER 96/END

AFTERWORD

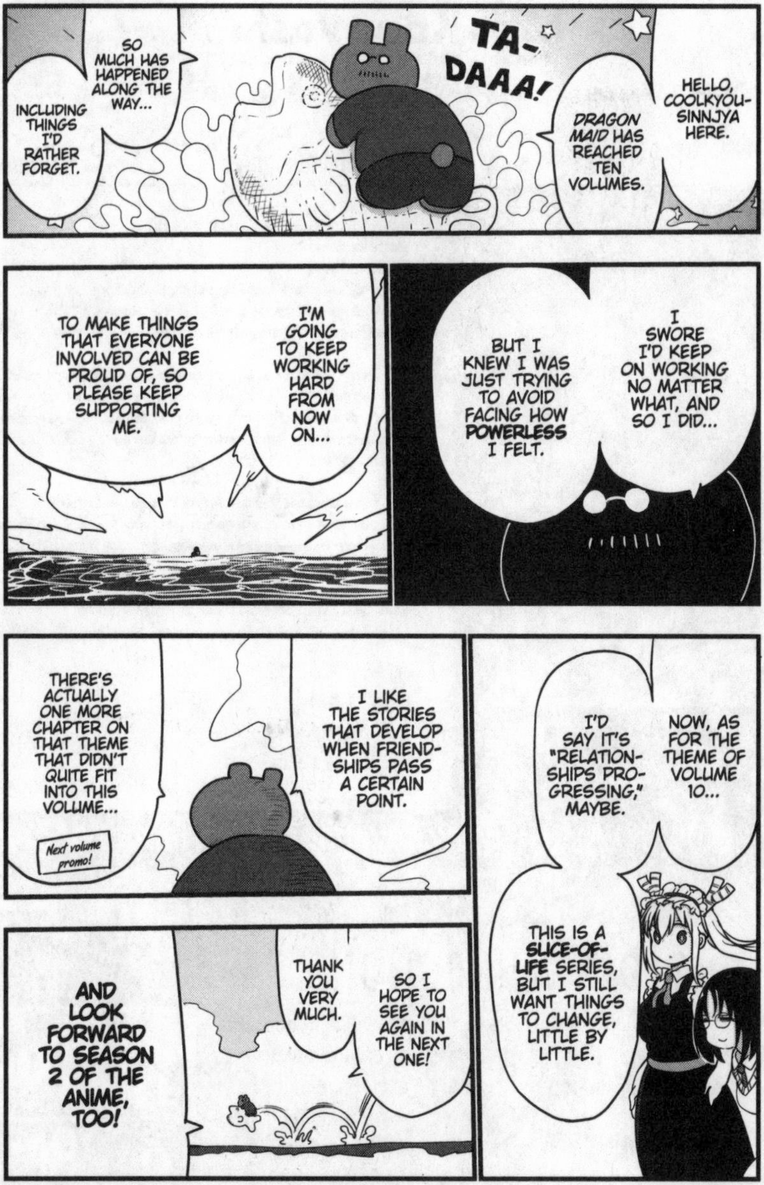

HELLO, COOLKYOU-SINNJYA HERE.
DRAGON MAID HAS REACHED TEN VOLUMES.
TA-DAAA!
SO MUCH HAS HAPPENED ALONG THE WAY...
INCLUDING THINGS I'D RATHER FORGET.
I SWORE I'D KEEP ON WORKING NO MATTER WHAT, AND SO I DID...
BUT I KNEW I WAS JUST TRYING TO AVOID FACING HOW **POWERLESS** I FELT.
I'M GOING TO KEEP WORKING HARD FROM NOW ON...
TO MAKE THINGS THAT EVERYONE INVOLVED CAN BE PROUD OF, SO PLEASE KEEP SUPPORTING ME.
NOW, AS FOR THE THEME OF VOLUME 10...
I'D SAY IT'S "RELATIONSHIPS PROGRESSING," MAYBE.
THIS IS A **SLICE-OF-LIFE** SERIES, BUT I STILL WANT THINGS TO CHANGE, LITTLE BY LITTLE.
I LIKE THE STORIES THAT DEVELOP WHEN FRIENDSHIPS PASS A CERTAIN POINT.
THERE'S ACTUALLY ONE MORE CHAPTER ON THAT THEME THAT DIDN'T QUITE FIT INTO THIS VOLUME...
Next volume promo!
SO I HOPE TO SEE YOU AGAIN IN THE NEXT ONE!
THANK YOU VERY MUCH.
AND LOOK FORWARD TO SEASON 2 OF THE ANIME, TOO!

Assistants: Namazenmai-sama, Giovanni Works-sama

SEVEN SEAS ENTERTAINMENT PRESENTS

Miss Kobayashi's Dragon Maid

VOL. 10

story and art by coolkyousinnjya

TRANSLATION
Jenny McKeon

ADAPTATION
Shanti Whitesides

LETTERING
Jennifer Skarupa

LOGO DESIGN
KC Fabellon

COVER DESIGN
Nicky Lim

PROOFREADING
Stephanie Cohen
Dawn Davis

PREPRESS TECHNICIAN
Rhiannon Rasmussen-Silverstein

PRODUCTION MANAGER
Lissa Pattillo

MANAGING EDITOR
Julie Davis

ASSOCIATE PUBLISHER
Adam Arnold

PUBLISHER
Jason DeAngelis

MISS KOBAYASHI'S DRAGON MAID VOL. 10

First published in Japan in 2020 by Futabasha Publishers Ltd., Tokyo.
English version published by Seven Seas Entertainment.
Under license from Futabasha Publishers Ltd.

Seven Seas press and purchase enquiries can be sent to Marketing Manager Lianne Sentar at press@gomanga.com. Information regarding the distribution and purchase of digital editions is available from Digital Manager CK Russell at digital@gomanga.com.

ISBN: 978-1-64505-784-0

Printed in Canada

First Printing: March 2021

10 9 8 7 6 5 4 3 2 1

FOLLOW US ONLINE: ***www.sevenseasentertainment.com***

READING DIRECTIONS

This book reads from ***right to left***, Japanese style. If this is your first time reading manga, you start reading from the top right panel on each page and take it from there. If you get lost, just follow the numbered diagram here. It may seem backwards at first, but you'll get the hang of it! Have fun!!

1
2
3
4
5
6
7
8
9

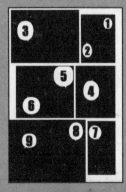